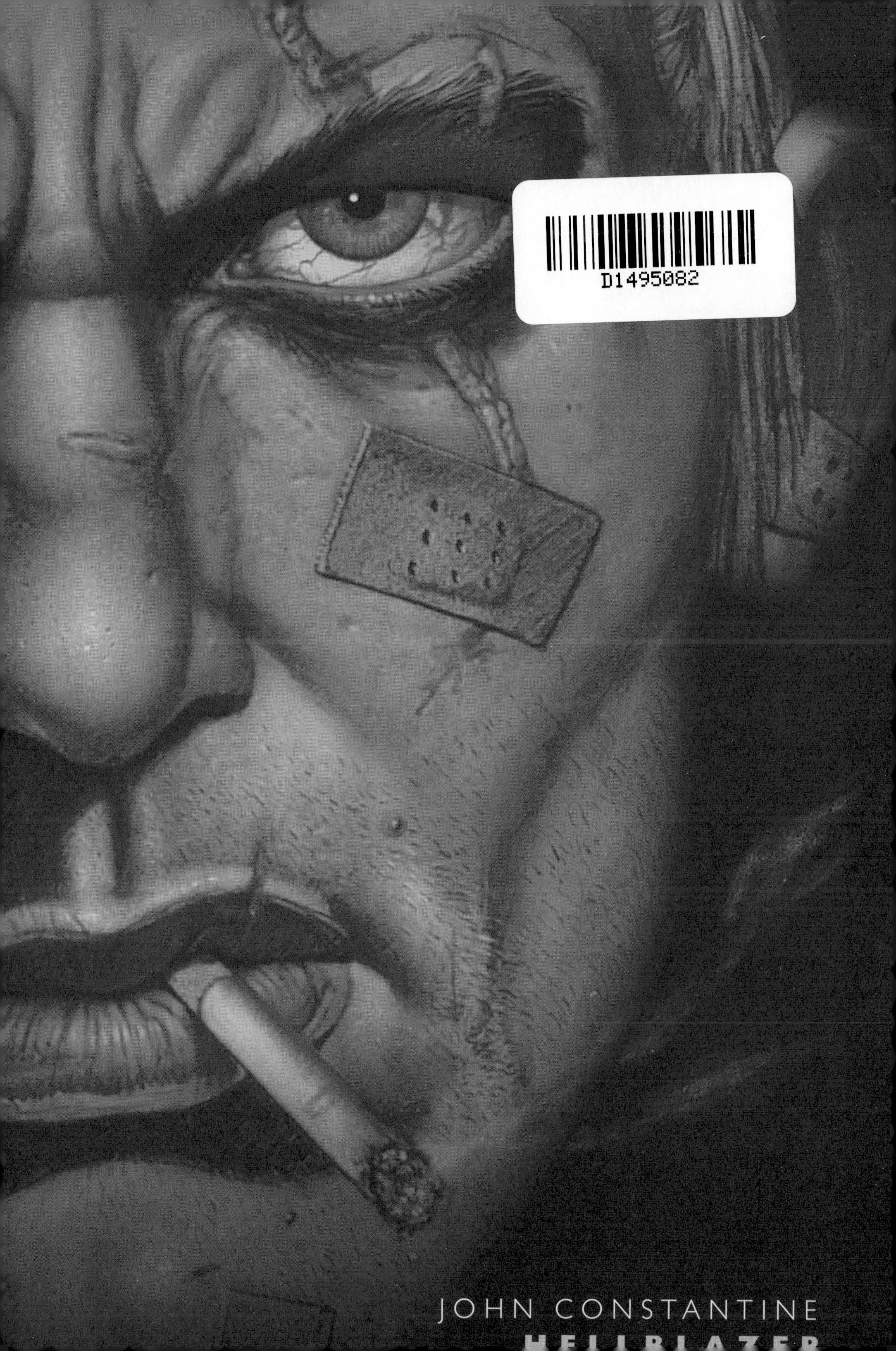

JOHN CONSTANTINE

HELLBLAZER

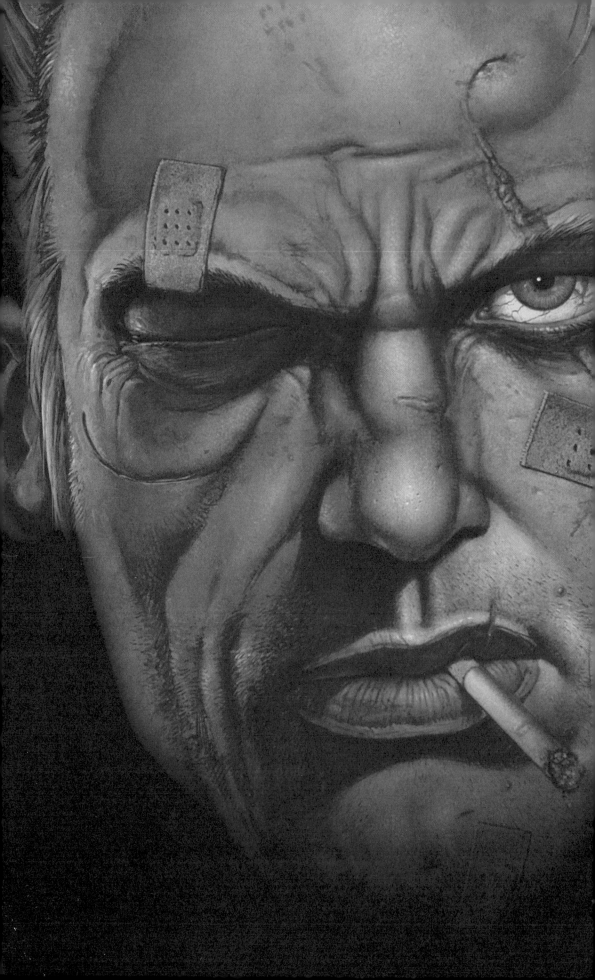

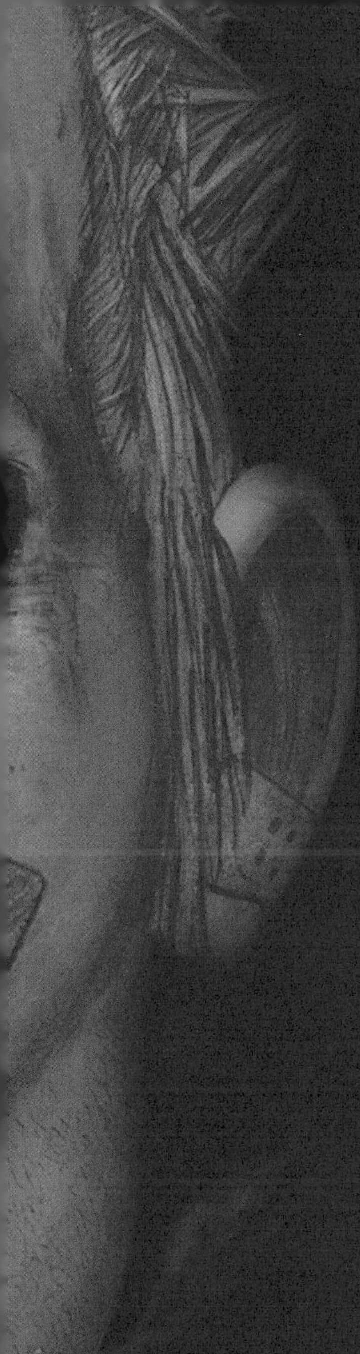

JOHN CONSTANTINE
HELLBLAZER
HOOKED

Peter Milligan writer

HOOKED
Giuseppe Camuncoli layouts
Stefano Landini finishes

THE COTTAGE
THE LONG CRAP FRIDAY
Simon Bisley artist

Jamie Grant colorist

Sal Cipriano letterer

Simon Bisley original series covers

THE JOHN CONSTANTINE HELLBLAZER
READER'S GUIDE

ORIGINAL SINS Collecting issues #1-9
THE DEVIL YOU KNOW Collecting issues #10-13, Annual #1 and The Horrorist 1-2
THE FEAR MACHINE Collecting issues #14-22
THE FAMILY MAN Collecting issues #23-24, 28-33
RARE CUTS Collecting issues #11, 25-26, 35, 56, 84
DANGEROUS HABITS Collecting issues #41-46
BLOODLINES Collecting issues #47-50, 52-55, 59-61
FEAR AND LOATHING Collecting issues #62-67
TAINTED LOVE Collecting issues #68-71, Special #1, Vertigo Jam #1
DAMNATION'S FLAME Collecting issues #72-77
RAKE AT THE GATES OF HELL Collecting issues #78-83
SON OF MAN Collecting issues #129-133
HAUNTED Collecting issues #134-139
SETTING SUN Collecting issues #140-143
HARD TIME Collecting issues #146-150
GOOD INTENTIONS Collecting issues #151-156
FREEZES OVER Collecting issues #157-163
HIGHWATER Collecting issues #164-174
RED SEPULCHRE Collecting issues #175-180
BLACK FLOWERS Collecting issues #181-186
STARING AT THE WALL Collecting issues #187-193
STATIONS OF THE CROSS Collecting issues #194-200
REASONS TO BE CHEERFUL Collecting issues #201-206
THE GIFT Collecting issues #207-215
EMPATHY IS THE ENEMY Collecting issues #216-222
THE RED RIGHT HAND Collecting issues #223-228
JOYRIDE Collecting issues #230-237
THE LAUGHING MAGICIAN Collecting issues #238-242
THE ROOTS OF COINCIDENCE Collecting issues #243-244, 247-249
SCAB Collecting issues #250-255

Look for these other important **HELLBLAZER** collections:
LADY CONSTANTINE
PAPA MIDNITE
CHAS — THE KNOWLEDGE
ALL HIS ENGINES

SHELLY BOND Editor-original series BRANDON MONTCLARE Assist. Editor-original series BOB HARRAS Group Editor-Collected Editions
SEAN MACKIEWICZ Editor ROBBIN BROSTERMAN Design Director-Books

DC COMICS
DIANE NELSON President DAN DIDIO and JIM LEE Co-Publishers GEOFF JOHNS Chief Creative Officer
PATRICK CALDON EVP- Finance and Administration JOHN ROOD EVP-Sales, Marketing and Business Development
KAREN BERGER SVP-Executive Editor, Vertigo MARK CHIARELLO Art Director AMY GENKINS SVP-Business and Legal Affairs
STEVE ROTTERDAM SVP-Sales and Marketing JOHN CUNNINGHAM VP-Marketing TERRI CUNNINGHAM VP-Managing Editor
ALISON GILL VP-Manufacturing DAVID HYDE VP-Publicity SUE POHJA VP-Book Trade Sales
ALYSSE SOLL VP-Advertising and Custom Publishing BOB WAYNE VP-Sales

Cover illustration by Simon Bisley.

JOHN CONSTANTINE, HELLBLAZER: HOOKED
Published by DC Comics. Cover and compilation Copyright © 2010 DC Comics. All Rights Reserved. Originally published in single magazine form as
HELLBLAZER #256-260. Copyright © 2009 DC Comics. All Rights Reserved. All characters, their distinctive likenesses and related elements featured in
this publication are trademarks of DC Comics. The stories, characters and incidents featured in this publication are entirely fictional. DC Comics does not
read or accept unsolicited submissions of ideas, stories or artwork.

DC Comics, 1700 Broadway, New York, NY 10019. A Warner Bros. Entertainment Company. First Printing.
Printed in the USA.
ISBN: 978-1-4012-2728-9

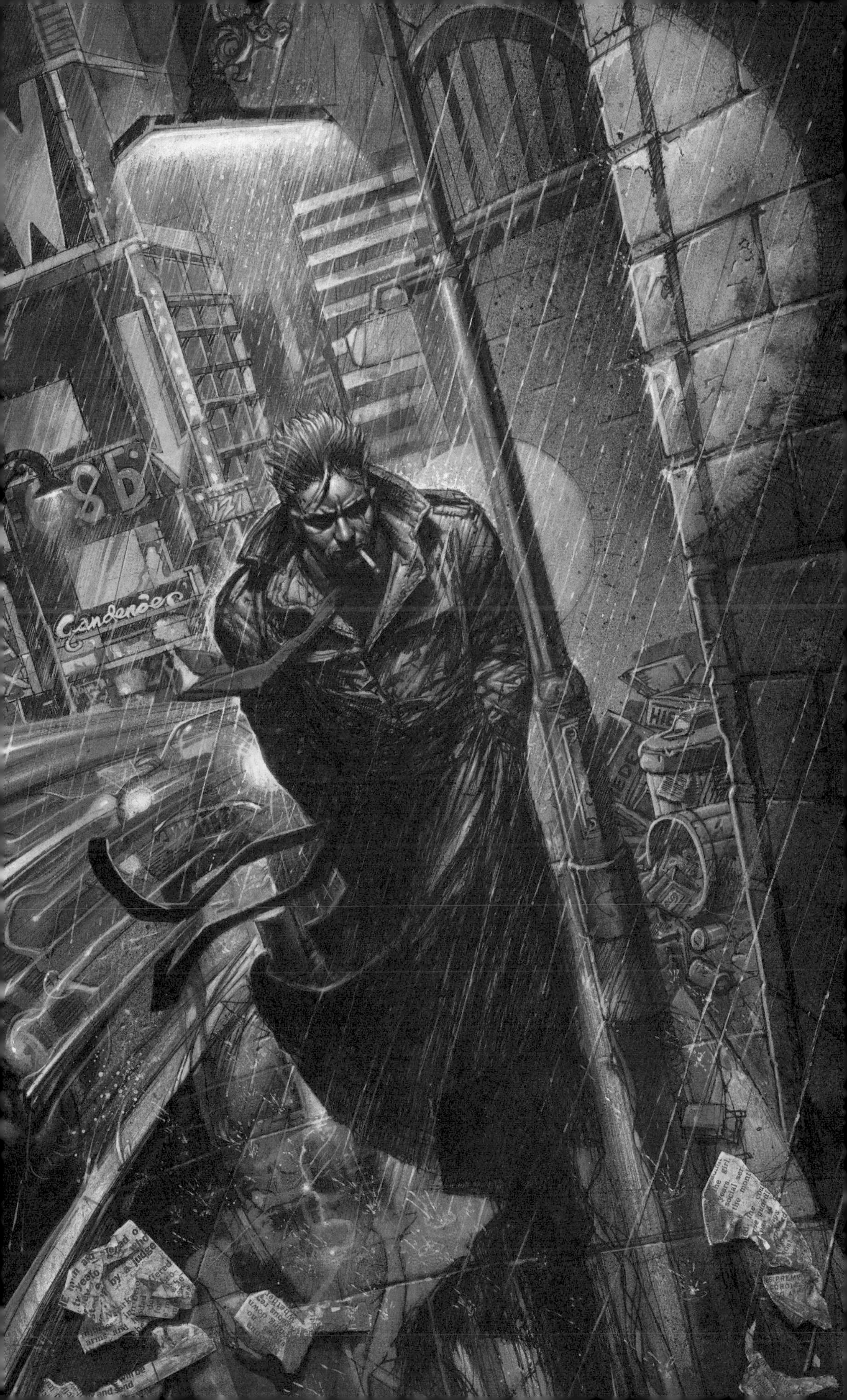
86

Hooked, Part One
There's Something About Phoebe

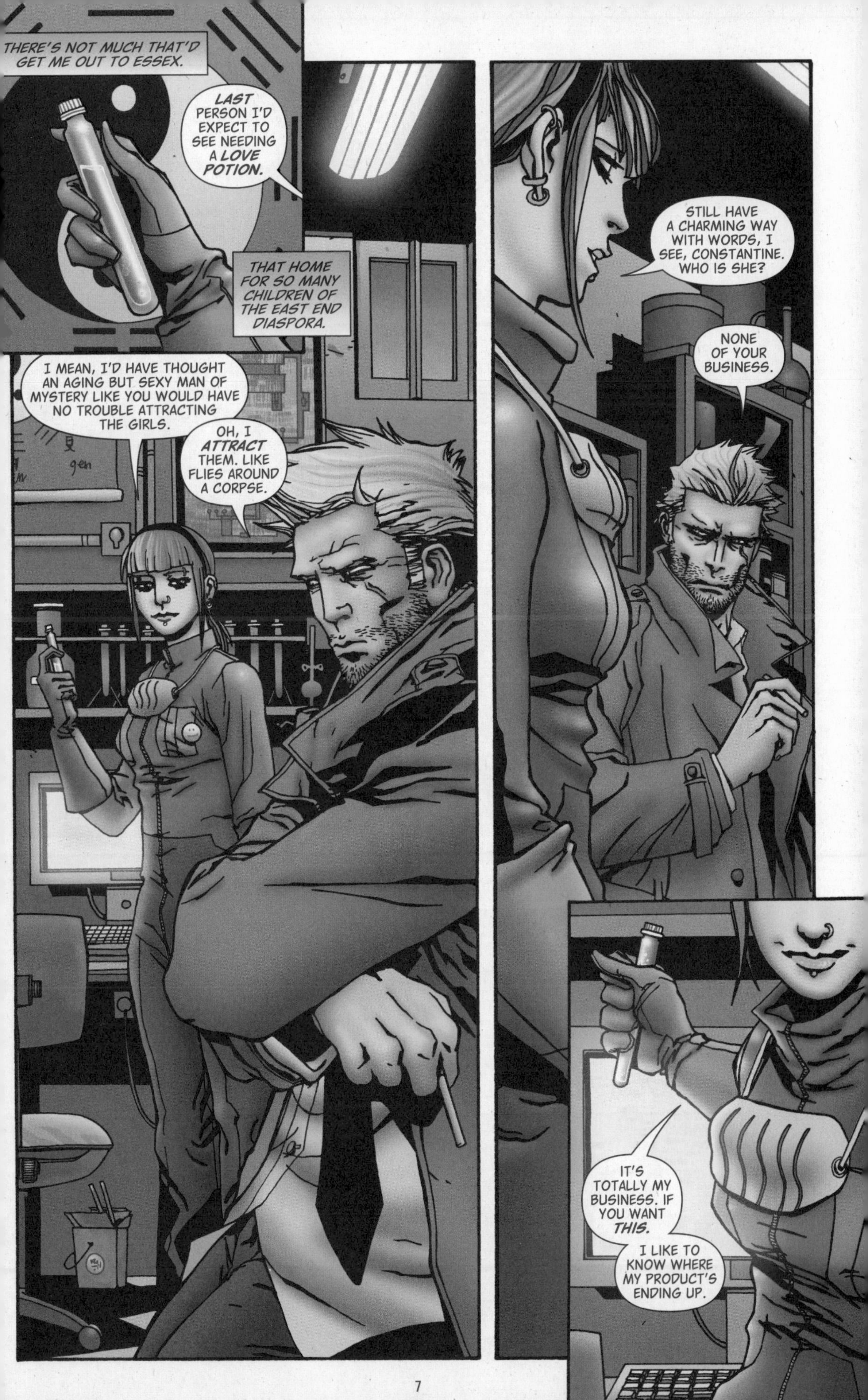
THERE'S NOT MUCH THAT'D GET ME OUT TO ESSEX.
LAST PERSON I'D EXPECT TO SEE NEEDING A LOVE POTION.
THAT HOME FOR SO MANY CHILDREN OF THE EAST END DIASPORA.
I MEAN, I'D HAVE THOUGHT AN AGING BUT SEXY MAN OF MYSTERY LIKE YOU WOULD HAVE NO TROUBLE ATTRACTING THE GIRLS.
OH, I ATTRACT THEM. LIKE FLIES AROUND A CORPSE.
STILL HAVE A CHARMING WAY WITH WORDS, I SEE, CONSTANTINE. WHO IS SHE?
NONE OF YOUR BUSINESS.
IT'S TOTALLY MY BUSINESS. IF YOU WANT THIS.
I LIKE TO KNOW WHERE MY PRODUCT'S ENDING UP.

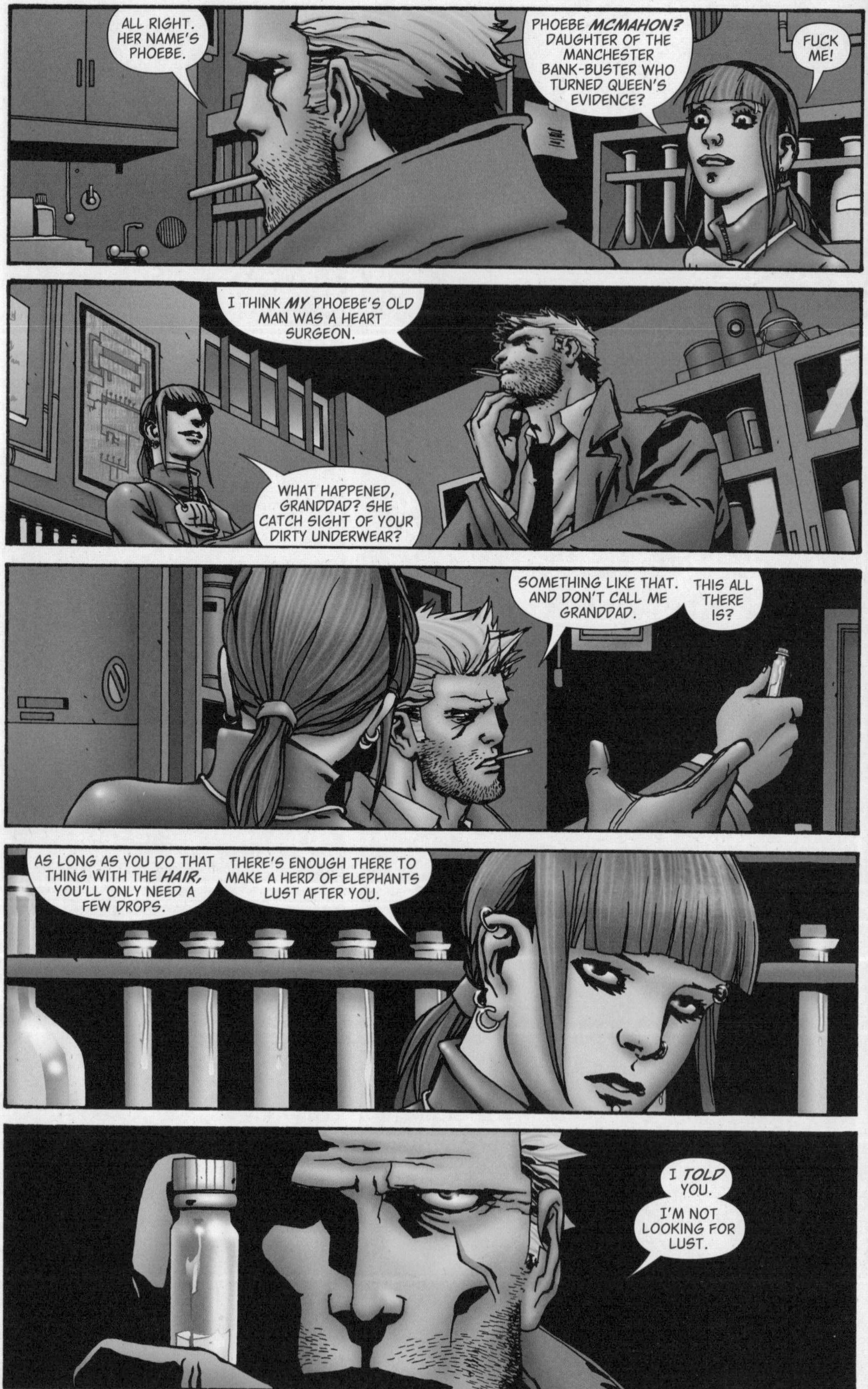
ALL RIGHT. HER NAME'S PHOEBE.
PHOEBE *MCMAHON?* DAUGHTER OF THE MANCHESTER BANK-BUSTER WHO TURNED QUEEN'S EVIDENCE?
FUCK ME!
I THINK *MY* PHOEBE'S OLD MAN WAS A HEART SURGEON.
WHAT HAPPENED, GRANDDAD? SHE CATCH SIGHT OF YOUR DIRTY UNDERWEAR?
SOMETHING LIKE THAT. AND DON'T CALL ME GRANDDAD.
THIS ALL THERE IS?
AS LONG AS YOU DO THAT THING WITH THE *HAIR,* YOU'LL ONLY NEED A FEW DROPS.
THERE'S ENOUGH THERE TO MAKE A HERD OF ELEPHANTS LUST AFTER YOU.
I *TOLD* YOU.
I'M NOT LOOKING FOR LUST.

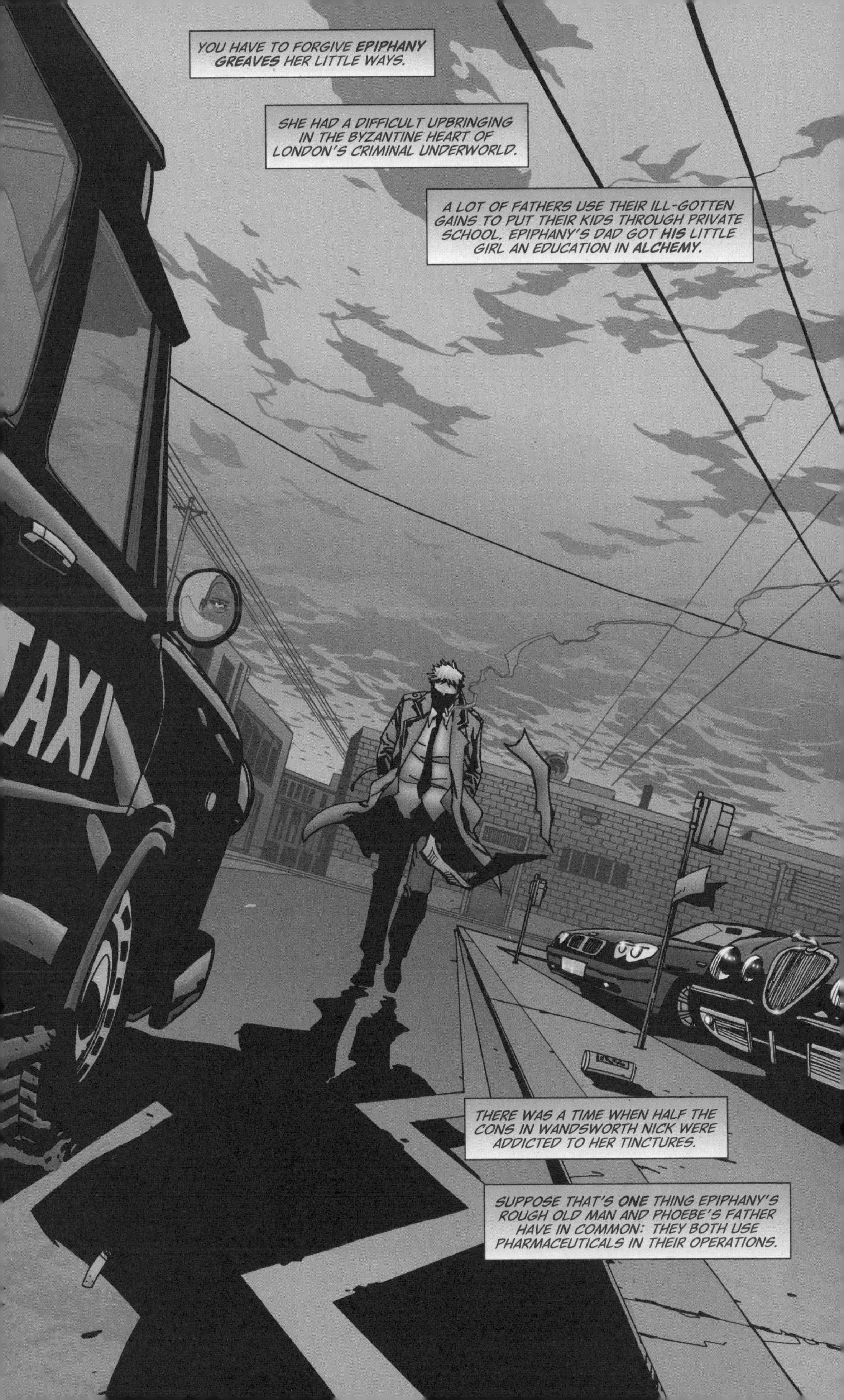
YOU HAVE TO FORGIVE EPIPHANY GREAVES HER LITTLE WAYS.
SHE HAD A DIFFICULT UPBRINGING IN THE BYZANTINE HEART OF LONDON'S CRIMINAL UNDERWORLD.
A LOT OF FATHERS USE THEIR ILL-GOTTEN GAINS TO PUT THEIR KIDS THROUGH PRIVATE SCHOOL. EPIPHANY'S DAD GOT HIS LITTLE GIRL AN EDUCATION IN ALCHEMY.
TAXI
THERE WAS A TIME WHEN HALF THE CONS IN WANDSWORTH NICK WERE ADDICTED TO HER TINCTURES.
SUPPOSE THAT'S ONE THING EPIPHANY'S ROUGH OLD MAN AND PHOEBE'S FATHER HAVE IN COMMON: THEY BOTH USE PHARMACEUTICALS IN THEIR OPERATIONS.

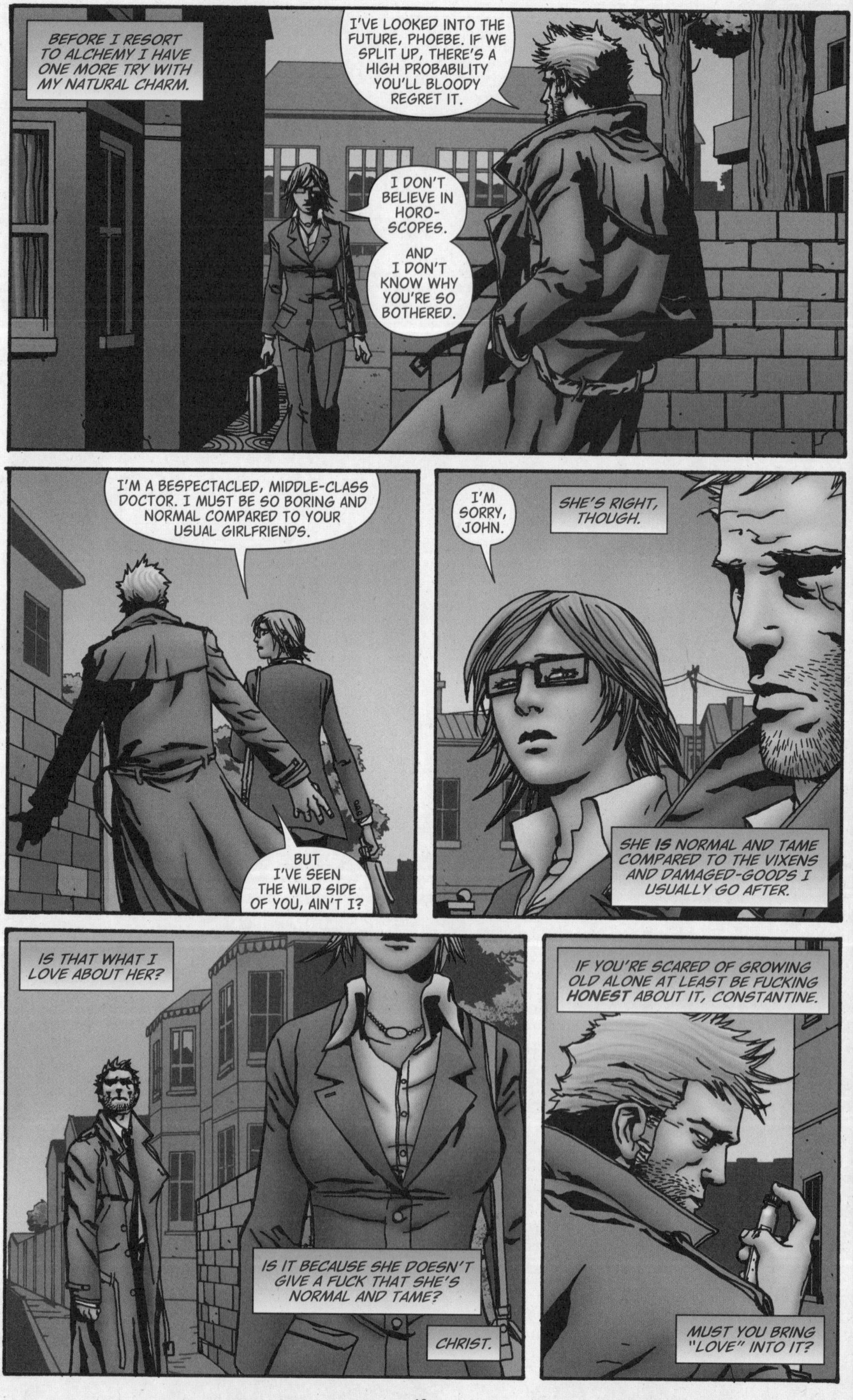
BEFORE I RESORT TO ALCHEMY I HAVE ONE MORE TRY WITH MY NATURAL CHARM.
I'VE LOOKED INTO THE FUTURE, PHOEBE. IF WE SPLIT UP, THERE'S A HIGH PROBABILITY YOU'LL BLOODY REGRET IT.
I DON'T BELIEVE IN HORO-SCOPES.
AND I DON'T KNOW WHY YOU'RE SO BOTHERED.
I'M A BESPECTACLED, MIDDLE-CLASS DOCTOR. I MUST BE SO BORING AND NORMAL COMPARED TO YOUR USUAL GIRLFRIENDS.
BUT I'VE SEEN THE WILD SIDE OF YOU, AIN'T I?
I'M SORRY, JOHN.
SHE'S RIGHT, THOUGH.
SHE IS NORMAL AND TAME COMPARED TO THE VIXENS AND DAMAGED-GOODS I USUALLY GO AFTER.
IS THAT WHAT I LOVE ABOUT HER?
IS IT BECAUSE SHE DOESN'T GIVE A FUCK THAT SHE'S NORMAL AND TAME?
CHRIST.
IF YOU'RE SCARED OF GROWING OLD ALONE AT LEAST BE FUCKING HONEST ABOUT IT, CONSTANTINE.
MUST YOU BRING "LOVE" INTO IT?

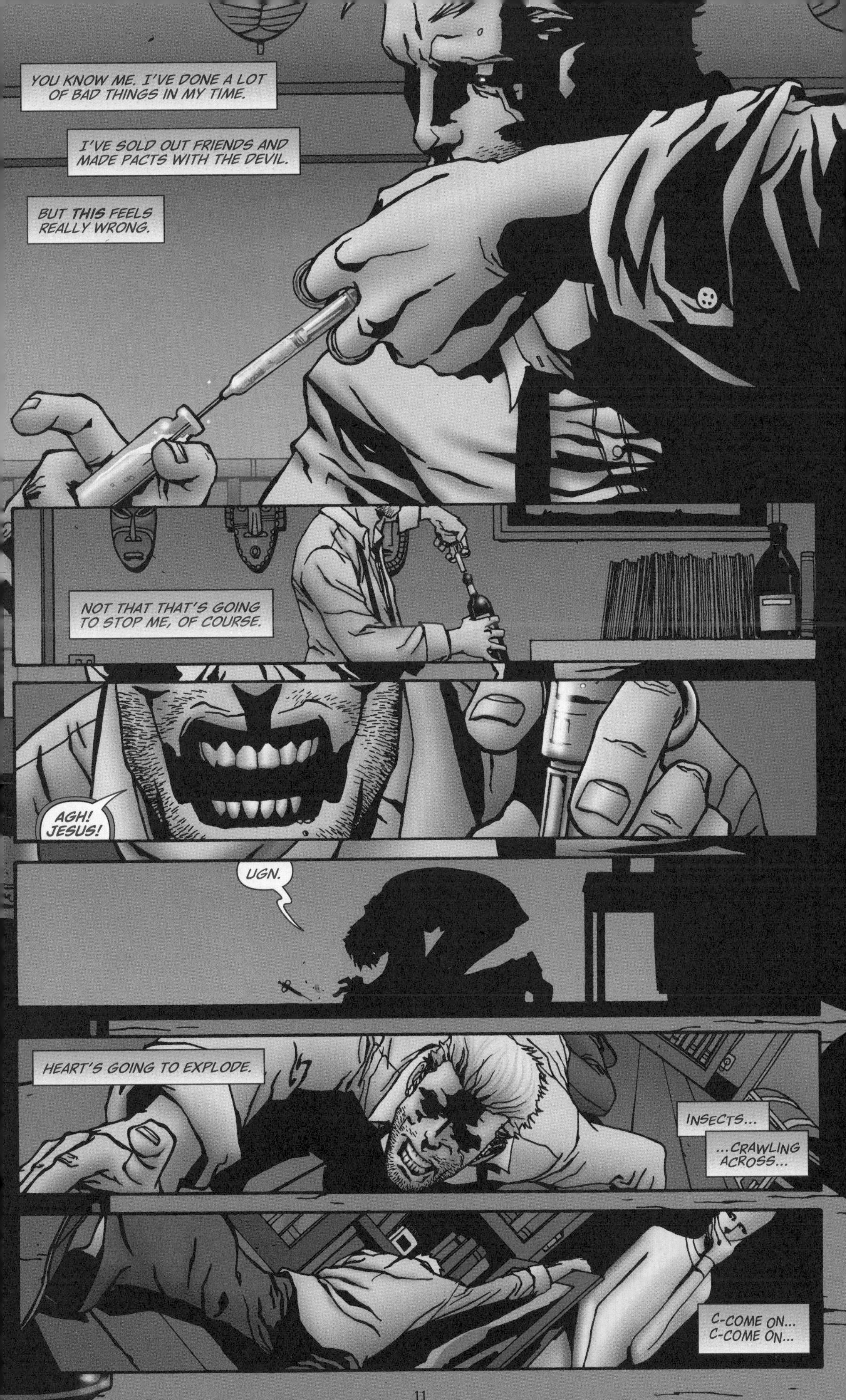
YOU KNOW ME. I'VE DONE A LOT OF BAD THINGS IN MY TIME.
I'VE SOLD OUT FRIENDS AND MADE PACTS WITH THE DEVIL.
BUT THIS FEELS REALLY WRONG.
NOT THAT THAT'S GOING TO STOP ME, OF COURSE.
AGH! JESUS!
UGN.
HEART'S GOING TO EXPLODE.
INSECTS...
...CRAWLING ACROSS...
C-COME ON... C-COME ON...

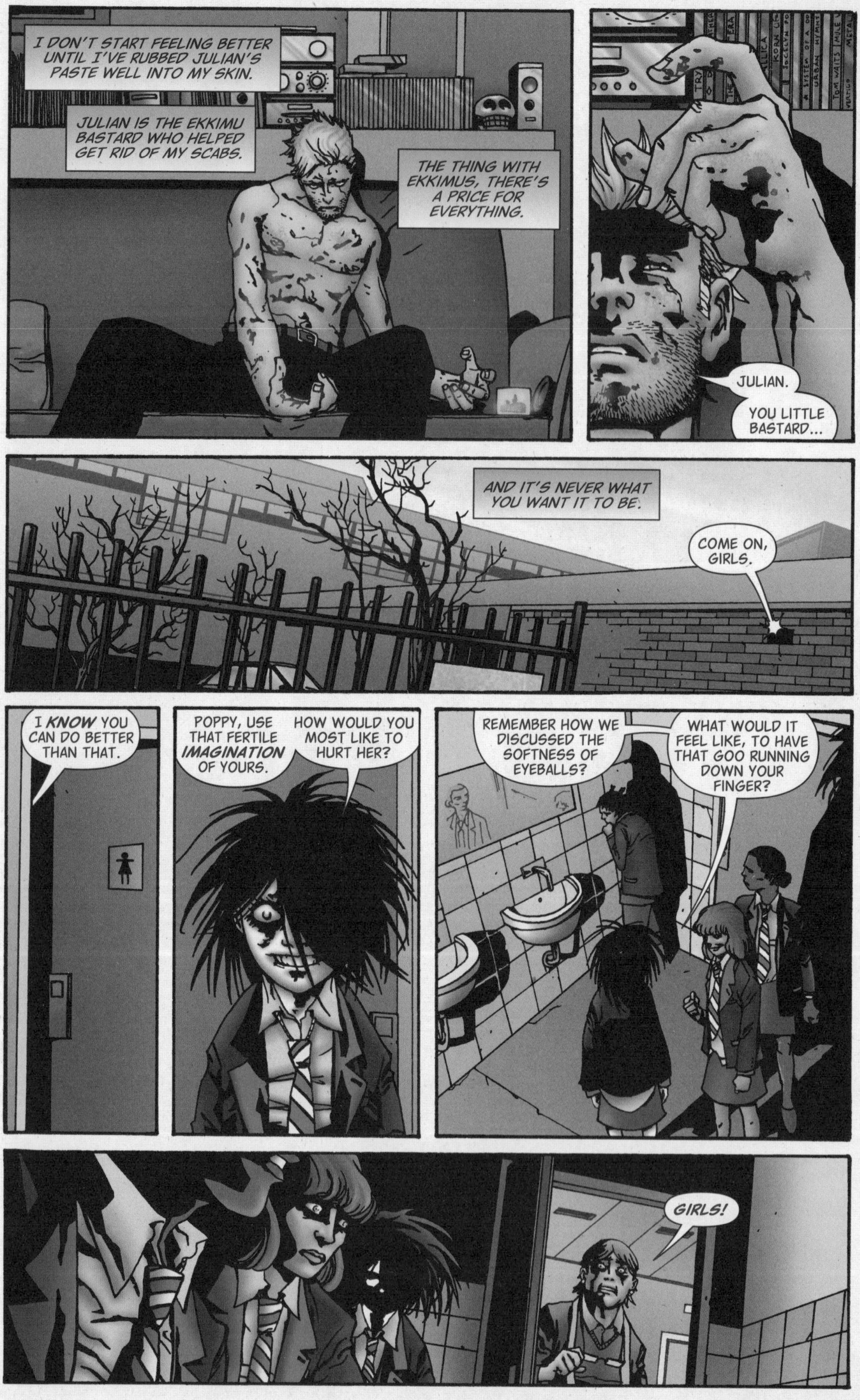
I DON'T START FEELING BETTER UNTIL I'VE RUBBED JULIAN'S PASTE WELL INTO MY SKIN.
JULIAN IS THE EKKIMU BASTARD WHO HELPED GET RID OF MY SCABS.
THE THING WITH EKKIMUS, THERE'S A PRICE FOR EVERYTHING.
JULIAN.
YOU LITTLE BASTARD...
AND IT'S NEVER WHAT YOU WANT IT TO BE.
COME ON, GIRLS.
I KNOW YOU CAN DO BETTER THAN THAT.
POPPY, USE THAT FERTILE IMAGINATION OF YOURS.
HOW WOULD YOU MOST LIKE TO HURT HER?
REMEMBER HOW WE DISCUSSED THE SOFTNESS OF EYEBALLS?
WHAT WOULD IT FEEL LIKE, TO HAVE THAT GOO RUNNING DOWN YOUR FINGER?
GIRLS!

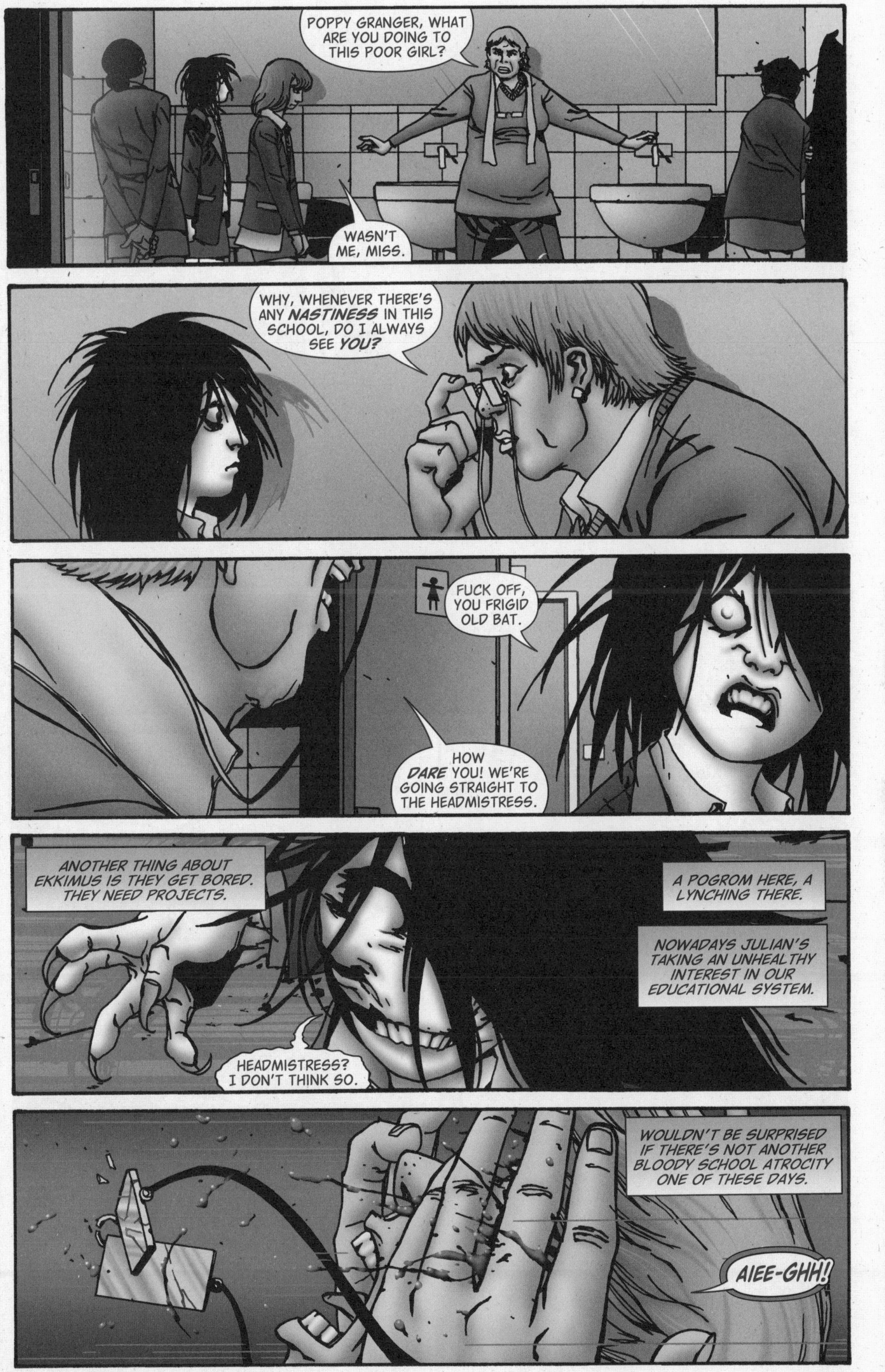
POPPY GRANGER, WHAT ARE YOU DOING TO THIS POOR GIRL?
WASN'T ME, MISS.
WHY, WHENEVER THERE'S ANY NASTINESS IN THIS SCHOOL, DO I ALWAYS SEE YOU?
FUCK OFF, YOU FRIGID OLD BAT.
HOW DARE YOU! WE'RE GOING STRAIGHT TO THE HEADMISTRESS.
ANOTHER THING ABOUT EKKIMUS IS THEY GET BORED. THEY NEED PROJECTS.
A POGROM HERE, A LYNCHING THERE.
NOWADAYS JULIAN'S TAKING AN UNHEALTHY INTEREST IN OUR EDUCATIONAL SYSTEM.
HEADMISTRESS? I DON'T THINK SO.
WOULDN'T BE SURPRISED IF THERE'S NOT ANOTHER BLOODY SCHOOL ATROCITY ONE OF THESE DAYS.
AIEE-GHH!

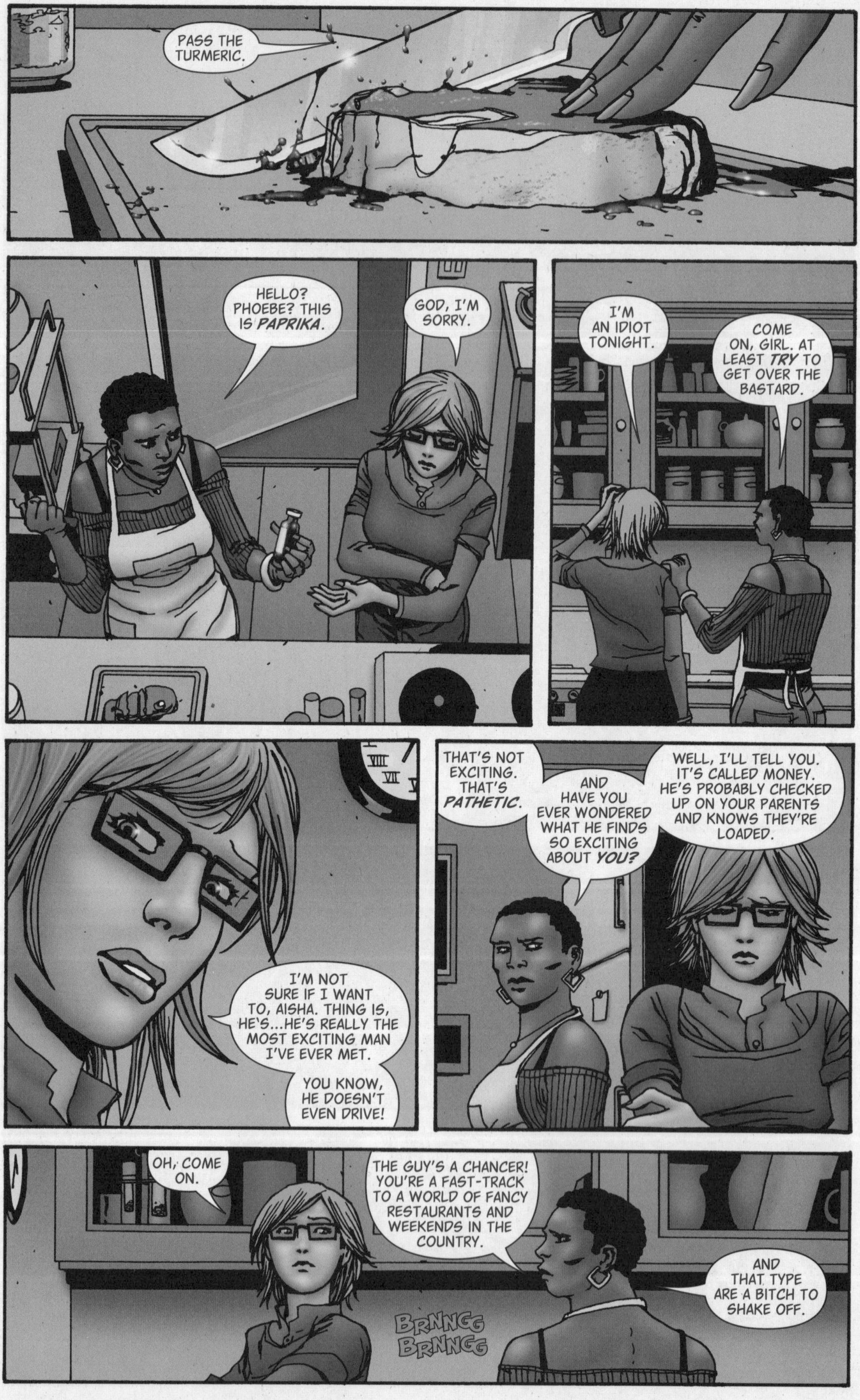
PASS THE TURMERIC.
HELLO? PHOEBE? THIS IS PAPRIKA.
GOD, I'M SORRY.
I'M AN IDIOT TONIGHT.
COME ON, GIRL. AT LEAST TRY TO GET OVER THE BASTARD.
I'M NOT SURE IF I WANT TO, AISHA. THING IS, HE'S...HE'S REALLY THE MOST EXCITING MAN I'VE EVER MET.
YOU KNOW, HE DOESN'T EVEN DRIVE!
THAT'S NOT EXCITING. THAT'S PATHETIC.
AND HAVE YOU EVER WONDERED WHAT HE FINDS SO EXCITING ABOUT YOU?
WELL, I'LL TELL YOU. IT'S CALLED MONEY. HE'S PROBABLY CHECKED UP ON YOUR PARENTS AND KNOWS THEY'RE LOADED.
OH, COME ON.
THE GUY'S A CHANCER! YOU'RE A FAST-TRACK TO A WORLD OF FANCY RESTAURANTS AND WEEKENDS IN THE COUNTRY.
AND THAT TYPE ARE A BITCH TO SHAKE OFF.
BRNNGG BRNNGG

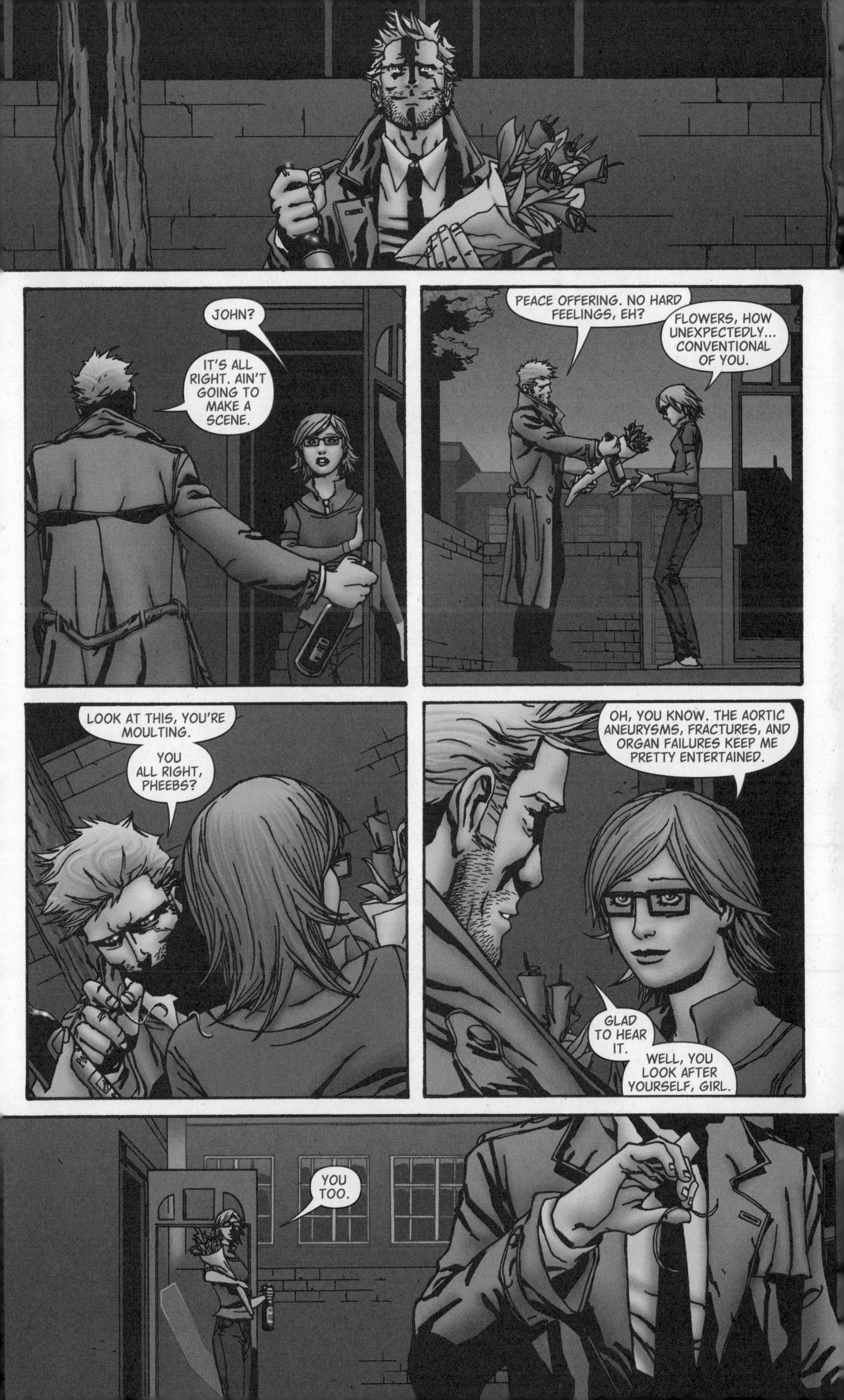
JOHN?
IT'S ALL RIGHT. AIN'T GOING TO MAKE A SCENE.
PEACE OFFERING. NO HARD FEELINGS, EH?
FLOWERS, HOW UNEXPECTEDLY... CONVENTIONAL OF YOU.
LOOK AT THIS, YOU'RE MOULTING.
YOU ALL RIGHT, PHEEBS?
OH, YOU KNOW. THE AORTIC ANEURYSMS, FRACTURES, AND ORGAN FAILURES KEEP ME PRETTY ENTERTAINED.
GLAD TO HEAR IT.
WELL, YOU LOOK AFTER YOURSELF, GIRL.
YOU TOO.

ONE HAIR, EPIPHANY SAID.

ONE PRECIOUS HAIR.

MAGIC.

PROBLEM.

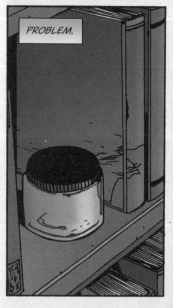

BIG FUCKING PROBLEM.

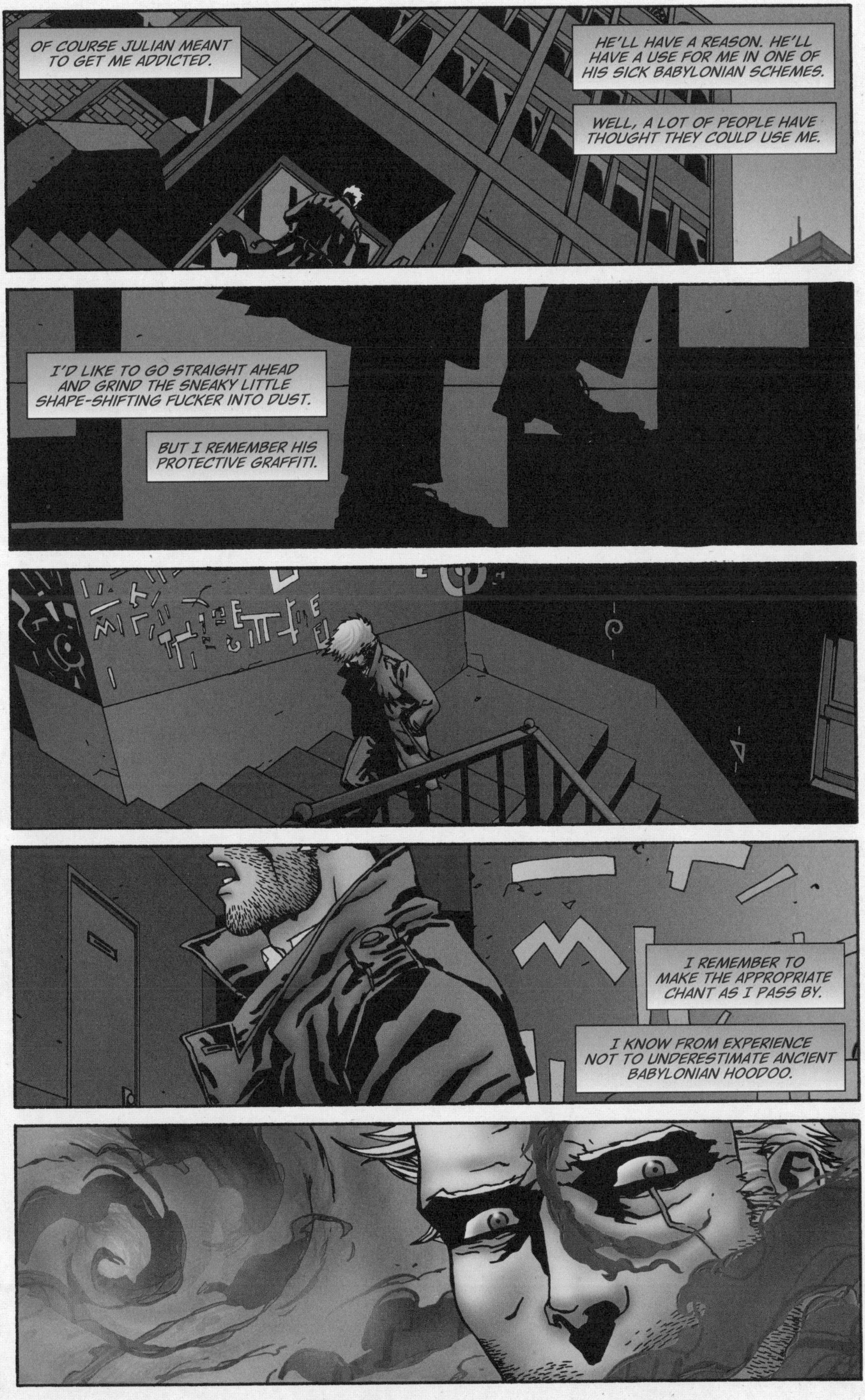
OF COURSE JULIAN MEANT TO GET ME ADDICTED.
HE'LL HAVE A REASON. HE'LL HAVE A USE FOR ME IN ONE OF HIS SICK BABYLONIAN SCHEMES.
WELL, A LOT OF PEOPLE HAVE THOUGHT THEY COULD USE ME.
I'D LIKE TO GO STRAIGHT AHEAD AND GRIND THE SNEAKY LITTLE SHAPE-SHIFTING FUCKER INTO DUST.
BUT I REMEMBER HIS PROTECTIVE GRAFFITI.
I REMEMBER TO MAKE THE APPROPRIATE CHANT AS I PASS BY.
I KNOW FROM EXPERIENCE NOT TO UNDERESTIMATE ANCIENT BABYLONIAN HOODOO.

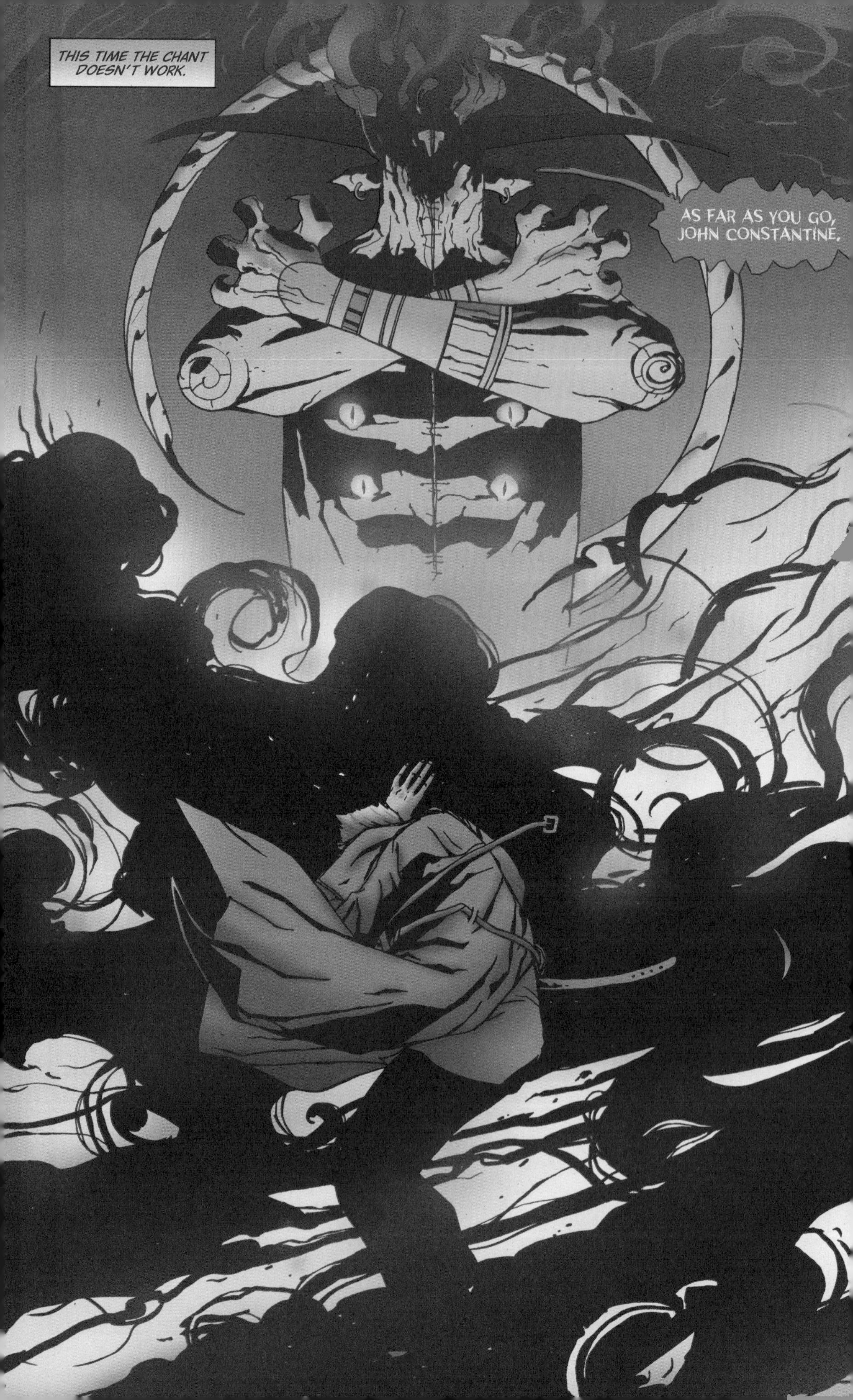
THIS TIME THE CHANT DOESN'T WORK.
AS FAR AS YOU GO, JOHN CONSTANTINE.

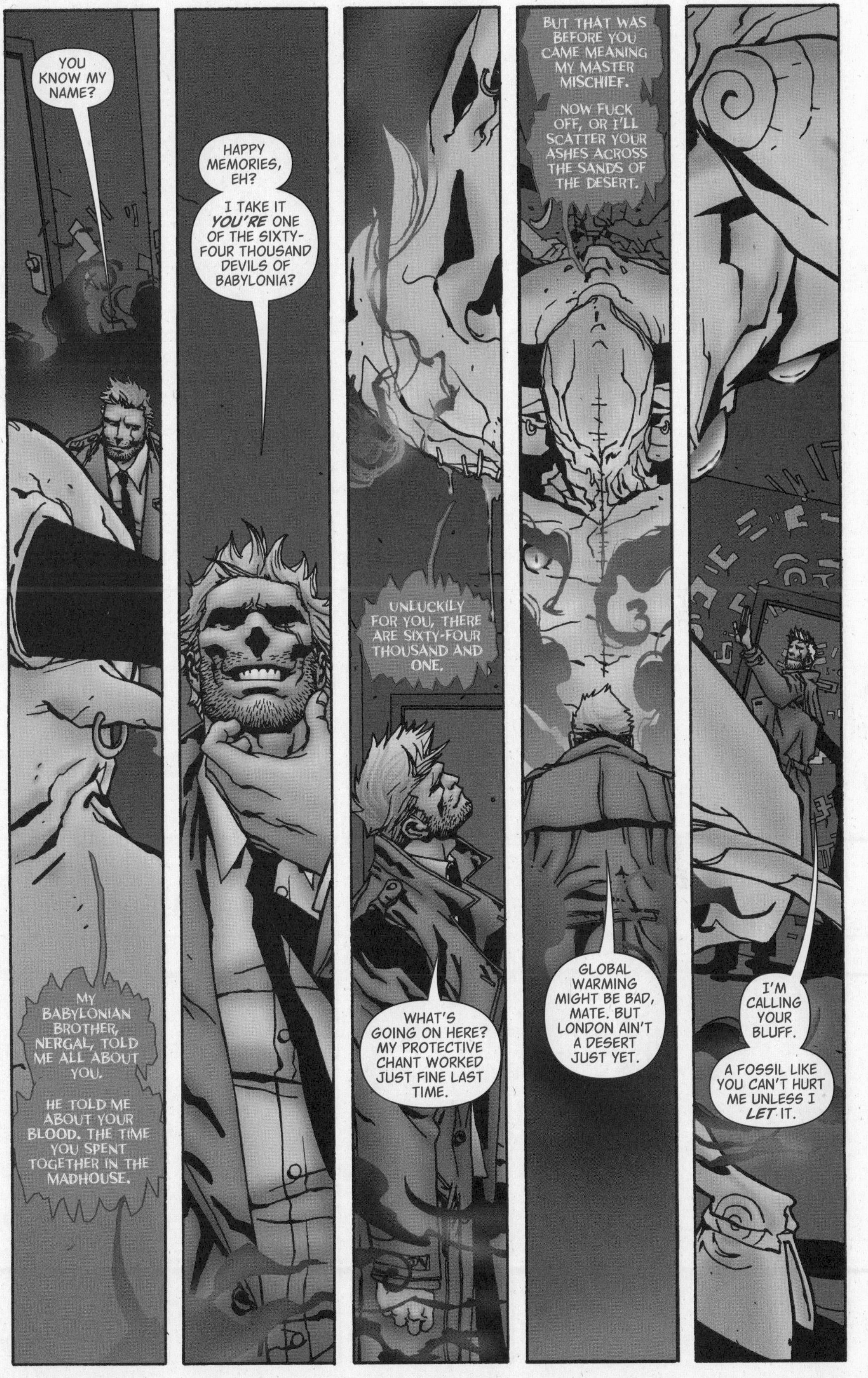
YOU KNOW MY NAME?
MY BABYLONIAN BROTHER, NERGAL, TOLD ME ALL ABOUT YOU.
HE TOLD ME ABOUT YOUR BLOOD. THE TIME YOU SPENT TOGETHER IN THE MADHOUSE.
HAPPY MEMORIES, EH?
I TAKE IT *YOU'RE* ONE OF THE SIXTY-FOUR THOUSAND DEVILS OF BABYLONIA?
UNLUCKILY FOR YOU, THERE ARE SIXTY-FOUR THOUSAND AND ONE.
WHAT'S GOING ON HERE? MY PROTECTIVE CHANT WORKED JUST FINE LAST TIME.
BUT THAT WAS BEFORE YOU CAME MEANING MY MASTER MISCHIEF.
NOW FUCK OFF, OR I'LL SCATTER YOUR ASHES ACROSS THE SANDS OF THE DESERT.
GLOBAL WARMING MIGHT BE BAD, MATE. BUT LONDON AIN'T A DESERT JUST YET.
I'M CALLING YOUR BLUFF.
A FOSSIL LIKE YOU CAN'T HURT ME UNLESS I *LET* IT.

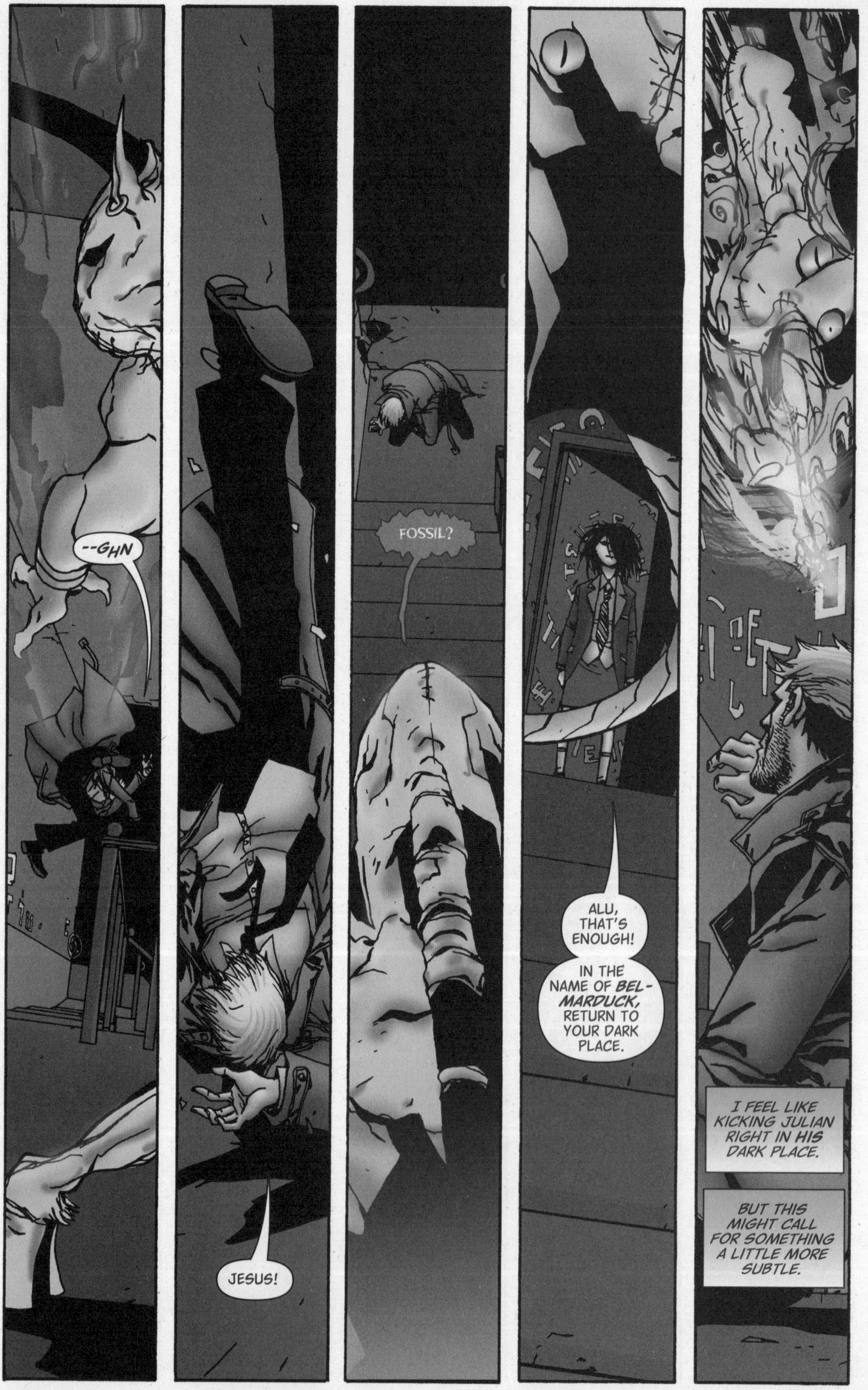
--GHN
JESUS!
FOSSIL?
ALU, THAT'S ENOUGH!
IN THE NAME OF BEL-MARDUCK, RETURN TO YOUR DARK PLACE.
I FEEL LIKE KICKING JULIAN RIGHT IN HIS DARK PLACE.
BUT THIS MIGHT CALL FOR SOMETHING A LITTLE MORE SUBTLE.

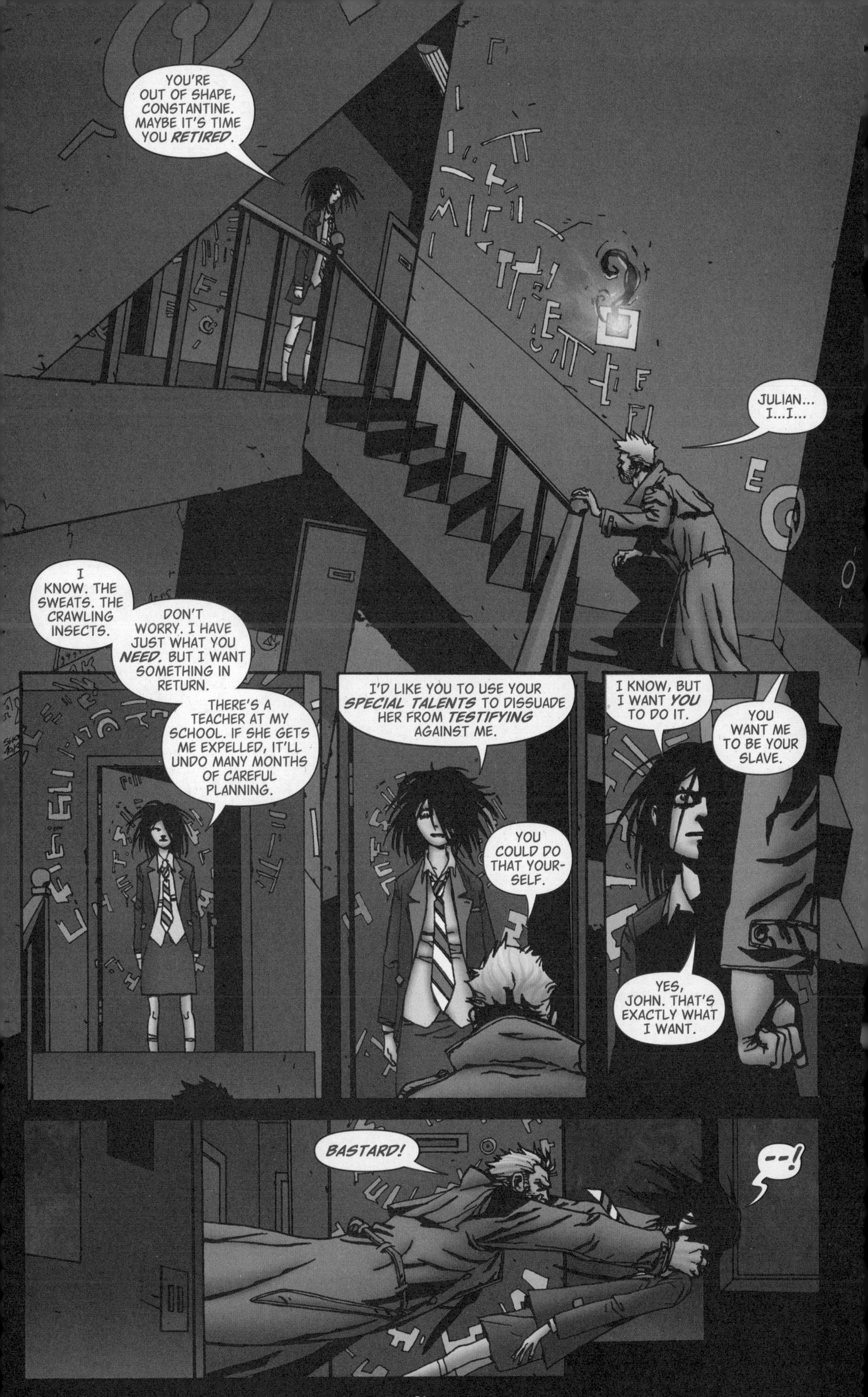
YOU'RE OUT OF SHAPE, CONSTANTINE. MAYBE IT'S TIME YOU RETIRED.
JULIAN... I...I...
I KNOW. THE SWEATS. THE CRAWLING INSECTS.
DON'T WORRY. I HAVE JUST WHAT YOU NEED. BUT I WANT SOMETHING IN RETURN.
THERE'S A TEACHER AT MY SCHOOL. IF SHE GETS ME EXPELLED, IT'LL UNDO MANY MONTHS OF CAREFUL PLANNING.
I'D LIKE YOU TO USE YOUR SPECIAL TALENTS TO DISSUADE HER FROM TESTIFYING AGAINST ME.
YOU COULD DO THAT YOURSELF.
I KNOW, BUT I WANT YOU TO DO IT.
YOU WANT ME TO BE YOUR SLAVE.
YES, JOHN. THAT'S EXACTLY WHAT I WANT.
BASTARD!
--!

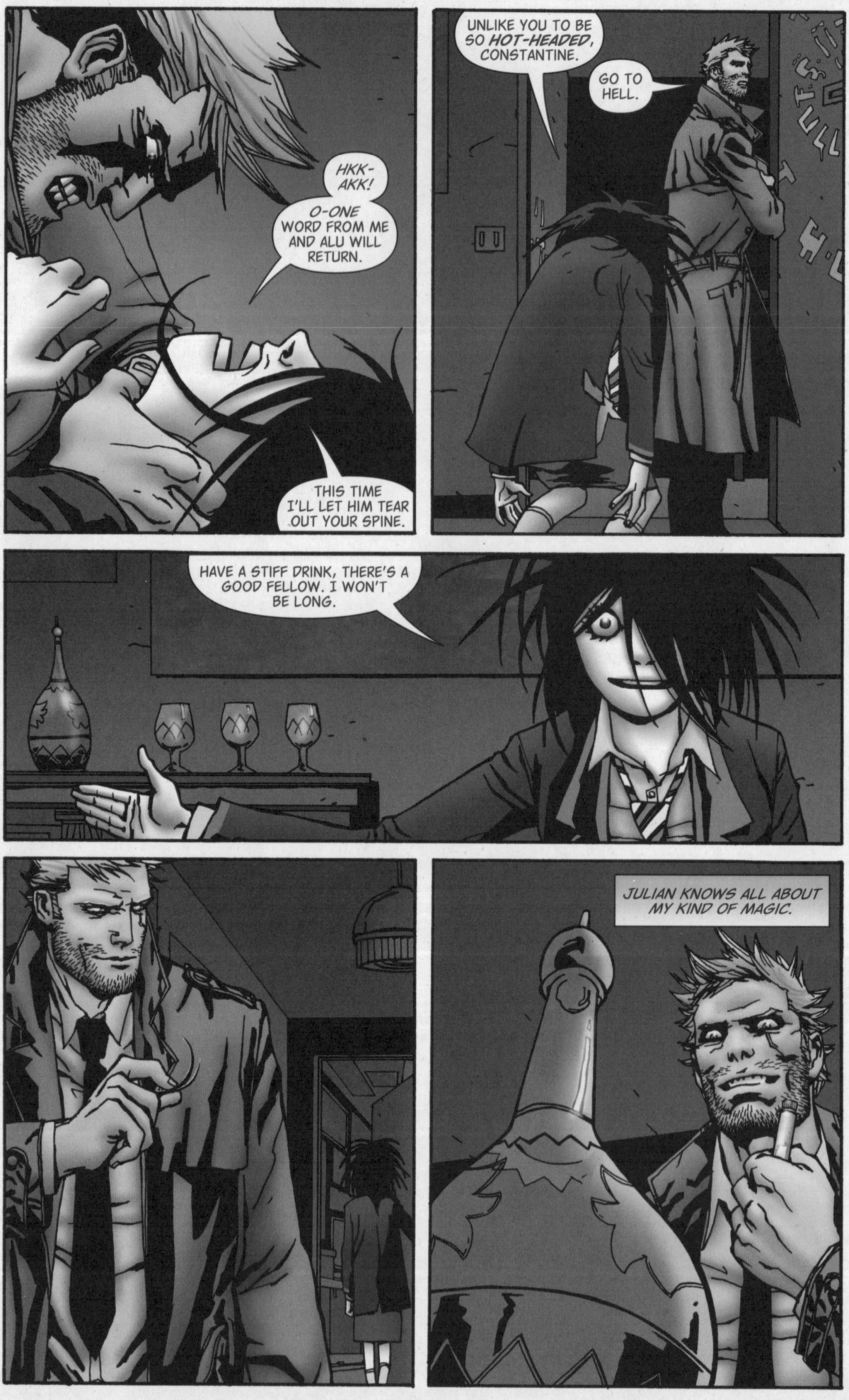
HKK-AKK!
O-ONE WORD FROM ME AND ALU WILL RETURN.
THIS TIME I'LL LET HIM TEAR OUT YOUR SPINE.
UNLIKE YOU TO BE SO *HOT-HEADED*, CONSTANTINE.
GO TO HELL.
HAVE A STIFF DRINK, THERE'S A GOOD FELLOW. I WON'T BE LONG.
JULIAN KNOWS ALL ABOUT MY KIND OF MAGIC.

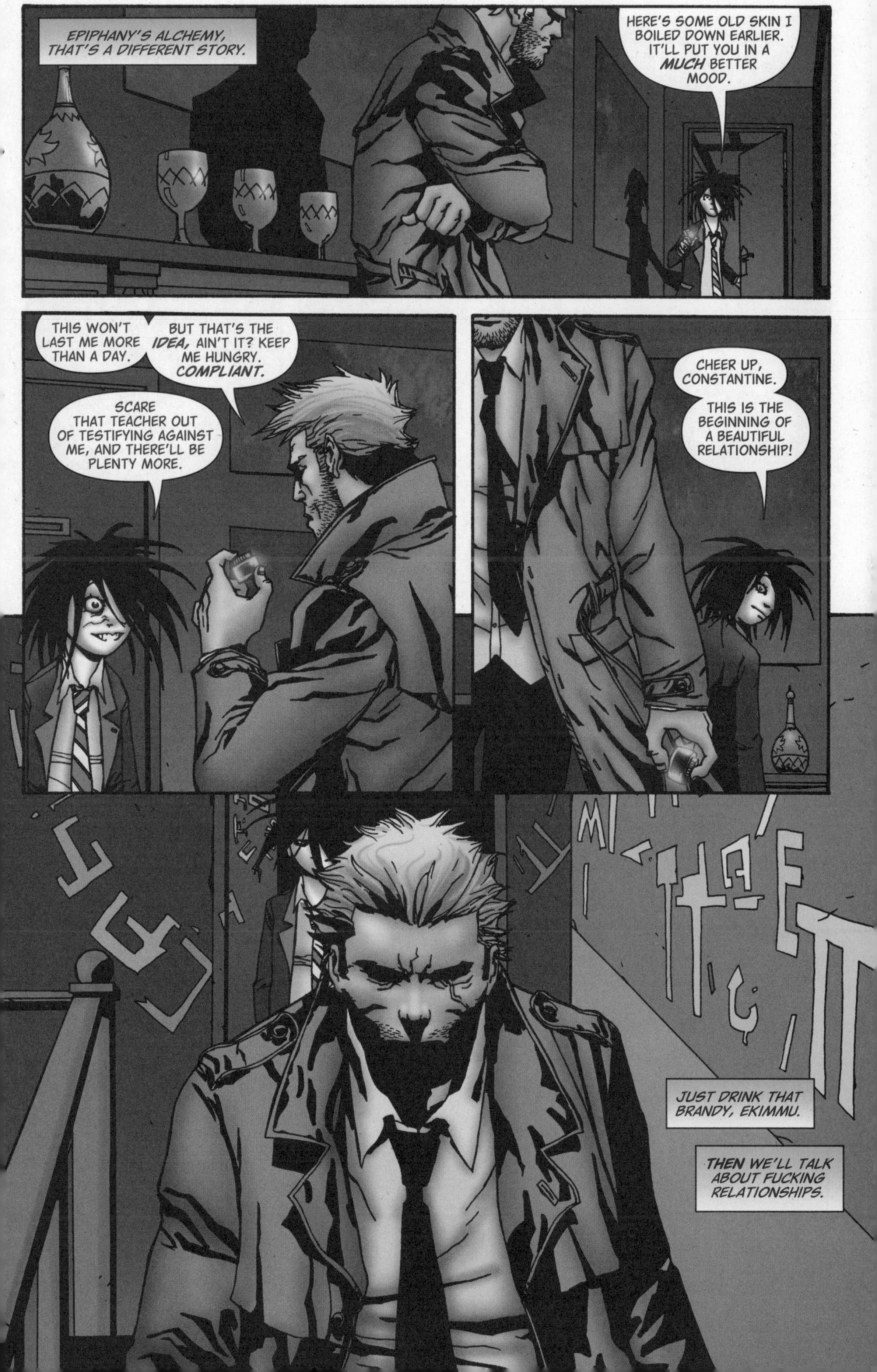
EPIPHANY'S ALCHEMY, THAT'S A DIFFERENT STORY.
HERE'S SOME OLD SKIN I BOILED DOWN EARLIER. IT'LL PUT YOU IN A MUCH BETTER MOOD.
THIS WON'T LAST ME MORE THAN A DAY.
BUT THAT'S THE IDEA, AIN'T IT? KEEP ME HUNGRY. COMPLIANT.
SCARE THAT TEACHER OUT OF TESTIFYING AGAINST ME, AND THERE'LL BE PLENTY MORE.
CHEER UP, CONSTANTINE.
THIS IS THE BEGINNING OF A BEAUTIFUL RELATIONSHIP!
JUST DRINK THAT BRANDY, EKIMMU.
THEN WE'LL TALK ABOUT FUCKING RELATIONSHIPS.

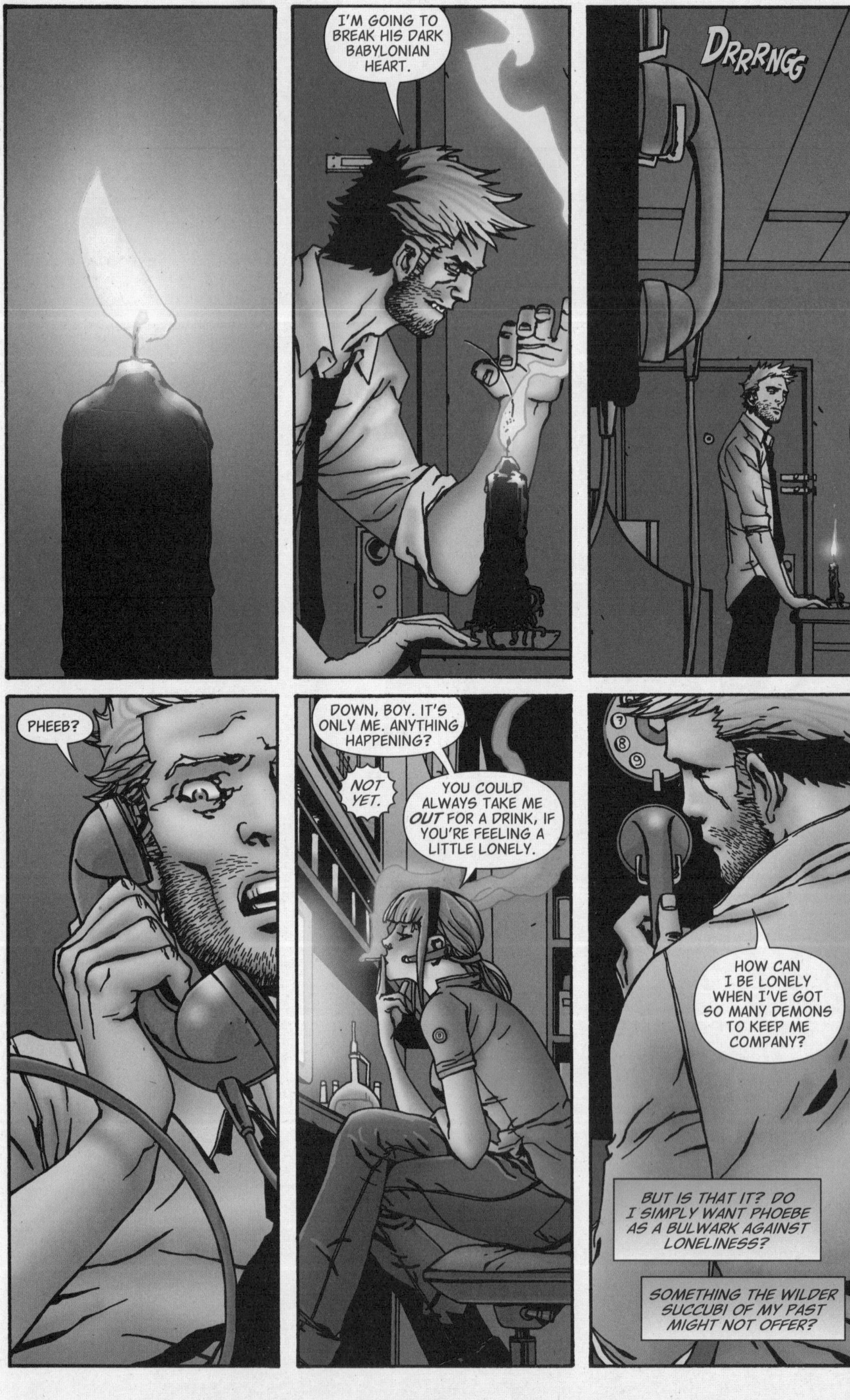
I'M GOING TO BREAK HIS DARK BABYLONIAN HEART.
DRRRNGG
PHEEB?
DOWN, BOY. IT'S ONLY ME. ANYTHING HAPPENING?
NOT YET.
YOU COULD ALWAYS TAKE ME OUT FOR A DRINK, IF YOU'RE FEELING A LITTLE LONELY.
HOW CAN I BE LONELY WHEN I'VE GOT SO MANY DEMONS TO KEEP ME COMPANY?
BUT IS THAT IT? DO I SIMPLY WANT PHOEBE AS A BULWARK AGAINST LONELINESS?
SOMETHING THE WILDER SUCCUBI OF MY PAST MIGHT NOT OFFER?

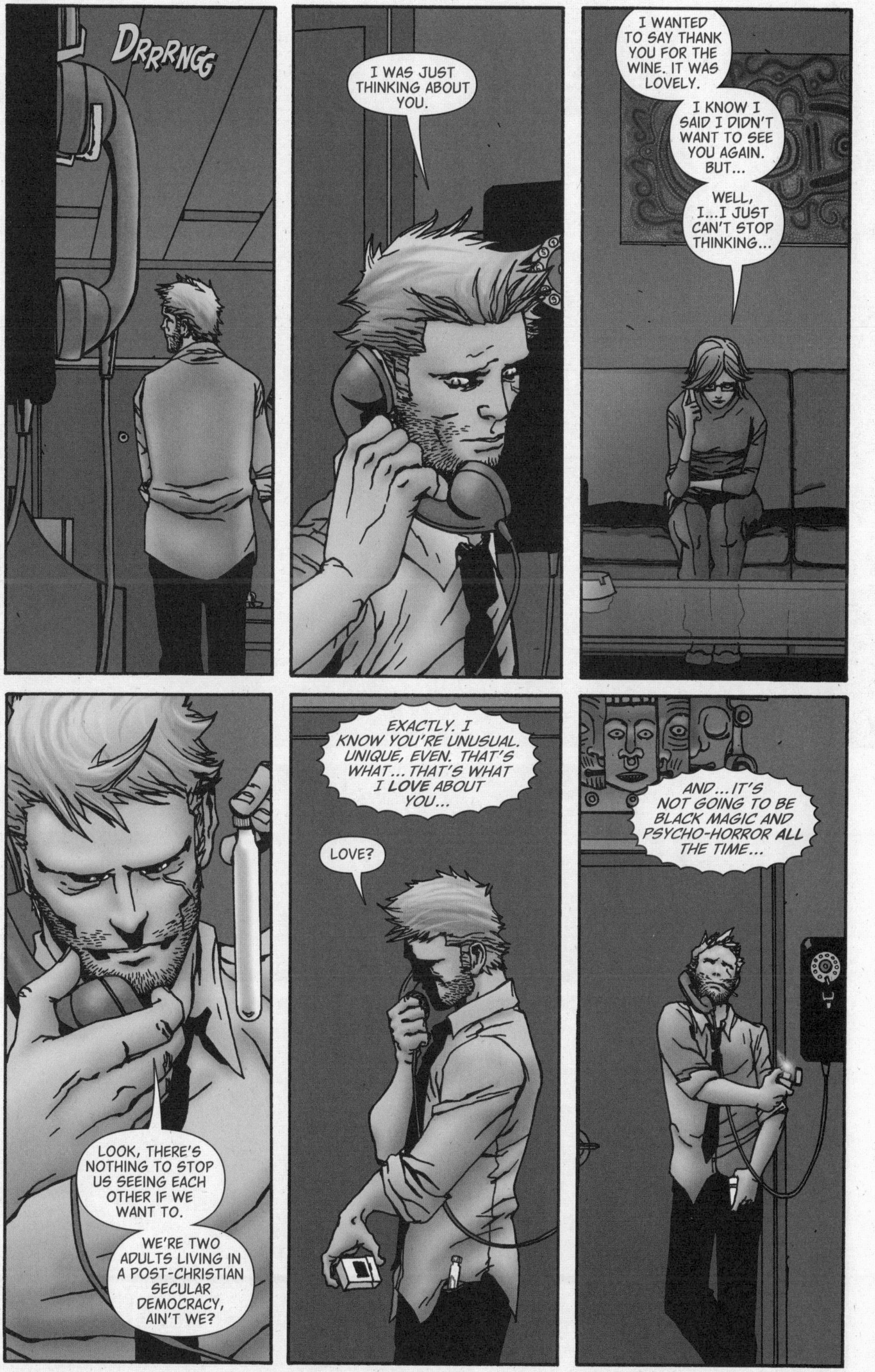
DRRRNGG
I WAS JUST THINKING ABOUT YOU.
I WANTED TO SAY THANK YOU FOR THE WINE. IT WAS LOVELY.
I KNOW I SAID I DIDN'T WANT TO SEE YOU AGAIN. BUT...
WELL, I...I JUST CAN'T STOP THINKING...
LOOK, THERE'S NOTHING TO STOP US SEEING EACH OTHER IF WE WANT TO.
WE'RE TWO ADULTS LIVING IN A POST-CHRISTIAN SECULAR DEMOCRACY, AIN'T WE?
EXACTLY. I KNOW YOU'RE UNUSUAL. UNIQUE, EVEN. THAT'S WHAT... THAT'S WHAT I LOVE ABOUT YOU...
LOVE?
AND... IT'S NOT GOING TO BE BLACK MAGIC AND PSYCHO-HORROR ALL THE TIME...

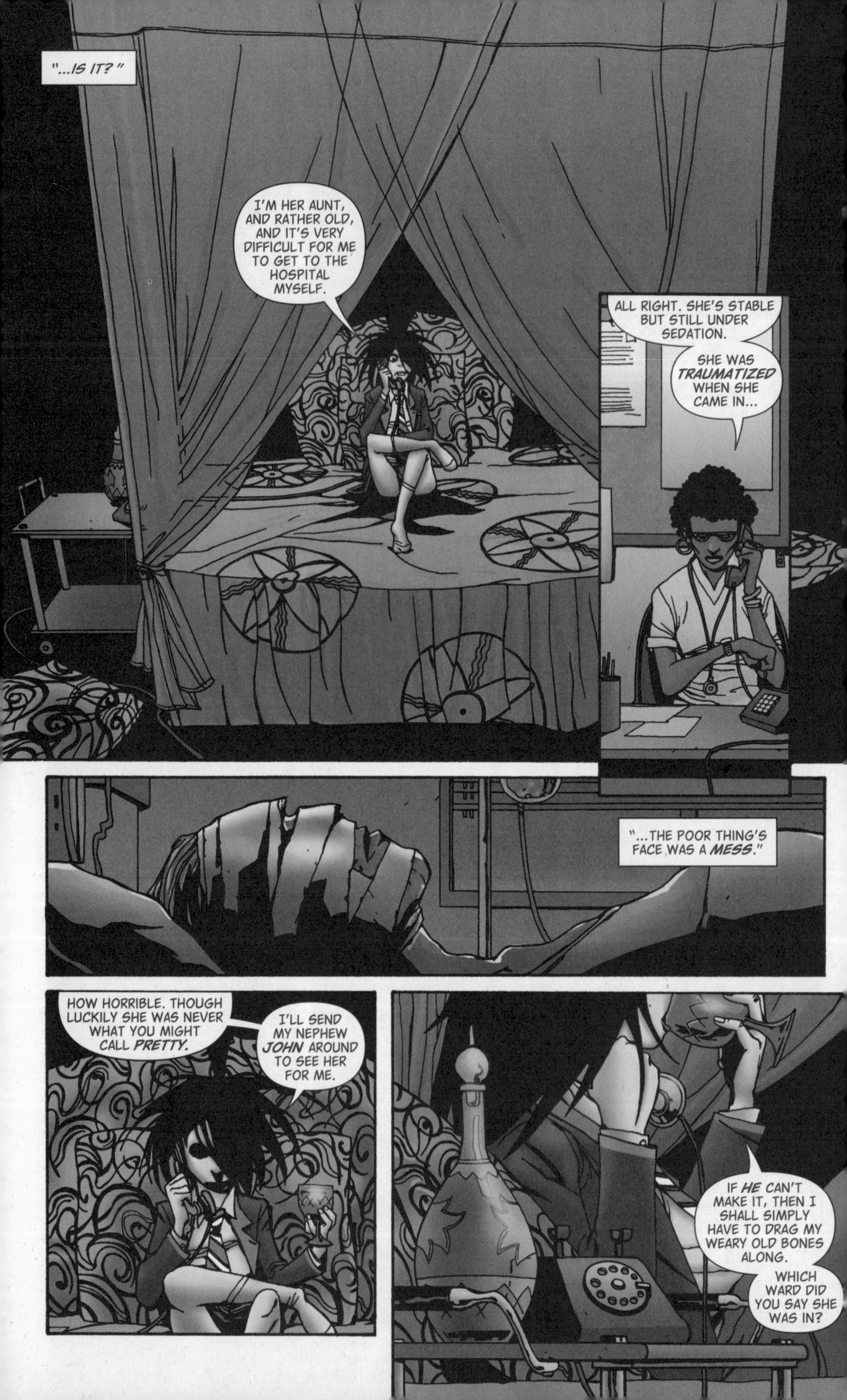
"...IS IT?"
I'M HER AUNT, AND RATHER OLD, AND IT'S VERY DIFFICULT FOR ME TO GET TO THE HOSPITAL MYSELF.
ALL RIGHT. SHE'S STABLE BUT STILL UNDER SEDATION.
SHE WAS TRAUMATIZED WHEN SHE CAME IN...
"...THE POOR THING'S FACE WAS A MESS."
HOW HORRIBLE. THOUGH LUCKILY SHE WAS NEVER WHAT YOU MIGHT CALL PRETTY.
I'LL SEND MY NEPHEW JOHN AROUND TO SEE HER FOR ME.
IF HE CAN'T MAKE IT, THEN I SHALL SIMPLY HAVE TO DRAG MY WEARY OLD BONES ALONG.
WHICH WARD DID YOU SAY SHE WAS IN?

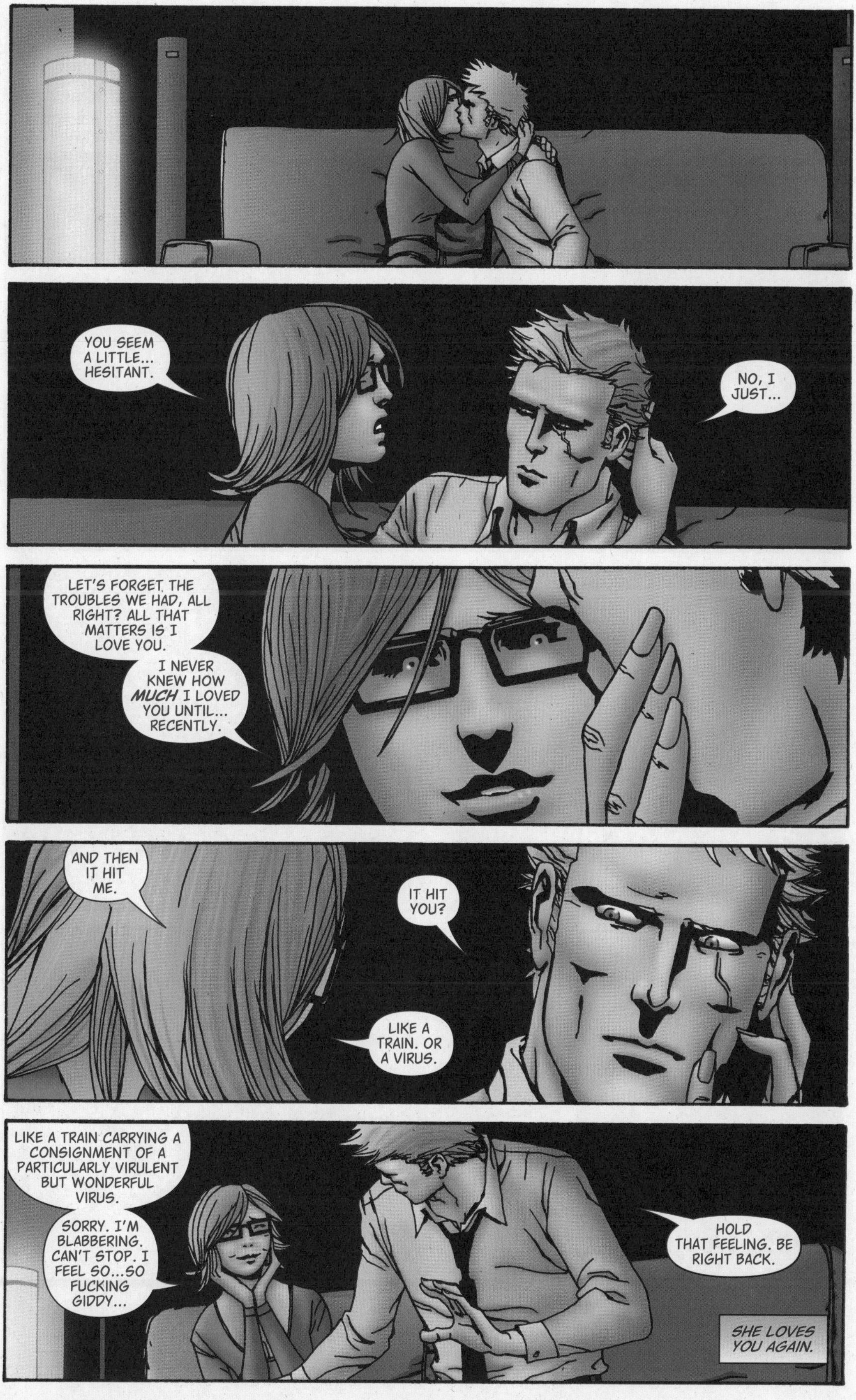
YOU SEEM A LITTLE... HESITANT.
NO, I JUST...
LET'S FORGET THE TROUBLES WE HAD, ALL RIGHT? ALL THAT MATTERS IS I LOVE YOU.
I NEVER KNEW HOW *MUCH* I LOVED YOU UNTIL... RECENTLY.
AND THEN IT HIT ME.
IT HIT YOU?
LIKE A TRAIN. OR A VIRUS.
LIKE A TRAIN CARRYING A CONSIGNMENT OF A PARTICULARLY VIRULENT BUT WONDERFUL VIRUS.
SORRY. I'M BLABBERING. CAN'T STOP. I FEEL SO...SO FUCKING GIDDY...
HOLD THAT FEELING. BE RIGHT BACK.
SHE LOVES YOU AGAIN.

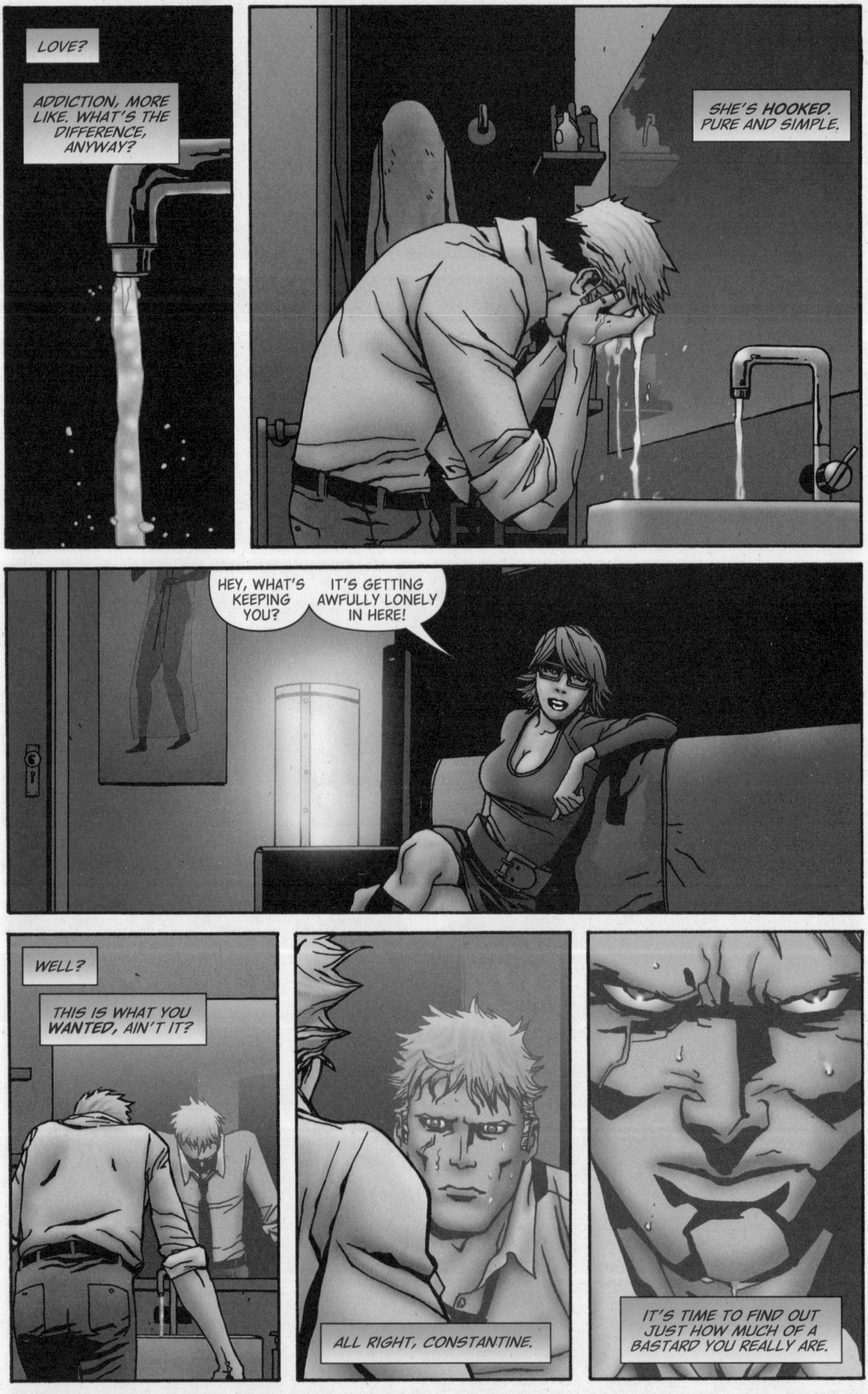
LOVE?
ADDICTION, MORE LIKE. WHAT'S THE DIFFERENCE, ANYWAY?
SHE'S HOOKED. PURE AND SIMPLE.
HEY, WHAT'S KEEPING YOU?
IT'S GETTING AWFULLY LONELY IN HERE!
WELL?
THIS IS WHAT YOU WANTED, AIN'T IT?
ALL RIGHT, CONSTANTINE.
IT'S TIME TO FIND OUT JUST HOW MUCH OF A BASTARD YOU REALLY ARE.

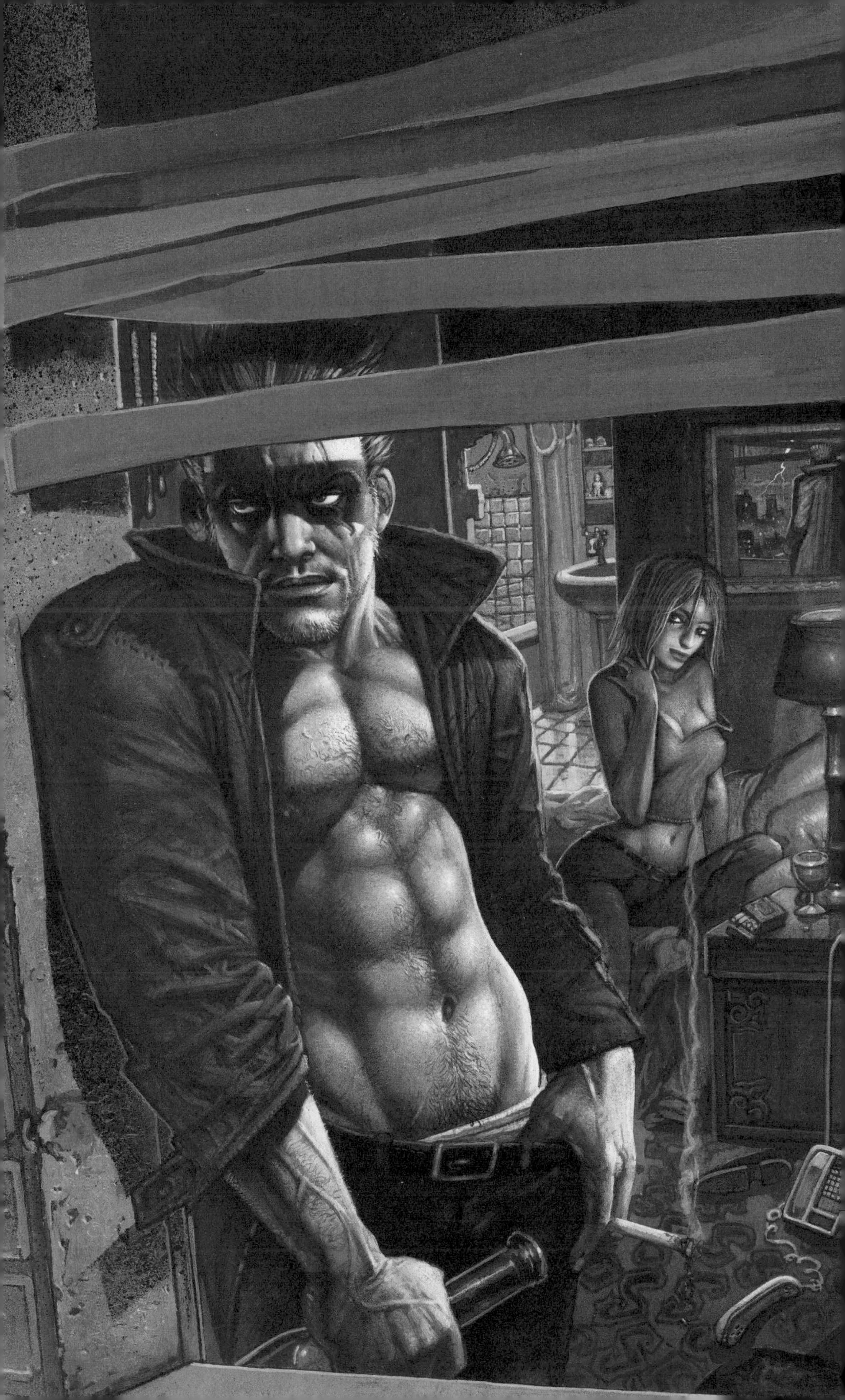

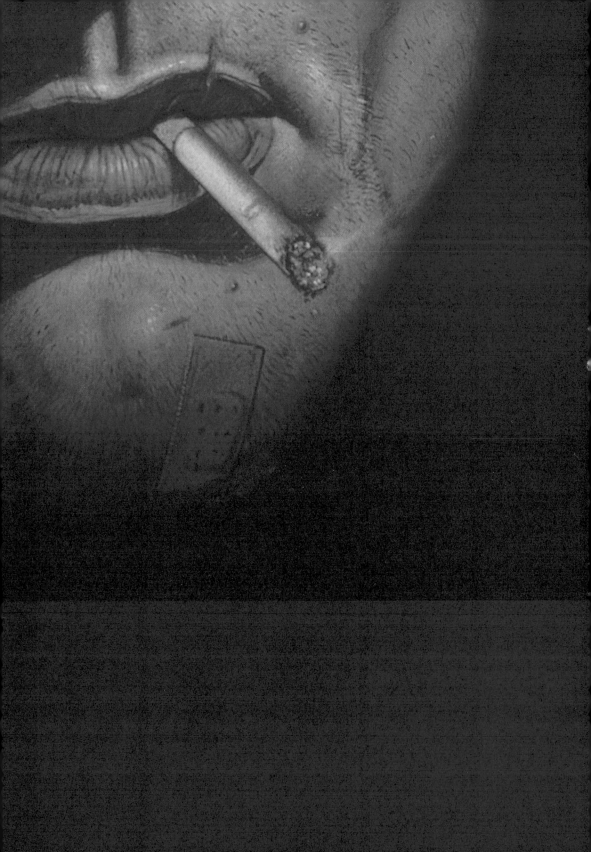

Hooked, Part Two
Temptation

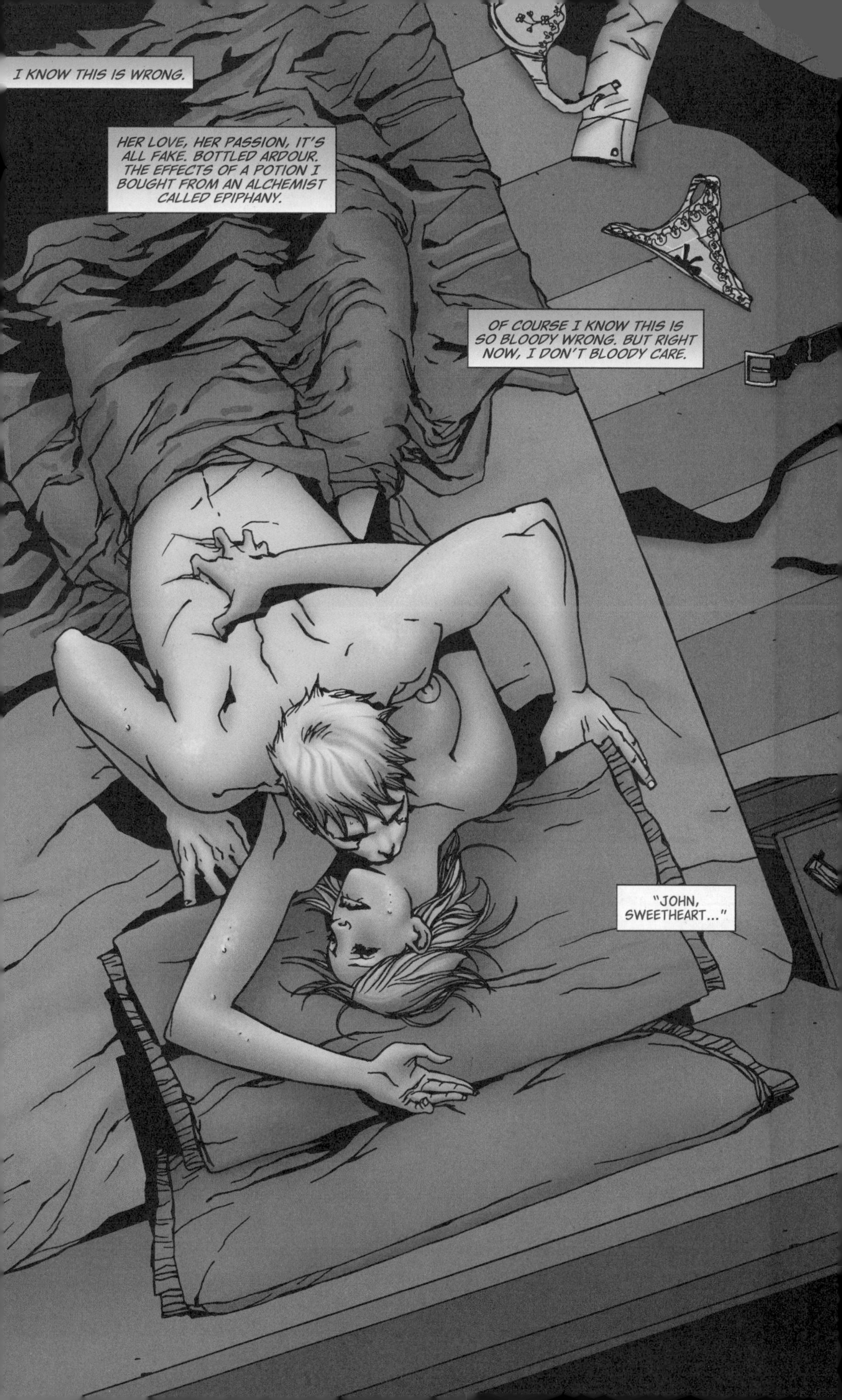
I KNOW THIS IS WRONG.
HER LOVE, HER PASSION, IT'S ALL FAKE. BOTTLED ARDOUR. THE EFFECTS OF A POTION I BOUGHT FROM AN ALCHEMIST CALLED EPIPHANY.
OF COURSE I KNOW THIS IS SO BLOODY WRONG. BUT RIGHT NOW, I DON'T BLOODY CARE.
"JOHN, SWEETHEART..."

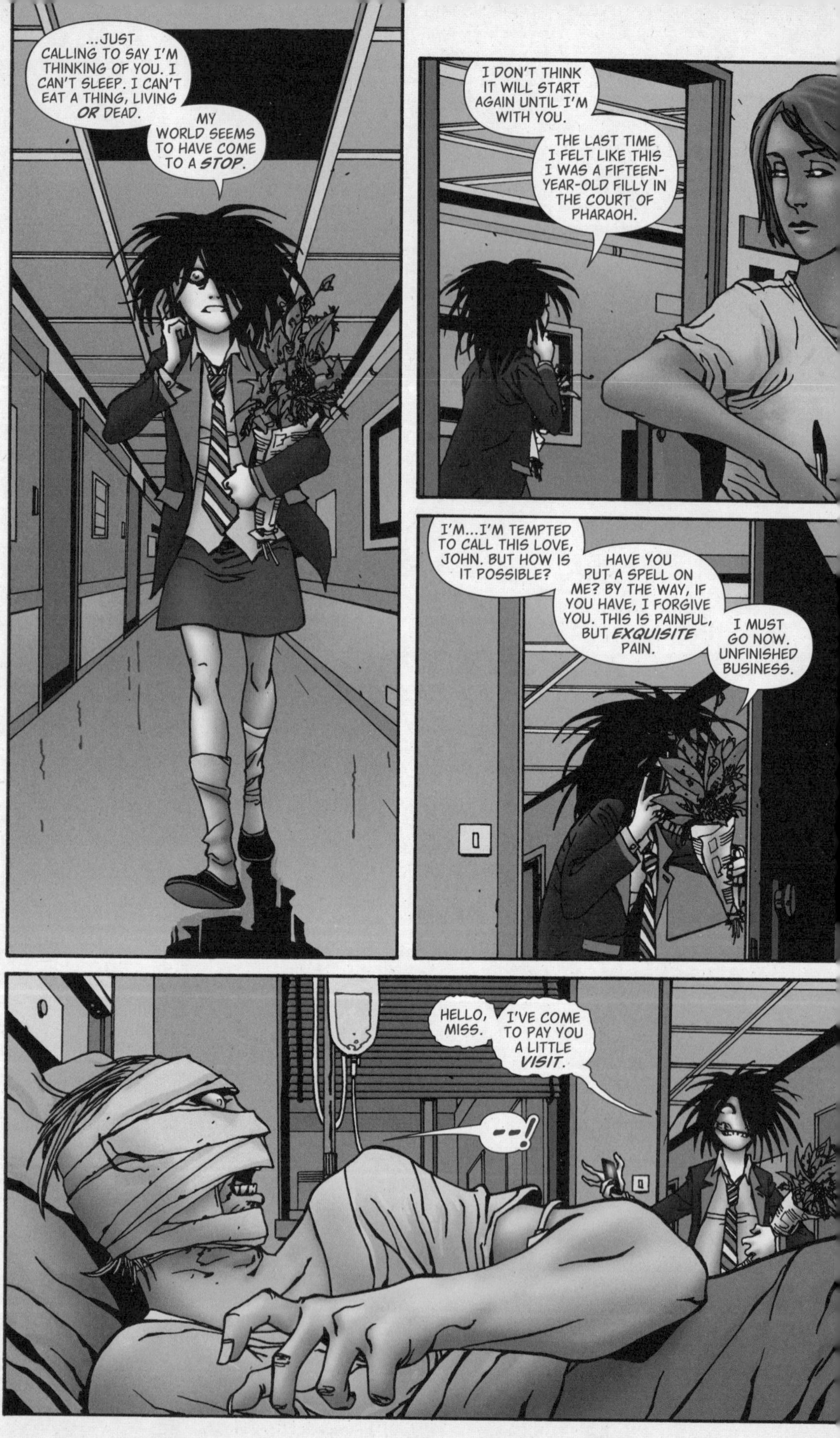

...JUST CALLING TO SAY I'M THINKING OF YOU. I CAN'T SLEEP. I CAN'T EAT A THING, LIVING OR DEAD.
MY WORLD SEEMS TO HAVE COME TO A STOP.
I DON'T THINK IT WILL START AGAIN UNTIL I'M WITH YOU.
THE LAST TIME I FELT LIKE THIS I WAS A FIFTEEN-YEAR-OLD FILLY IN THE COURT OF PHARAOH.
I'M...I'M TEMPTED TO CALL THIS LOVE, JOHN. BUT HOW IS IT POSSIBLE?
HAVE YOU PUT A SPELL ON ME? BY THE WAY, IF YOU HAVE, I FORGIVE YOU. THIS IS PAINFUL, BUT EXQUISITE PAIN.
I MUST GO NOW. UNFINISHED BUSINESS.
HELLO, MISS.
I'VE COME TO PAY YOU A LITTLE VISIT.
--!

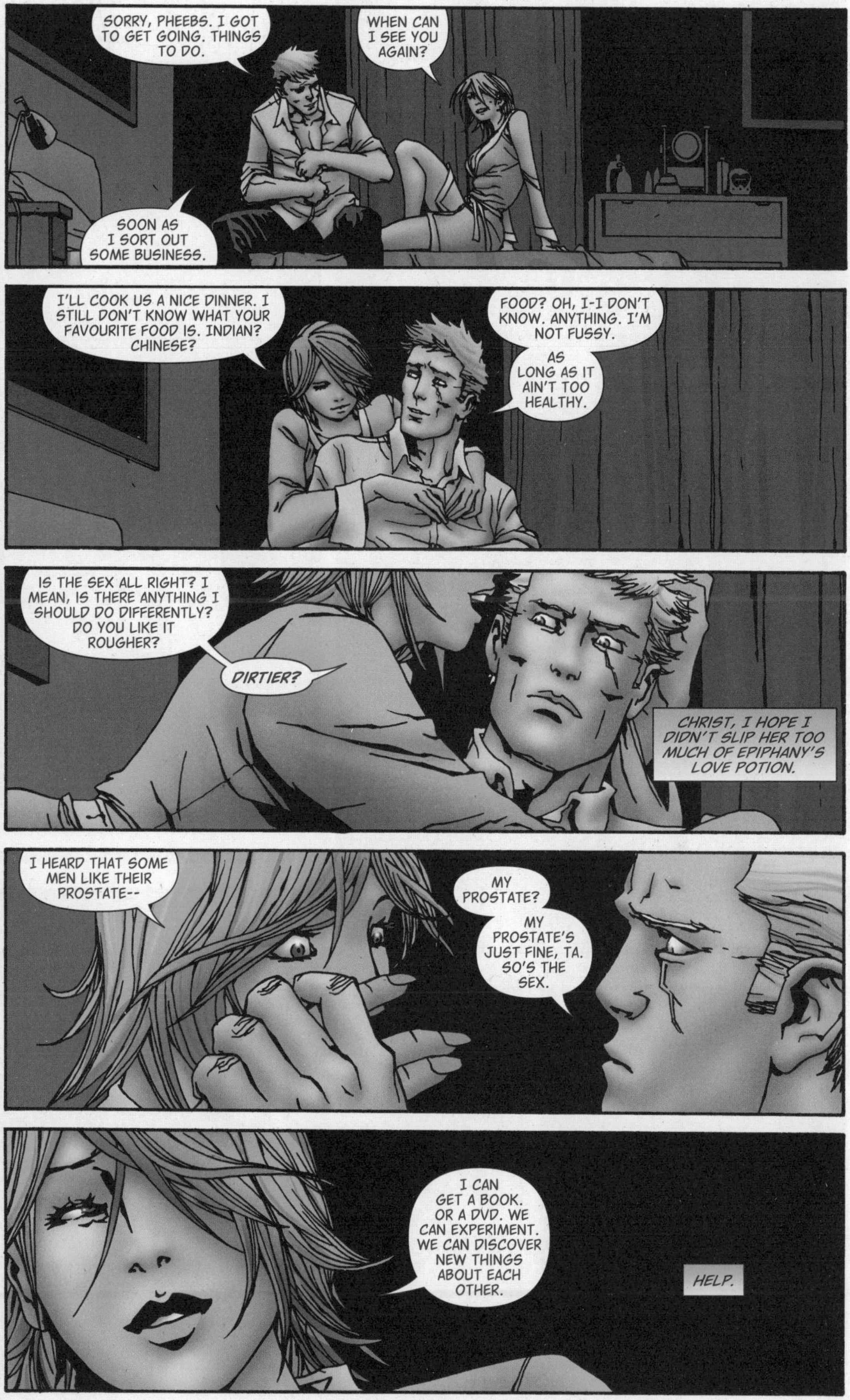
SORRY, PHEEBS. I GOT TO GET GOING. THINGS TO DO.
WHEN CAN I SEE YOU AGAIN?
SOON AS I SORT OUT SOME BUSINESS.
I'LL COOK US A NICE DINNER. I STILL DON'T KNOW WHAT YOUR FAVOURITE FOOD IS. INDIAN? CHINESE?
FOOD? OH, I-I DON'T KNOW. ANYTHING. I'M NOT FUSSY.
AS LONG AS IT AIN'T TOO HEALTHY.
IS THE SEX ALL RIGHT? I MEAN, IS THERE ANYTHING I SHOULD DO DIFFERENTLY? DO YOU LIKE IT ROUGHER?
DIRTIER?
CHRIST, I HOPE I DIDN'T SLIP HER TOO MUCH OF EPIPHANY'S LOVE POTION.
I HEARD THAT SOME MEN LIKE THEIR PROSTATE--
MY PROSTATE?
MY PROSTATE'S JUST FINE, TA. SO'S THE SEX.
I CAN GET A BOOK. OR A DVD. WE CAN EXPERIMENT. WE CAN DISCOVER NEW THINGS ABOUT EACH OTHER.
HELP.

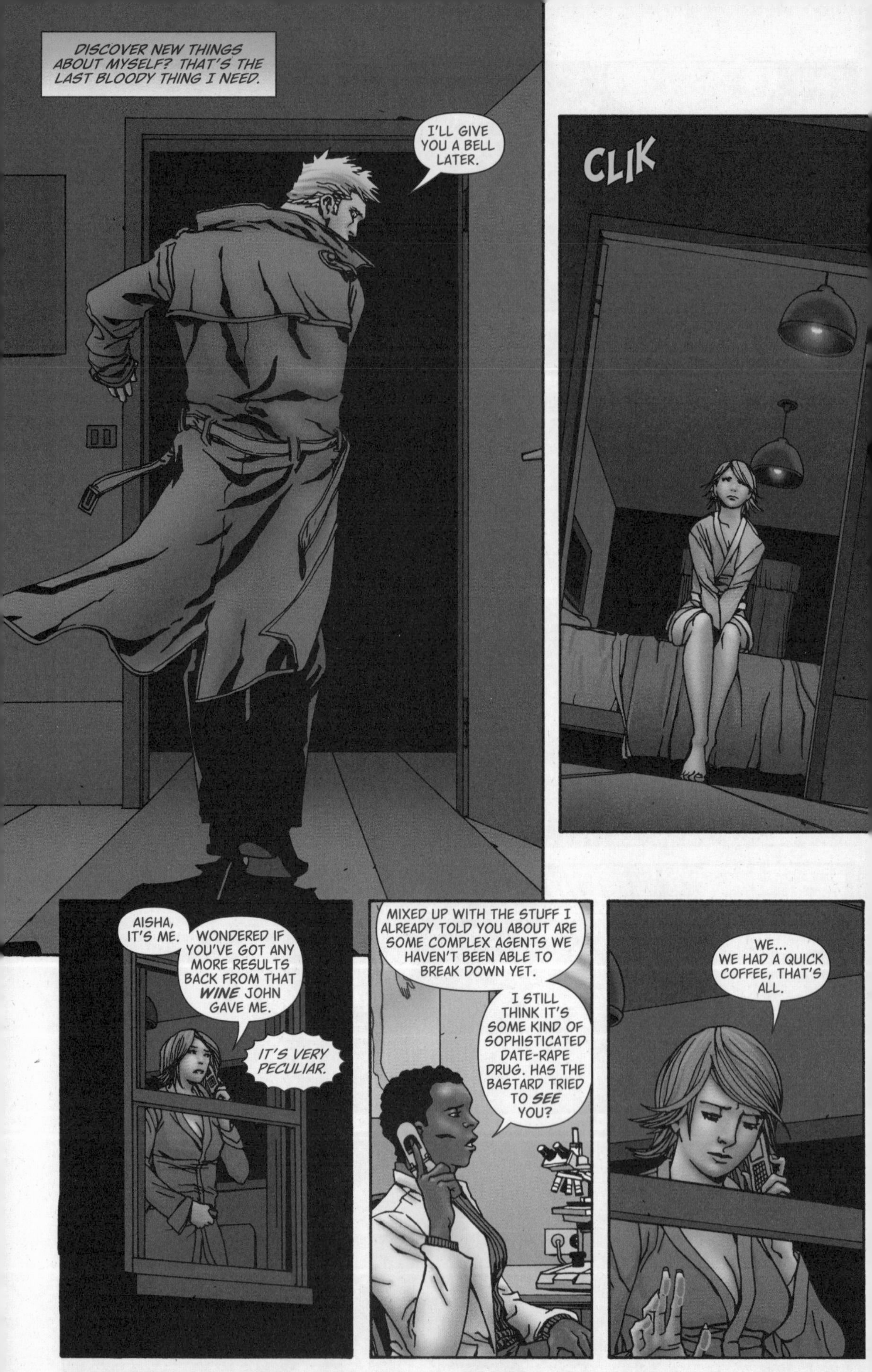
DISCOVER NEW THINGS ABOUT MYSELF? THAT'S THE LAST BLOODY THING I NEED.
I'LL GIVE YOU A BELL LATER.
CLIK
AISHA, IT'S ME.
WONDERED IF YOU'VE GOT ANY MORE RESULTS BACK FROM THAT WINE JOHN GAVE ME.
IT'S VERY PECULIAR.
MIXED UP WITH THE STUFF I ALREADY TOLD YOU ABOUT ARE SOME COMPLEX AGENTS WE HAVEN'T BEEN ABLE TO BREAK DOWN YET.
I STILL THINK IT'S SOME KIND OF SOPHISTICATED DATE-RAPE DRUG. HAS THE BASTARD TRIED TO SEE YOU?
WE... WE HAD A QUICK COFFEE, THAT'S ALL.

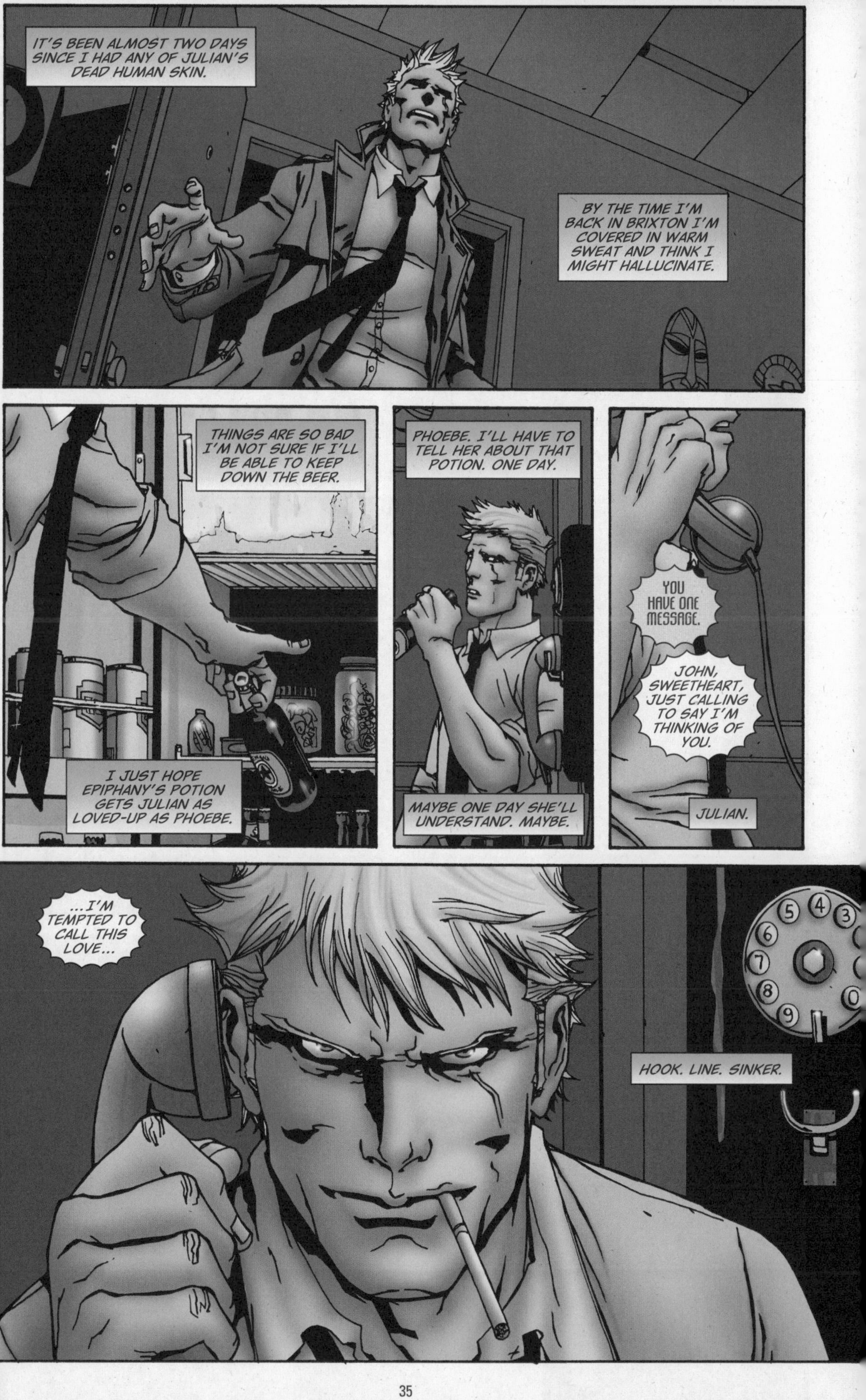
IT'S BEEN ALMOST TWO DAYS SINCE I HAD ANY OF JULIAN'S DEAD HUMAN SKIN.
BY THE TIME I'M BACK IN BRIXTON I'M COVERED IN WARM SWEAT AND THINK I MIGHT HALLUCINATE.
THINGS ARE SO BAD I'M NOT SURE IF I'LL BE ABLE TO KEEP DOWN THE BEER.
I JUST HOPE EPIPHANY'S POTION GETS JULIAN AS LOVED-UP AS PHOEBE.
PHOEBE. I'LL HAVE TO TELL HER ABOUT THAT POTION. ONE DAY.
MAYBE ONE DAY SHE'LL UNDERSTAND. MAYBE.
YOU HAVE ONE MESSAGE.
JOHN, SWEETHEART, JUST CALLING TO SAY I'M THINKING OF YOU.
JULIAN.
...I'M TEMPTED TO CALL THIS LOVE...
HOOK. LINE. SINKER.

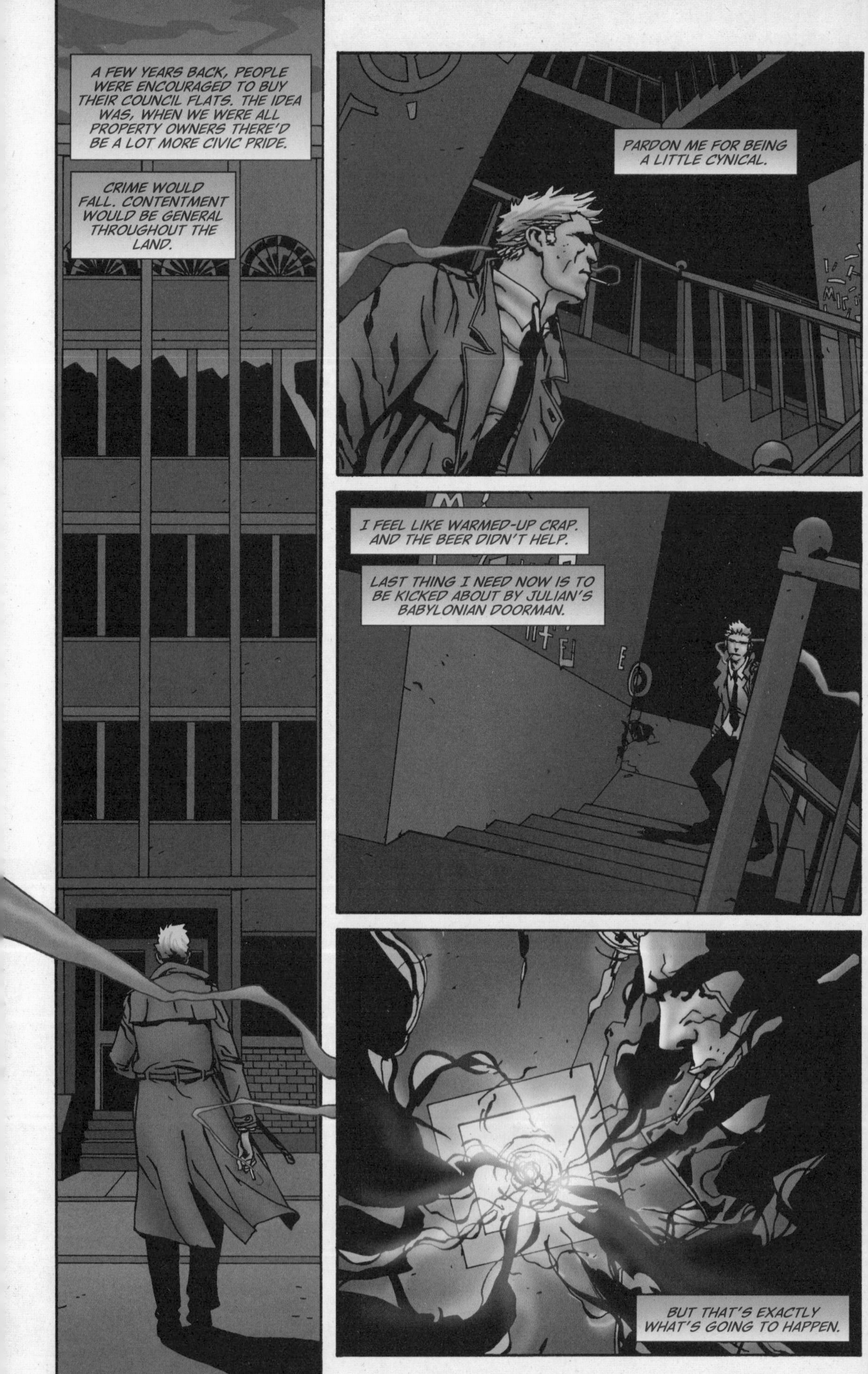
A FEW YEARS BACK, PEOPLE WERE ENCOURAGED TO BUY THEIR COUNCIL FLATS. THE IDEA WAS, WHEN WE WERE ALL PROPERTY OWNERS THERE'D BE A LOT MORE CIVIC PRIDE.
CRIME WOULD FALL. CONTENTMENT WOULD BE GENERAL THROUGHOUT THE LAND.
PARDON ME FOR BEING A LITTLE CYNICAL.
I FEEL LIKE WARMED-UP CRAP. AND THE BEER DIDN'T HELP.
LAST THING I NEED NOW IS TO BE KICKED ABOUT BY JULIAN'S BABYLONIAN DOORMAN.
BUT THAT'S EXACTLY WHAT'S GOING TO HAPPEN.

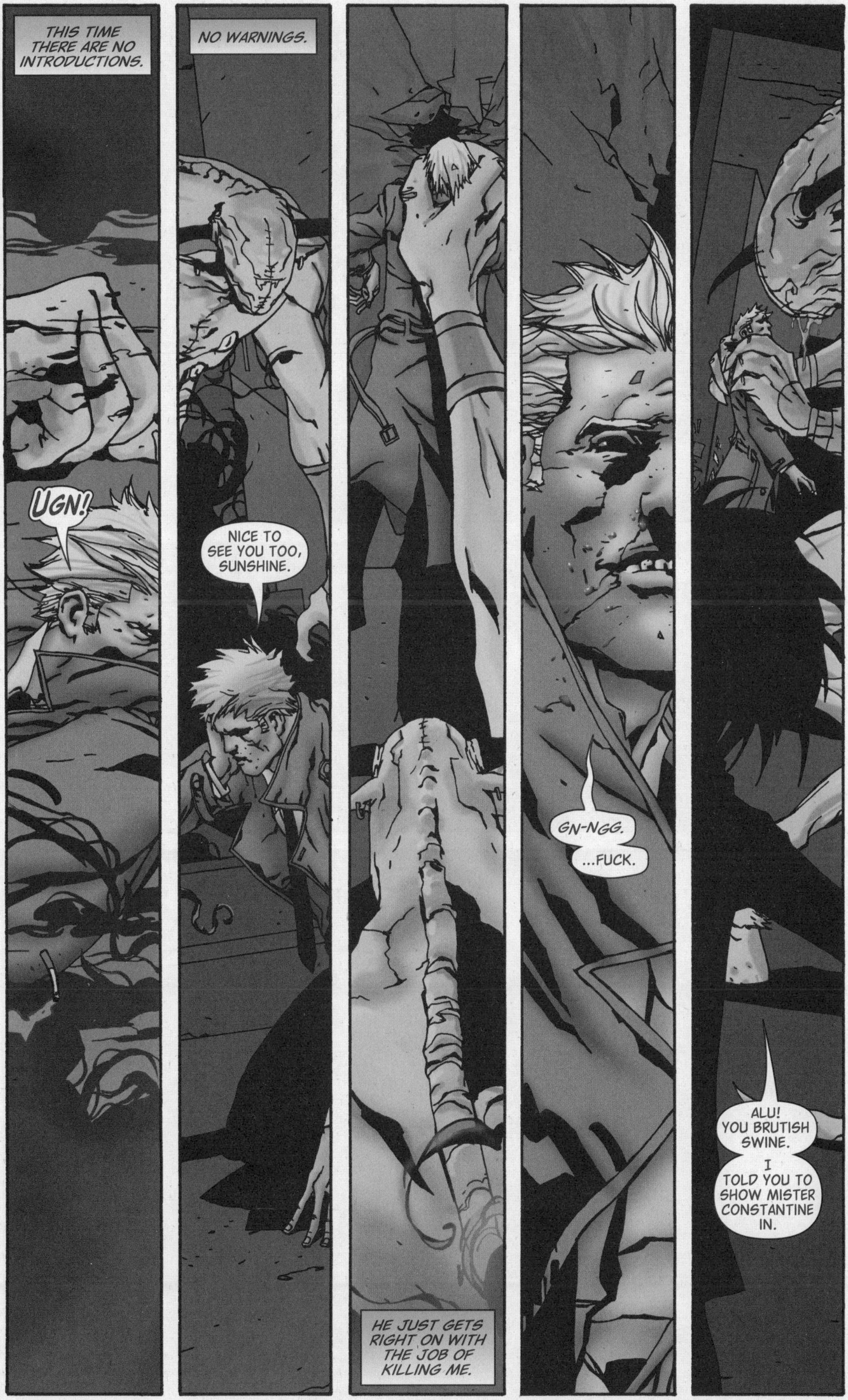
THIS TIME THERE ARE NO INTRODUCTIONS.
UGN!
NO WARNINGS.
NICE TO SEE YOU TOO, SUNSHINE.
HE JUST GETS RIGHT ON WITH THE JOB OF KILLING ME.
GN-NGG.
...FUCK.
ALU! YOU BRUTISH SWINE.
I TOLD YOU TO SHOW MISTER CONSTANTINE IN.

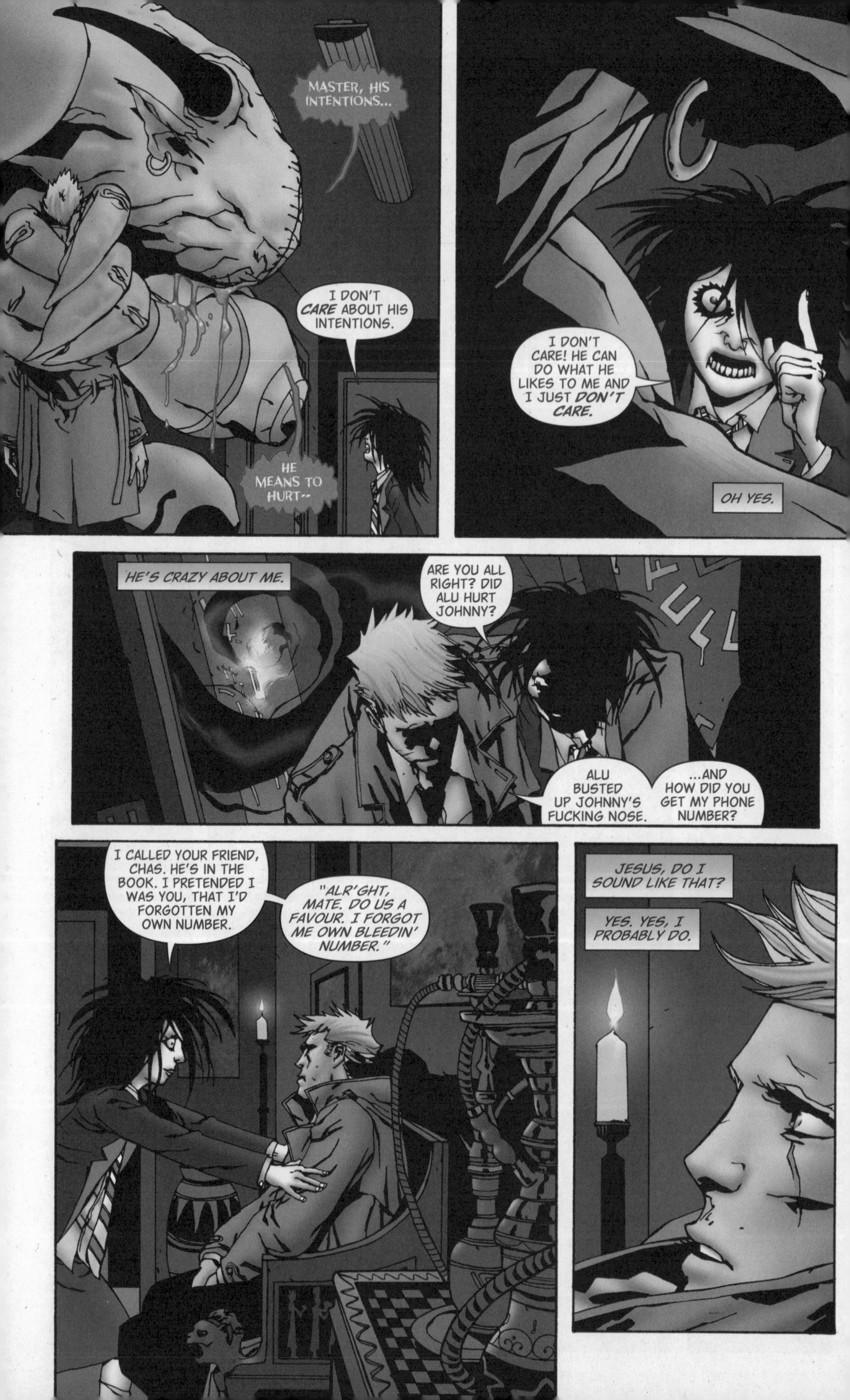
MASTER, HIS INTENTIONS...
I DON'T CARE ABOUT HIS INTENTIONS.
HE MEANS TO HURT--
I DON'T CARE! HE CAN DO WHAT HE LIKES TO ME AND I JUST DON'T CARE.
OH YES.
HE'S CRAZY ABOUT ME.
ARE YOU ALL RIGHT? DID ALU HURT JOHNNY?
ALU BUSTED UP JOHNNY'S FUCKING NOSE.
...AND HOW DID YOU GET MY PHONE NUMBER?
I CALLED YOUR FRIEND, CHAS. HE'S IN THE BOOK. I PRETENDED I WAS YOU, THAT I'D FORGOTTEN MY OWN NUMBER.
"ALR'GHT, MATE. DO US A FAVOUR. I FORGOT ME OWN BLEEDIN' NUMBER."
JESUS, DO I SOUND LIKE THAT?
YES. YES, I PROBABLY DO.

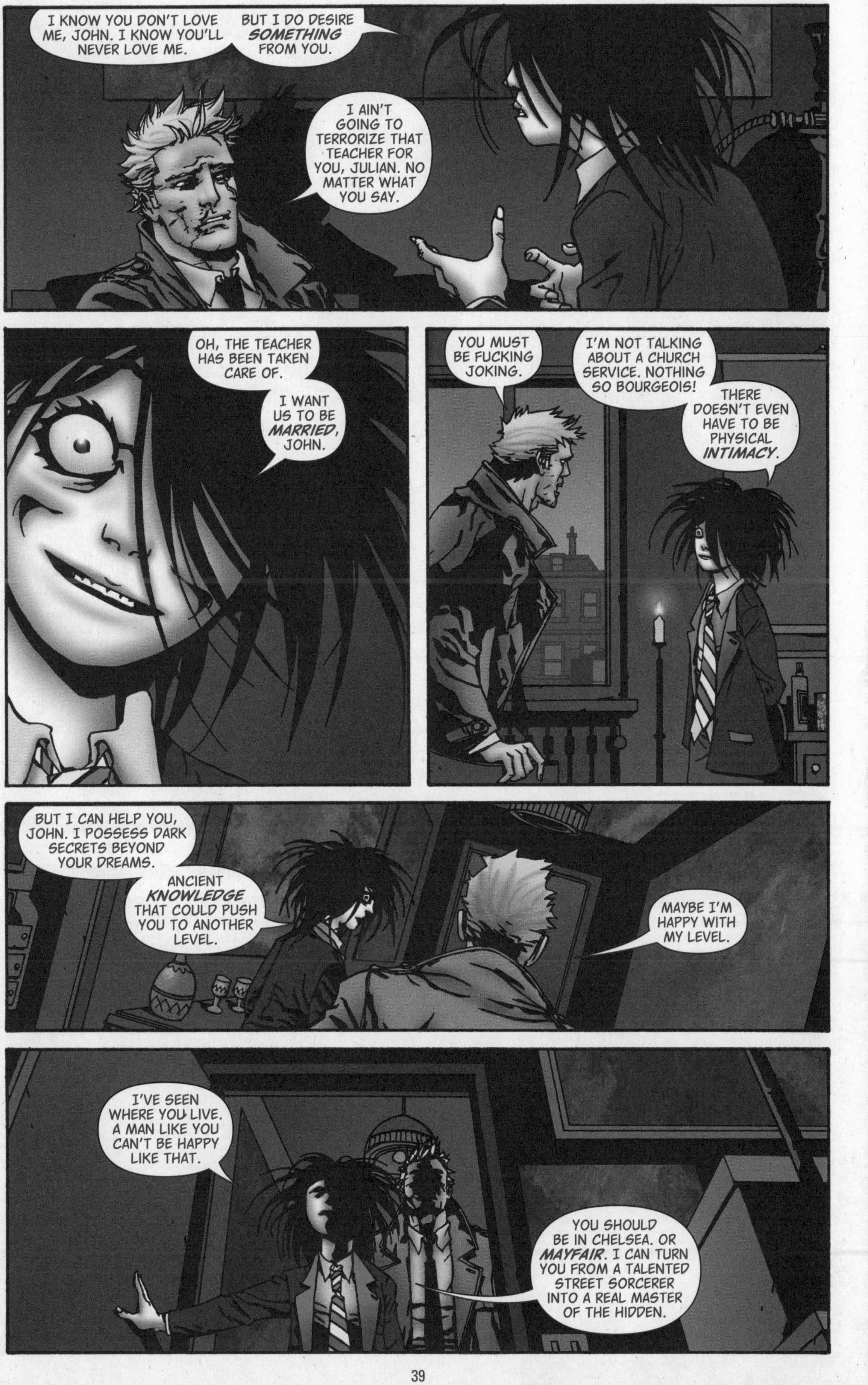
I KNOW YOU DON'T LOVE ME, JOHN. I KNOW YOU'LL NEVER LOVE ME.
BUT I DO DESIRE ***SOMETHING*** FROM YOU.
I AIN'T GOING TO TERRORIZE THAT TEACHER FOR YOU, JULIAN. NO MATTER WHAT YOU SAY.
OH, THE TEACHER HAS BEEN TAKEN CARE OF.
I WANT US TO BE ***MARRIED***, JOHN.
YOU MUST BE FUCKING JOKING.
I'M NOT TALKING ABOUT A CHURCH SERVICE. NOTHING SO BOURGEOIS!
THERE DOESN'T EVEN HAVE TO BE PHYSICAL ***INTIMACY***.
BUT I CAN HELP YOU, JOHN. I POSSESS DARK SECRETS BEYOND YOUR DREAMS.
ANCIENT ***KNOWLEDGE*** THAT COULD PUSH YOU TO ANOTHER LEVEL.
MAYBE I'M HAPPY WITH MY LEVEL.
I'VE SEEN WHERE YOU LIVE. A MAN LIKE YOU CAN'T BE HAPPY LIKE THAT.
YOU SHOULD BE IN CHELSEA. OR ***MAYFAIR***. I CAN TURN YOU FROM A TALENTED STREET SORCERER INTO A REAL MASTER OF THE HIDDEN.

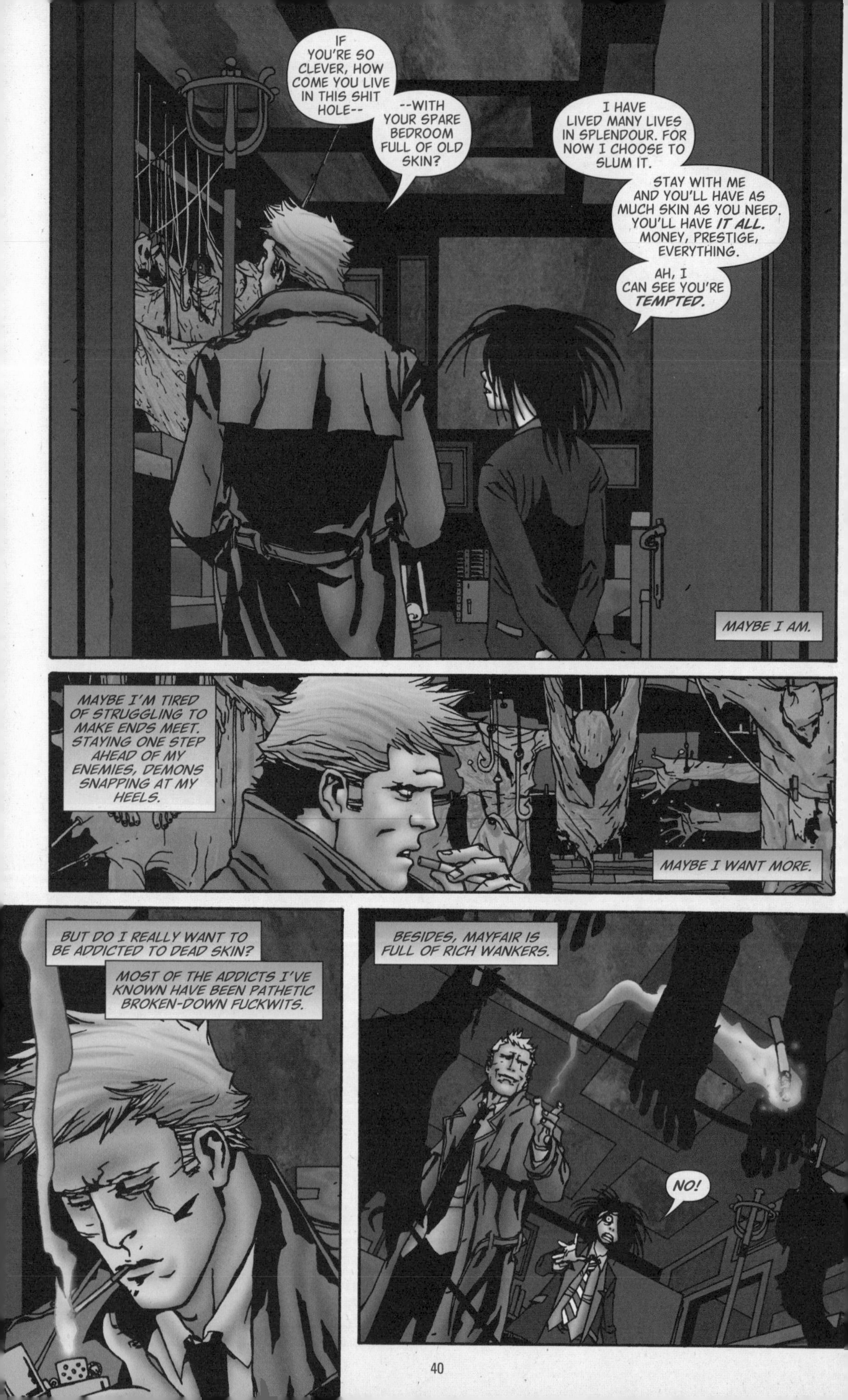
IF YOU'RE SO CLEVER, HOW COME YOU LIVE IN THIS SHIT HOLE--
--WITH YOUR SPARE BEDROOM FULL OF OLD SKIN?
I HAVE LIVED MANY LIVES IN SPLENDOUR. FOR NOW I CHOOSE TO SLUM IT.
STAY WITH ME AND YOU'LL HAVE AS MUCH SKIN AS YOU NEED. YOU'LL HAVE IT ALL. MONEY, PRESTIGE, EVERYTHING.
AH, I CAN SEE YOU'RE TEMPTED.
MAYBE I AM.
MAYBE I'M TIRED OF STRUGGLING TO MAKE ENDS MEET. STAYING ONE STEP AHEAD OF MY ENEMIES, DEMONS SNAPPING AT MY HEELS.
MAYBE I WANT MORE.
BUT DO I REALLY WANT TO BE ADDICTED TO DEAD SKIN?
MOST OF THE ADDICTS I'VE KNOWN HAVE BEEN PATHETIC BROKEN-DOWN FUCKWITS.
BESIDES, MAYFAIR IS FULL OF RICH WANKERS.
NO!

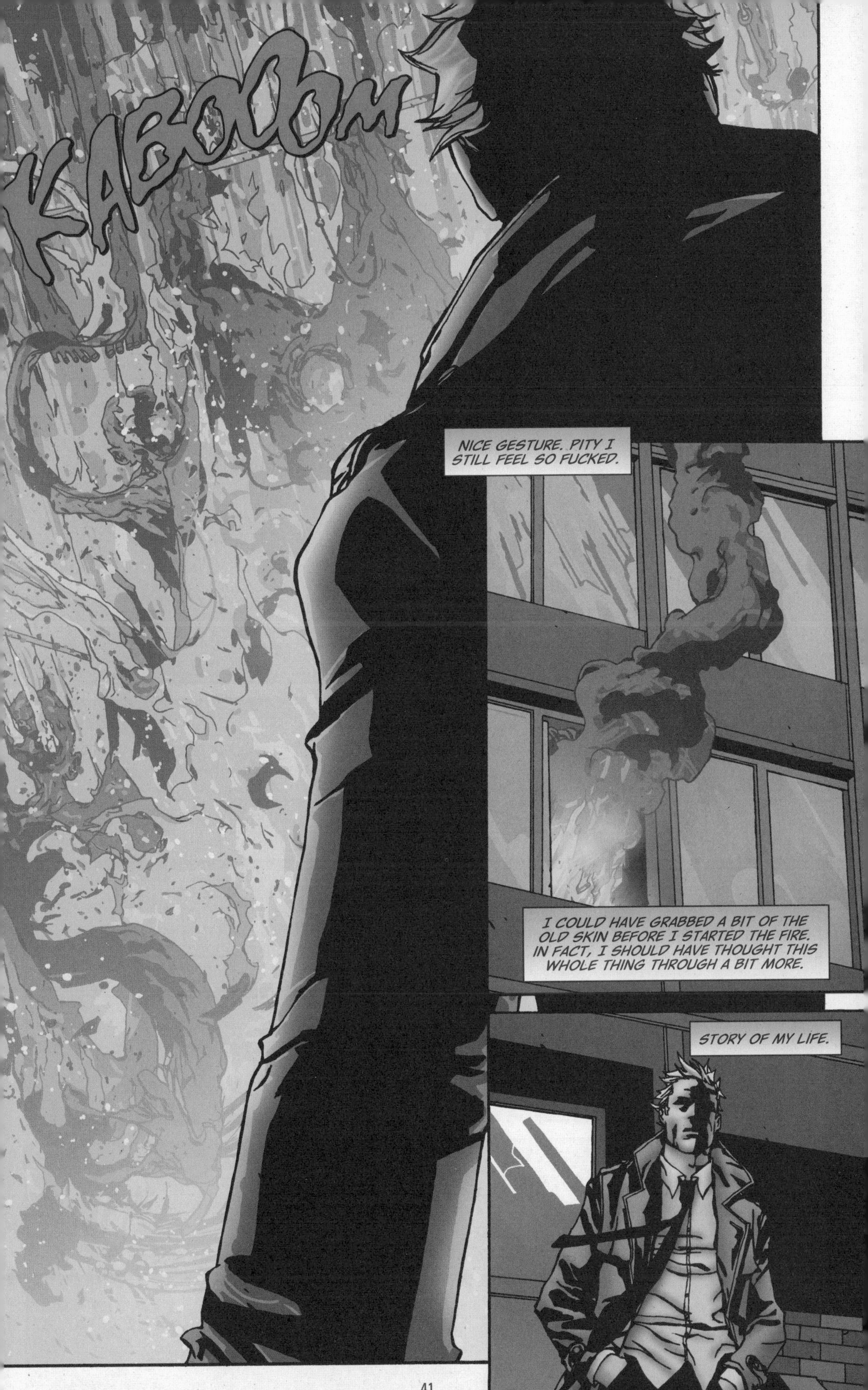
KABOOOM
NICE GESTURE. PITY I STILL FEEL SO FUCKED.
I COULD HAVE GRABBED A BIT OF THE OLD SKIN BEFORE I STARTED THE FIRE. IN FACT, I SHOULD HAVE THOUGHT THIS WHOLE THING THROUGH A BIT MORE.
STORY OF MY LIFE.

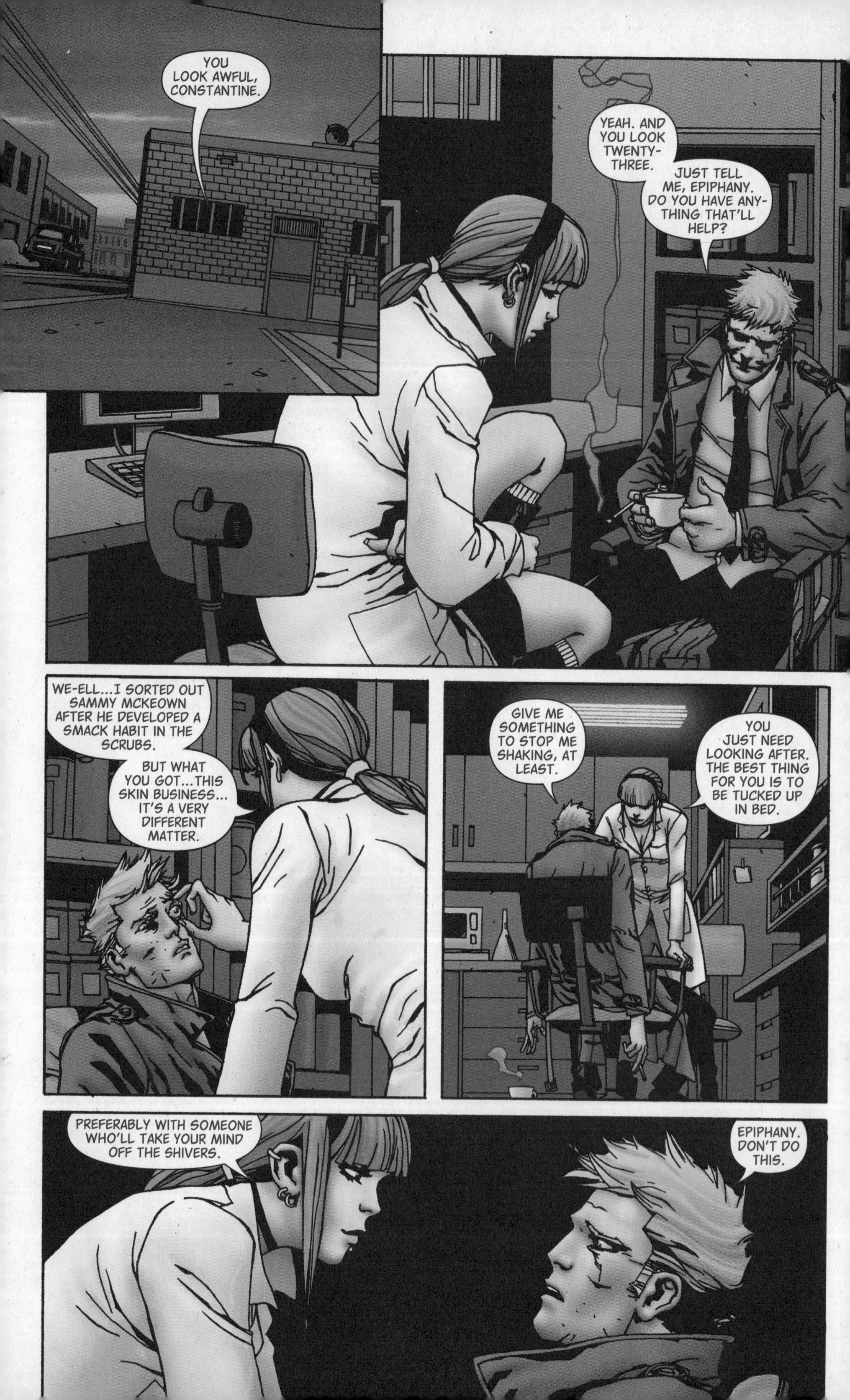
YOU LOOK AWFUL, CONSTANTINE.
YEAH. AND YOU LOOK TWENTY-THREE.
JUST TELL ME, EPIPHANY. DO YOU HAVE ANY-THING THAT'LL HELP?
WE-ELL...I SORTED OUT SAMMY MCKEOWN AFTER HE DEVELOPED A SMACK HABIT IN THE SCRUBS.
BUT WHAT YOU GOT...THIS SKIN BUSINESS... IT'S A VERY DIFFERENT MATTER.
GIVE ME SOMETHING TO STOP ME SHAKING, AT LEAST.
YOU JUST NEED LOOKING AFTER. THE BEST THING FOR YOU IS TO BE TUCKED UP IN BED.
PREFERABLY WITH SOMEONE WHO'LL TAKE YOUR MIND OFF THE SHIVERS.
EPIPHANY. DON'T DO THIS.

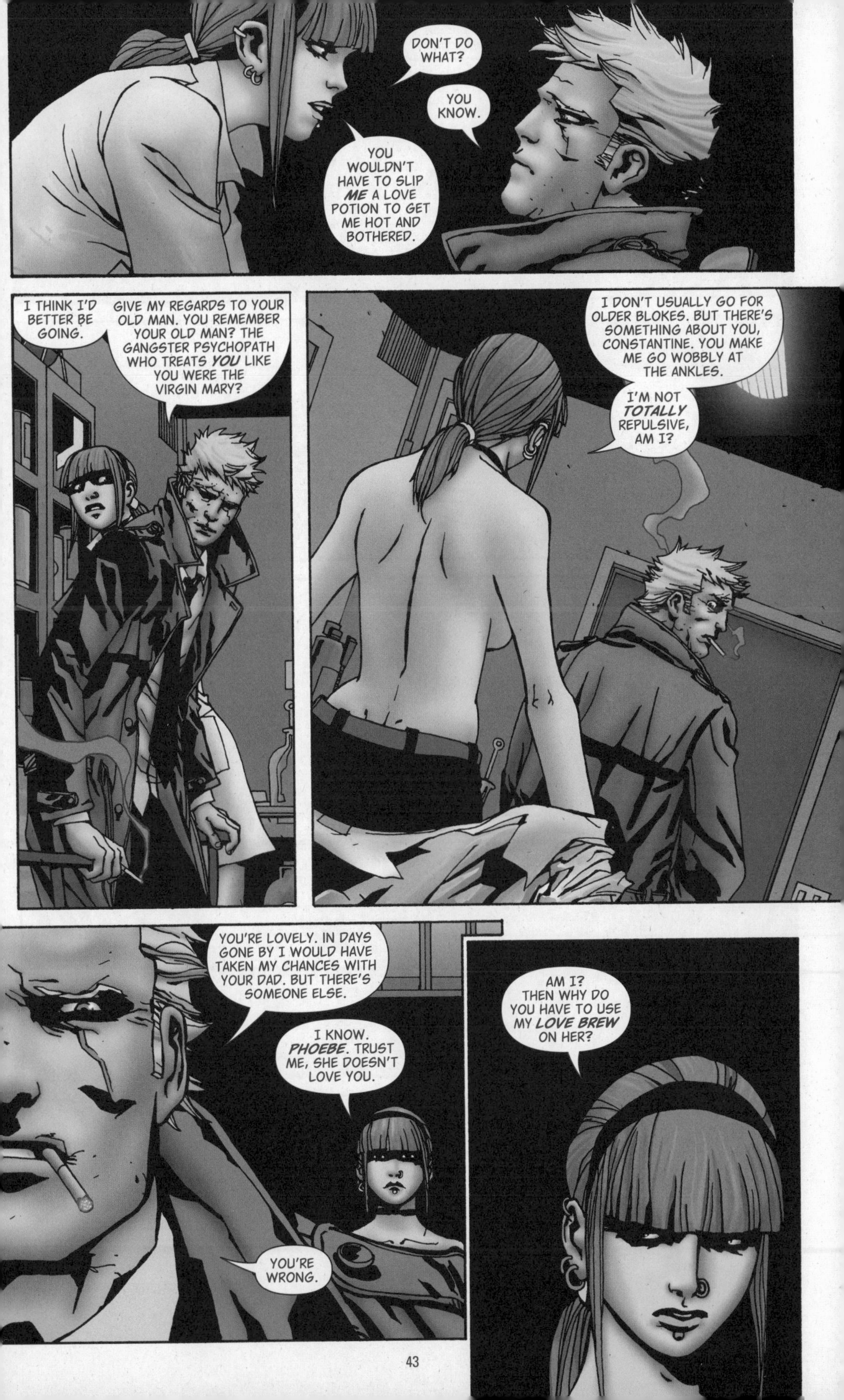
DON'T DO WHAT?
YOU KNOW.
YOU WOULDN'T HAVE TO SLIP ME A LOVE POTION TO GET ME HOT AND BOTHERED.
I THINK I'D BETTER BE GOING.
GIVE MY REGARDS TO YOUR OLD MAN. YOU REMEMBER YOUR OLD MAN? THE GANGSTER PSYCHOPATH WHO TREATS YOU LIKE YOU WERE THE VIRGIN MARY?
I DON'T USUALLY GO FOR OLDER BLOKES. BUT THERE'S SOMETHING ABOUT YOU, CONSTANTINE. YOU MAKE ME GO WOBBLY AT THE ANKLES.
I'M NOT TOTALLY REPULSIVE, AM I?
YOU'RE LOVELY. IN DAYS GONE BY I WOULD HAVE TAKEN MY CHANCES WITH YOUR DAD. BUT THERE'S SOMEONE ELSE.
I KNOW. PHOEBE. TRUST ME, SHE DOESN'T LOVE YOU.
YOU'RE WRONG.
AM I? THEN WHY DO YOU HAVE TO USE MY LOVE BREW ON HER?

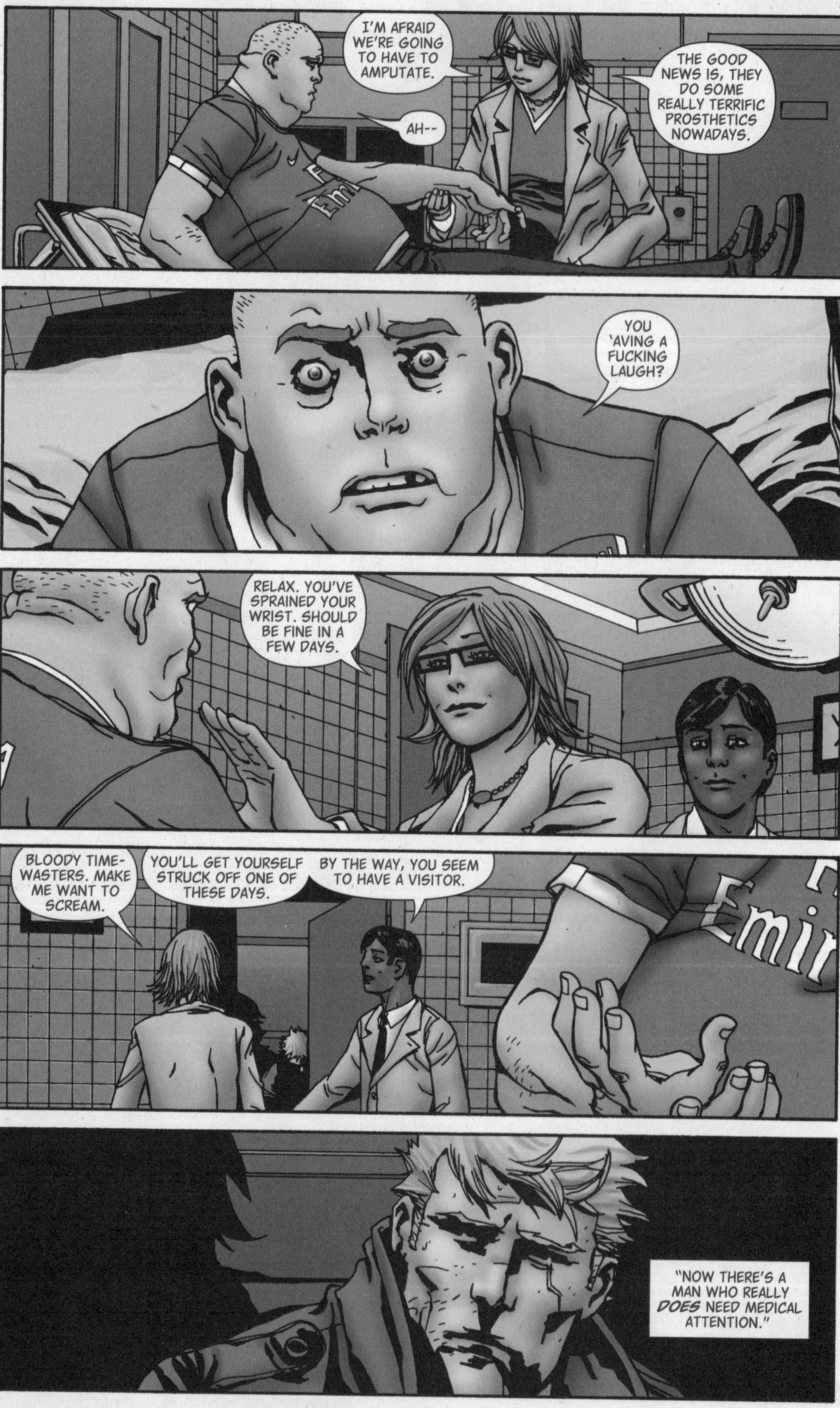
I'M AFRAID WE'RE GOING TO HAVE TO AMPUTATE.
AH--
THE GOOD NEWS IS, THEY DO SOME REALLY TERRIFIC PROSTHETICS NOWADAYS.
YOU 'AVING A FUCKING LAUGH?
RELAX. YOU'VE SPRAINED YOUR WRIST. SHOULD BE FINE IN A FEW DAYS.
BLOODY TIME-WASTERS. MAKE ME WANT TO SCREAM.
YOU'LL GET YOURSELF STRUCK OFF ONE OF THESE DAYS.
BY THE WAY, YOU SEEM TO HAVE A VISITOR.
"NOW THERE'S A MAN WHO REALLY *DOES* NEED MEDICAL ATTENTION."

I...I GOT TO TELL YOU SOMETHING, PHEEBS...

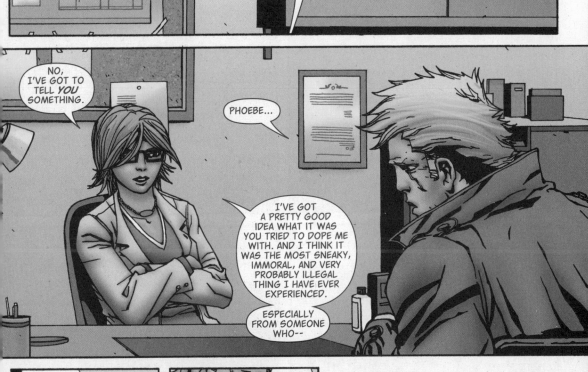

NO, I'VE GOT TO TELL *YOU* SOMETHING.

PHOEBE...

I'VE GOT A PRETTY GOOD IDEA WHAT IT WAS YOU TRIED TO DOPE ME WITH. AND I THINK IT WAS THE MOST SNEAKY, IMMORAL, AND VERY PROBABLY ILLEGAL THING I HAVE EVER EXPERIENCED.

ESPECIALLY FROM SOMEONE WHO--

YOU KNOW ABOUT--?

I HAD AISHA RUN SOME TESTS.

I COULD HANDLE YOU BEING A BASTARD. I JUST WASN'T PREPARED FOR YOU BEING SUCH A COMPLETE BASTARD TO *ME*.

SO YOU DIDN'T DRINK ANY?

NOT A DROP.

THEN ALL THAT, THE PASSION, THE STUFF ABOUT MY PROSTATE...

PRETTY CONVINCING, AREN'T I?

WELL, IT WASN'T THE FIRST TIME I'VE FAKED IT.

45

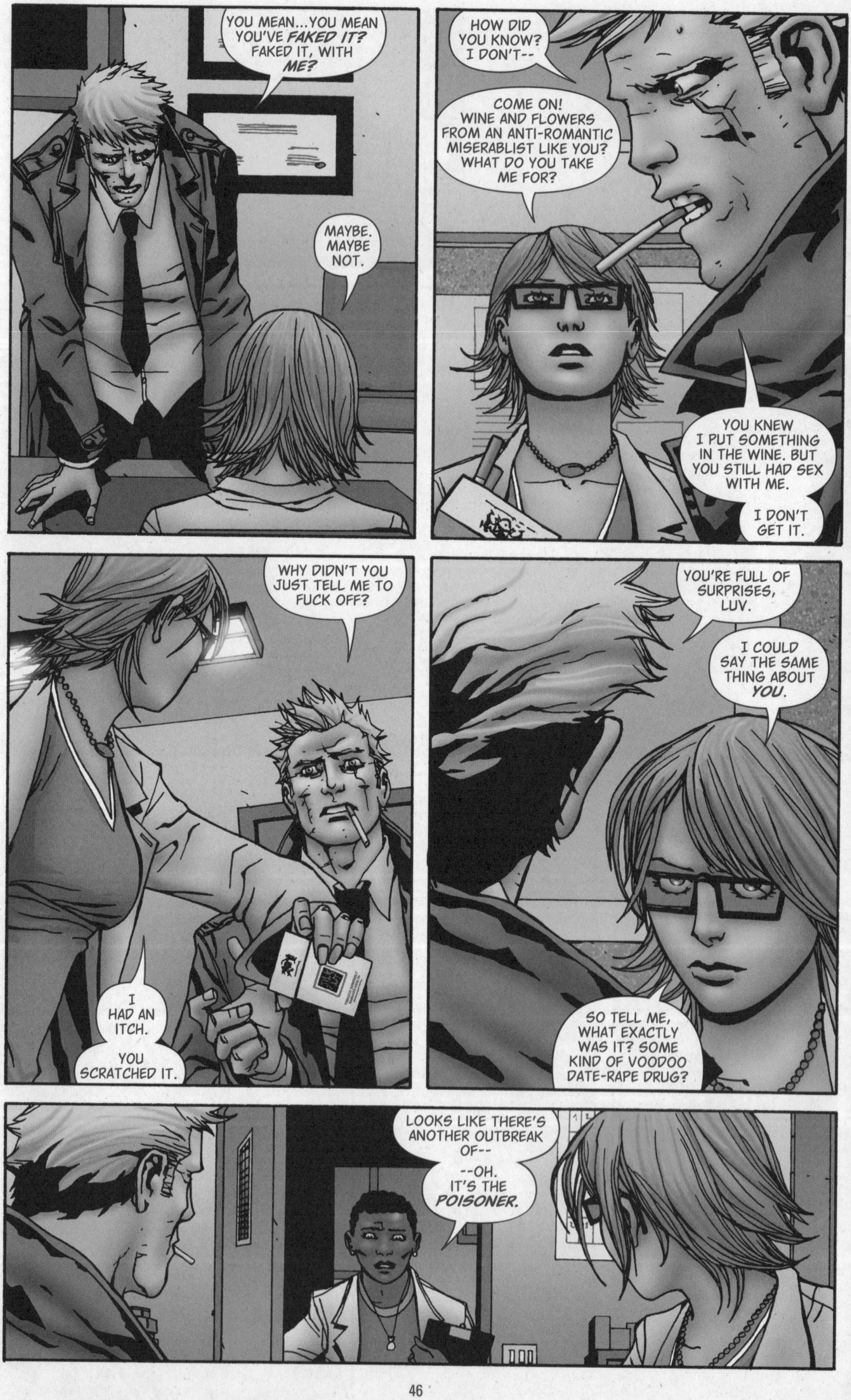

YOU MEAN...YOU MEAN YOU'VE FAKED IT? FAKED IT, WITH ME?
MAYBE. MAYBE NOT.
HOW DID YOU KNOW? I DON'T--
COME ON! WINE AND FLOWERS FROM AN ANTI-ROMANTIC MISERABLIST LIKE YOU? WHAT DO YOU TAKE ME FOR?
YOU KNEW I PUT SOMETHING IN THE WINE. BUT YOU STILL HAD SEX WITH ME.
I DON'T GET IT.
WHY DIDN'T YOU JUST TELL ME TO FUCK OFF?
I HAD AN ITCH.
YOU SCRATCHED IT.
YOU'RE FULL OF SURPRISES, LUV.
I COULD SAY THE SAME THING ABOUT YOU.
SO TELL ME, WHAT EXACTLY WAS IT? SOME KIND OF VOODOO DATE-RAPE DRUG?
LOOKS LIKE THERE'S ANOTHER OUTBREAK OF--
--OH. IT'S THE POISONER.

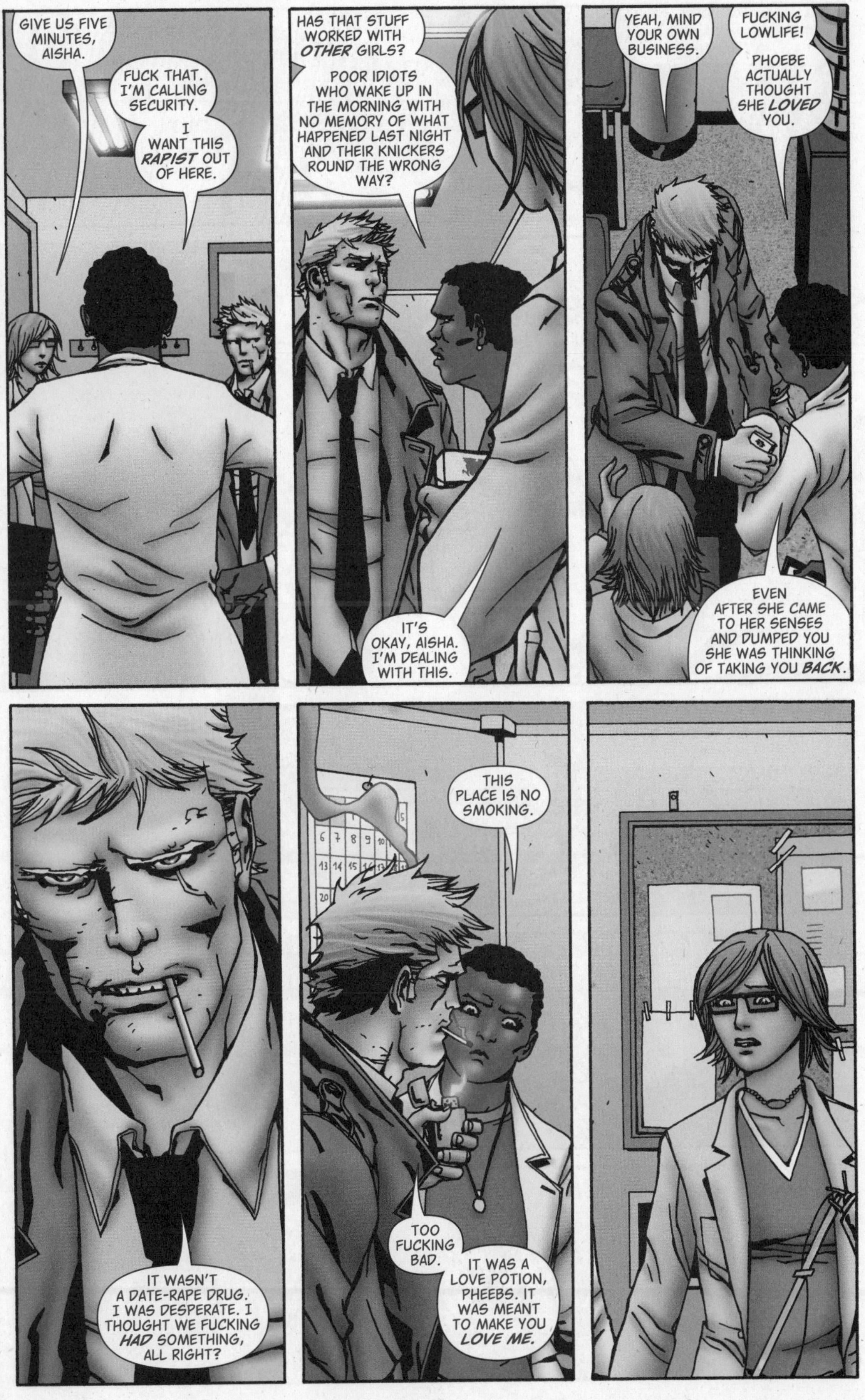
GIVE US FIVE MINUTES, AISHA.
FUCK THAT. I'M CALLING SECURITY.
I WANT THIS RAPIST OUT OF HERE.
HAS THAT STUFF WORKED WITH OTHER GIRLS?
POOR IDIOTS WHO WAKE UP IN THE MORNING WITH NO MEMORY OF WHAT HAPPENED LAST NIGHT AND THEIR KNICKERS ROUND THE WRONG WAY?
IT'S OKAY, AISHA. I'M DEALING WITH THIS.
YEAH, MIND YOUR OWN BUSINESS.
FUCKING LOWLIFE!
PHOEBE ACTUALLY THOUGHT SHE LOVED YOU.
EVEN AFTER SHE CAME TO HER SENSES AND DUMPED YOU SHE WAS THINKING OF TAKING YOU BACK.
IT WASN'T A DATE-RAPE DRUG. I WAS DESPERATE. I THOUGHT WE FUCKING HAD SOMETHING, ALL RIGHT?
THIS PLACE IS NO SMOKING.
TOO FUCKING BAD.
IT WAS A LOVE POTION, PHEEBS. IT WAS MEANT TO MAKE YOU LOVE ME.

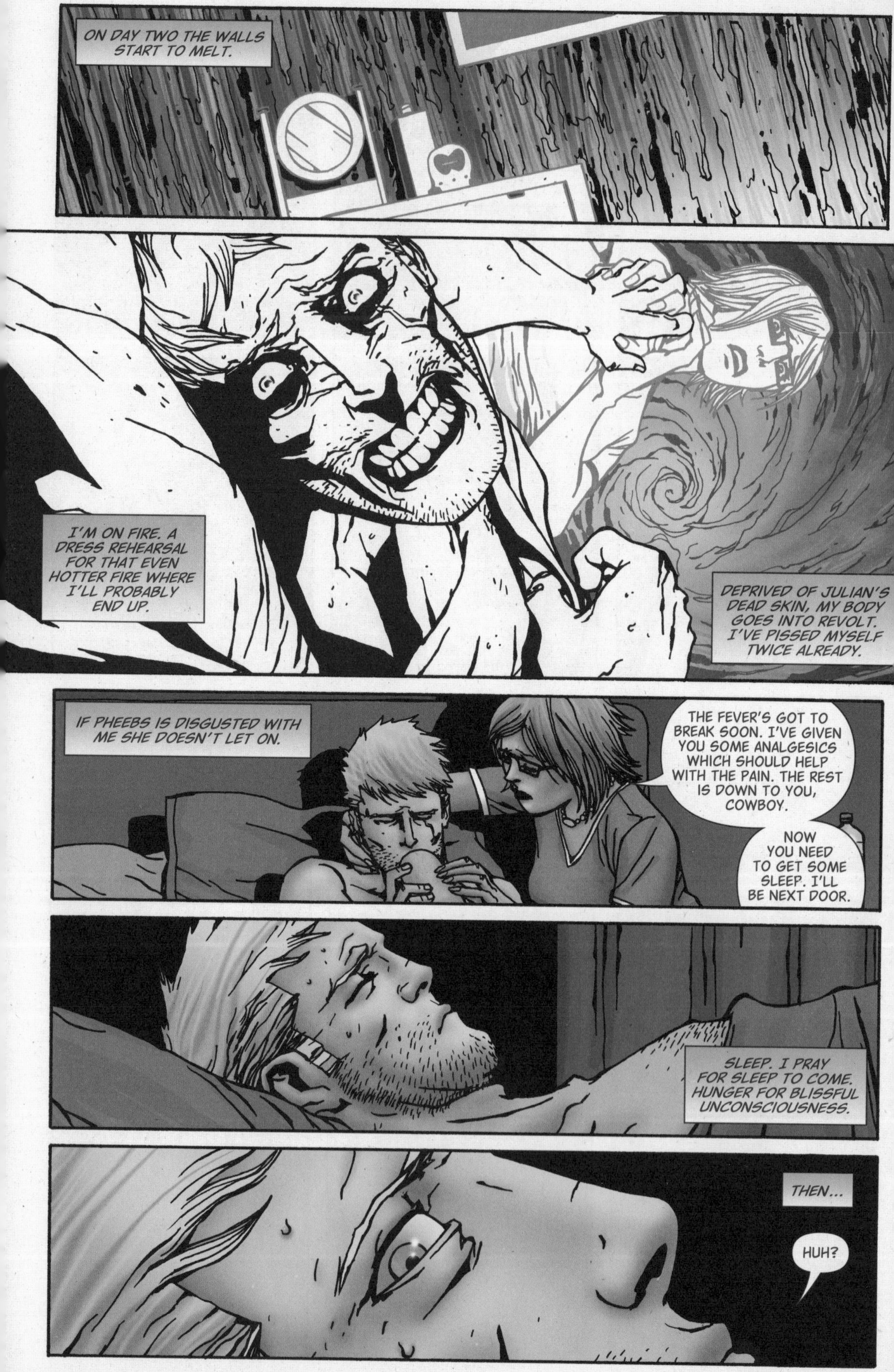
ON DAY TWO THE WALLS START TO MELT.
I'M ON FIRE. A DRESS REHEARSAL FOR THAT EVEN HOTTER FIRE WHERE I'LL PROBABLY END UP.
DEPRIVED OF JULIAN'S DEAD SKIN, MY BODY GOES INTO REVOLT. I'VE PISSED MYSELF TWICE ALREADY.
IF PHEEBS IS DISGUSTED WITH ME SHE DOESN'T LET ON.
THE FEVER'S GOT TO BREAK SOON. I'VE GIVEN YOU SOME ANALGESICS WHICH SHOULD HELP WITH THE PAIN. THE REST IS DOWN TO YOU, COWBOY.
NOW YOU NEED TO GET SOME SLEEP. I'LL BE NEXT DOOR.
SLEEP. I PRAY FOR SLEEP TO COME. HUNGER FOR BLISSFUL UNCONSCIOUSNESS.
THEN...
HUH?

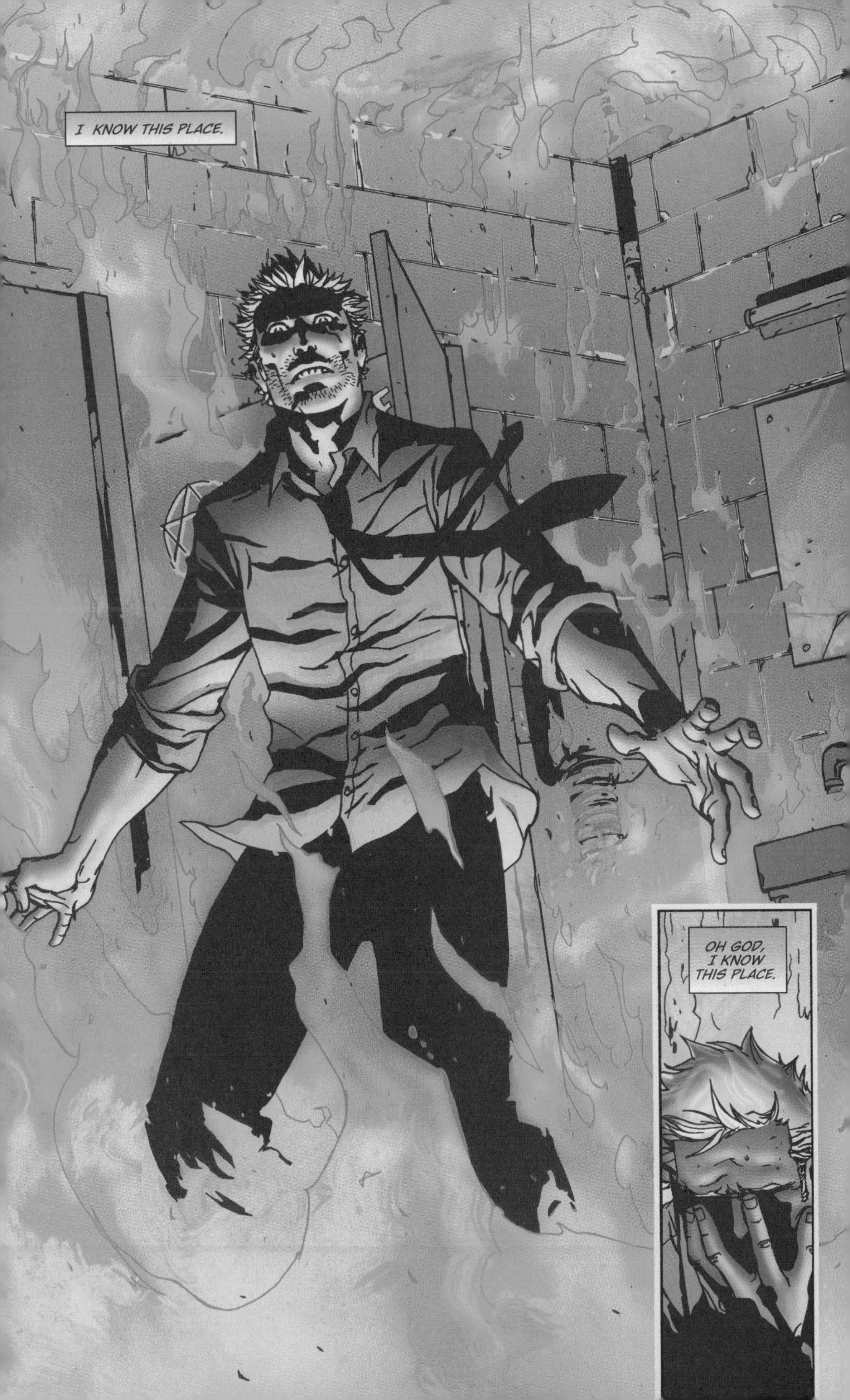
I KNOW THIS PLACE.
OH GOD, I KNOW THIS PLACE.

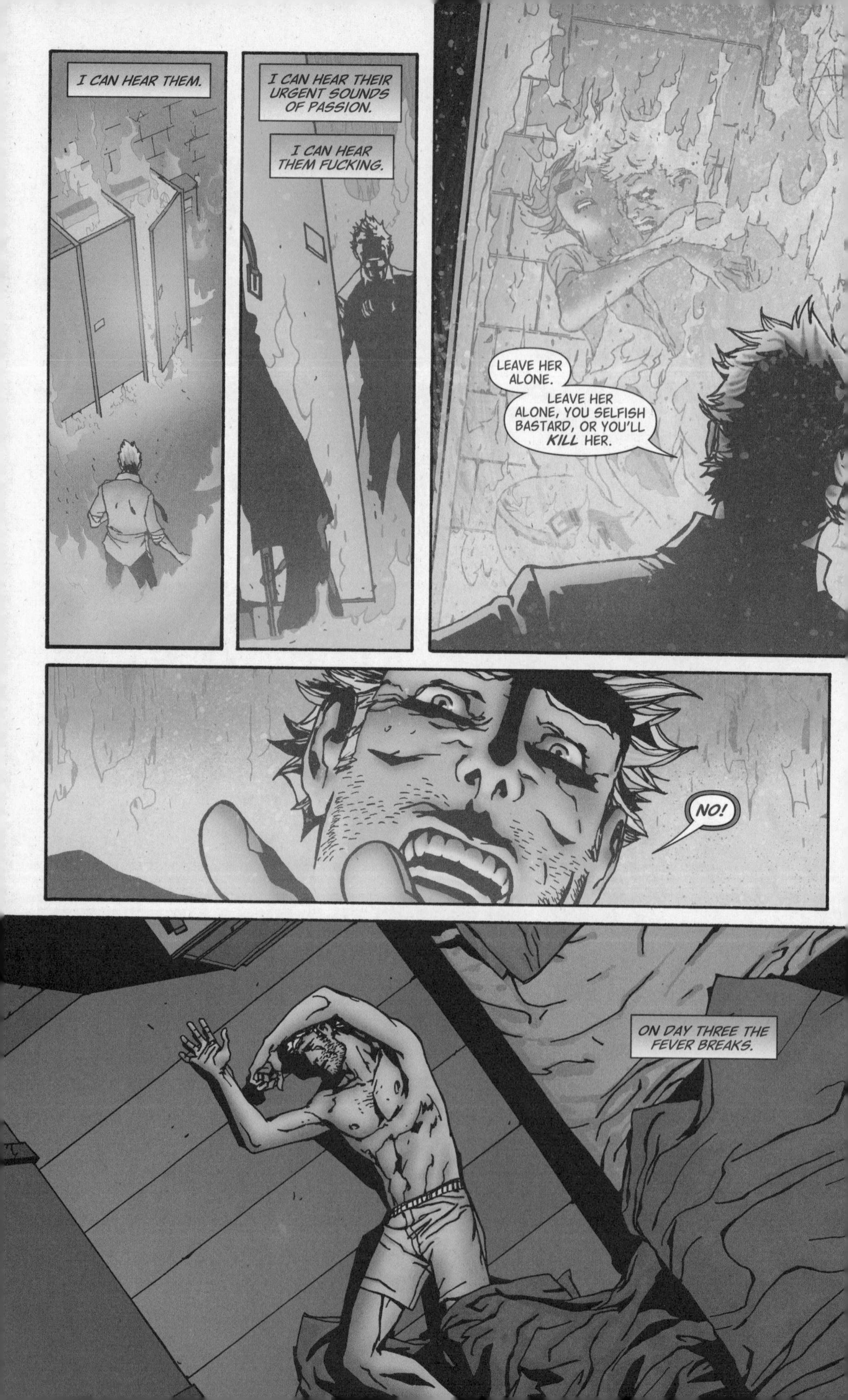
I CAN HEAR THEM.
I CAN HEAR THEIR URGENT SOUNDS OF PASSION.
I CAN HEAR THEM FUCKING.
LEAVE HER ALONE.
LEAVE HER ALONE, YOU SELFISH BASTARD, OR YOU'LL *KILL* HER.
NO!
ON DAY THREE THE FEVER BREAKS.

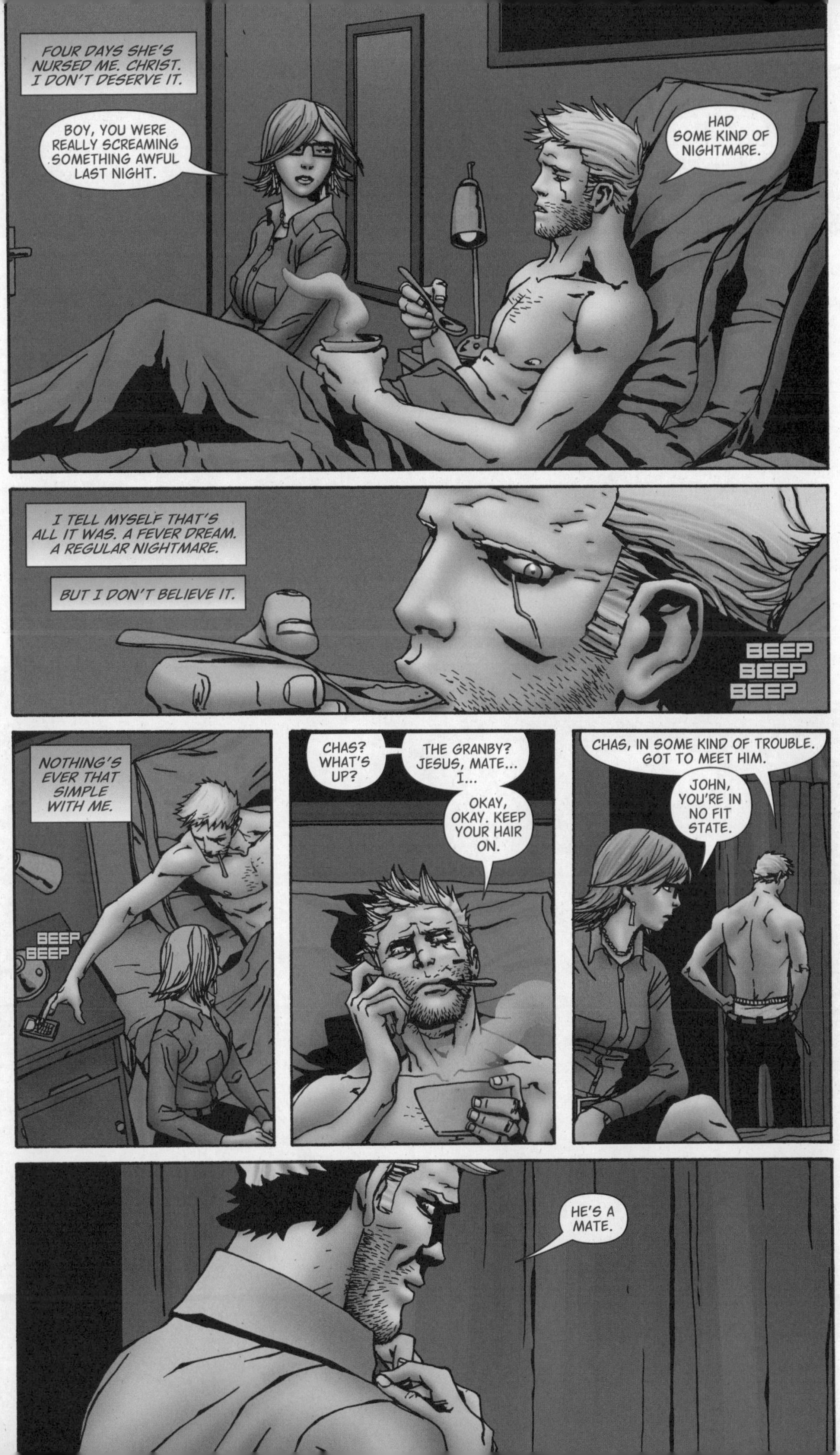
FOUR DAYS SHE'S NURSED ME. CHRIST. I DON'T DESERVE IT.
BOY, YOU WERE REALLY SCREAMING SOMETHING AWFUL LAST NIGHT.
HAD SOME KIND OF NIGHTMARE.
I TELL MYSELF THAT'S ALL IT WAS. A FEVER DREAM. A REGULAR NIGHTMARE.
BUT I DON'T BELIEVE IT.
BEEP BEEP BEEP
NOTHING'S EVER THAT SIMPLE WITH ME.
BEEP BEEP
CHAS? WHAT'S UP?
THE GRANBY? JESUS, MATE... I...
OKAY, OKAY. KEEP YOUR HAIR ON.
CHAS, IN SOME KIND OF TROUBLE. GOT TO MEET HIM.
JOHN, YOU'RE IN NO FIT STATE.
HE'S A MATE.

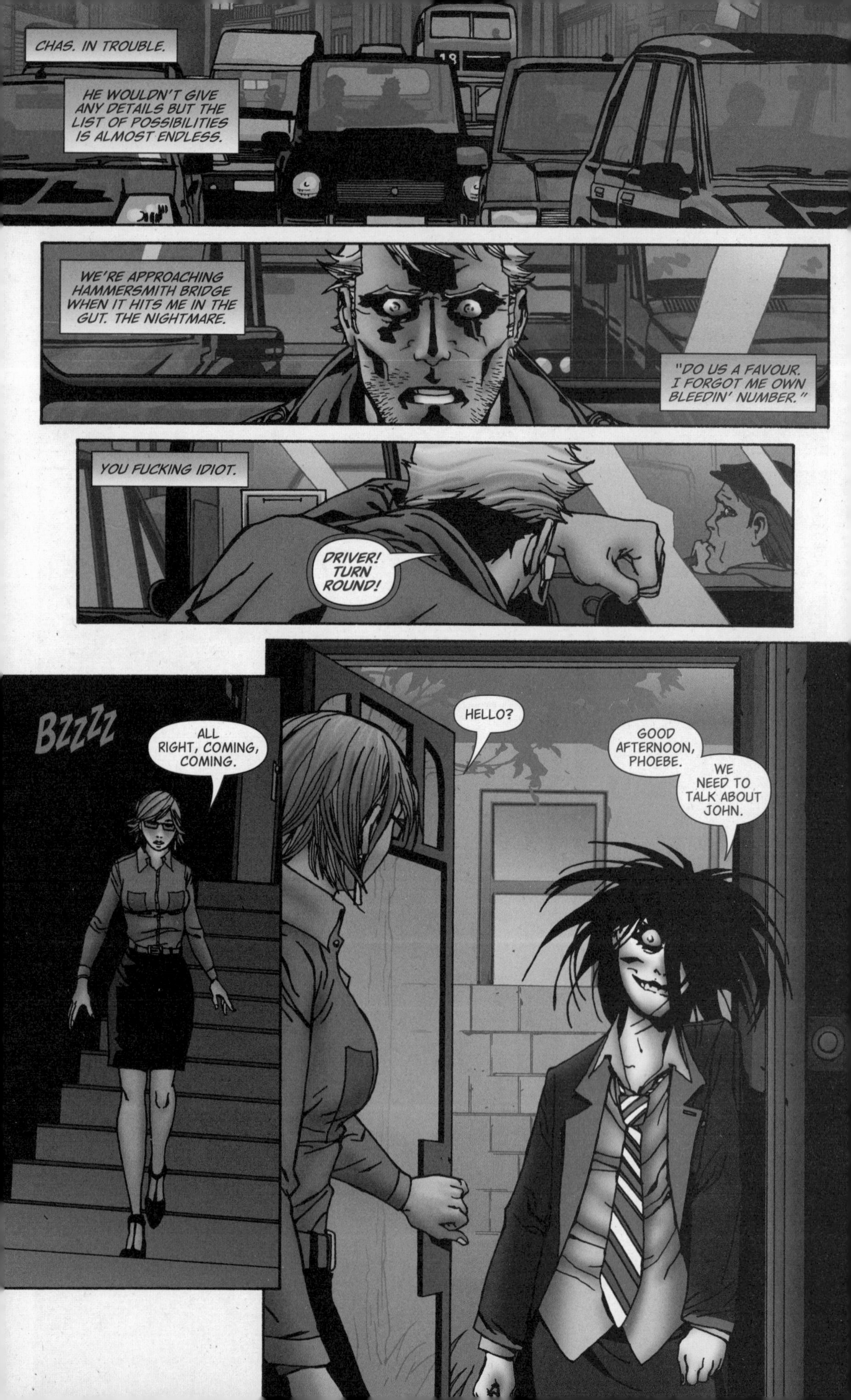
CHAS. IN TROUBLE.
HE WOULDN'T GIVE ANY DETAILS BUT THE LIST OF POSSIBILITIES IS ALMOST ENDLESS.
WE'RE APPROACHING HAMMERSMITH BRIDGE WHEN IT HITS ME IN THE GUT. THE NIGHTMARE.
"DO US A FAVOUR. I FORGOT ME OWN BLEEDIN' NUMBER."
YOU FUCKING IDIOT.
DRIVER! TURN ROUND!
BZZZZ
ALL RIGHT, COMING, COMING.
HELLO?
GOOD AFTERNOON, PHOEBE.
WE NEED TO TALK ABOUT JOHN.

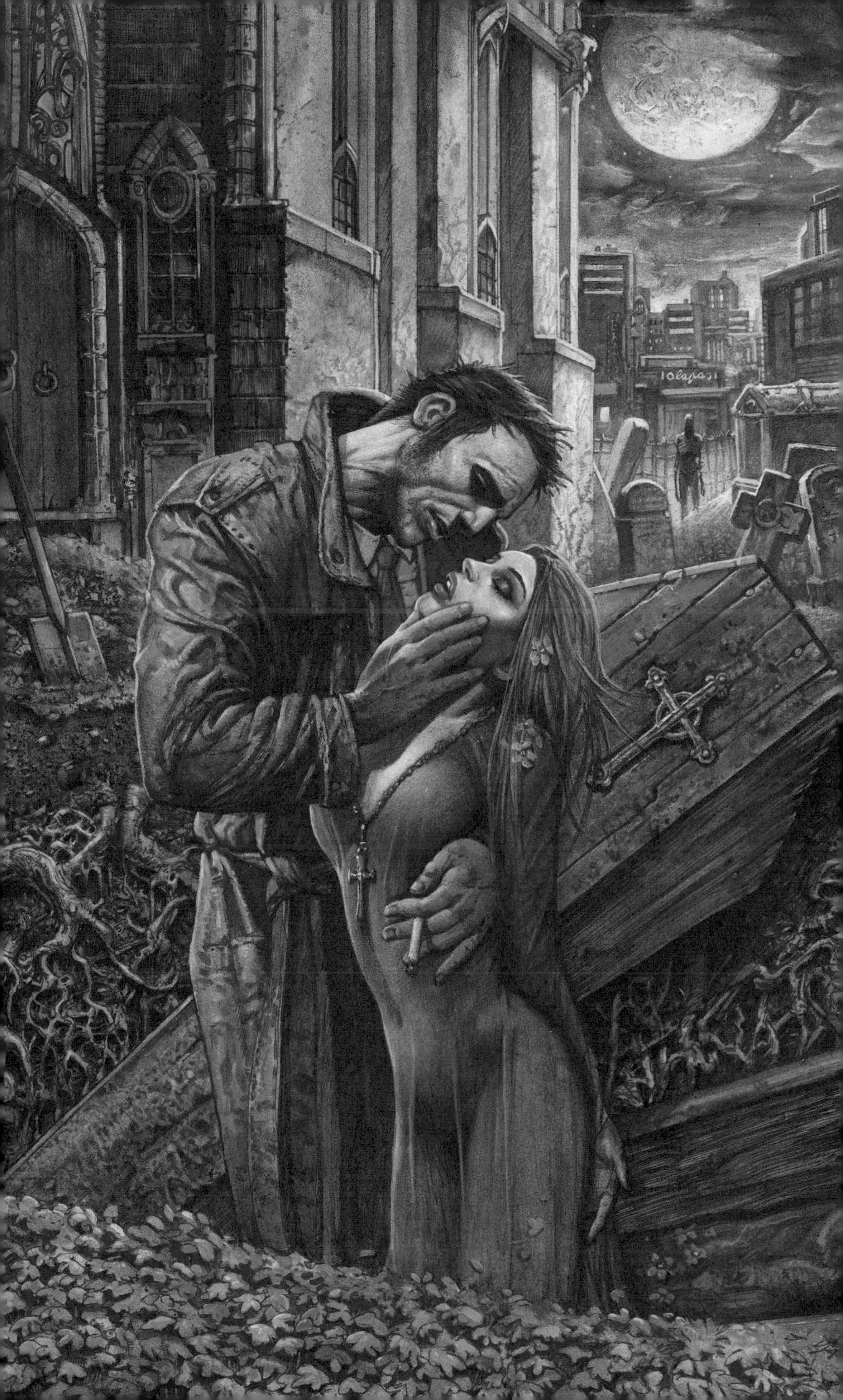

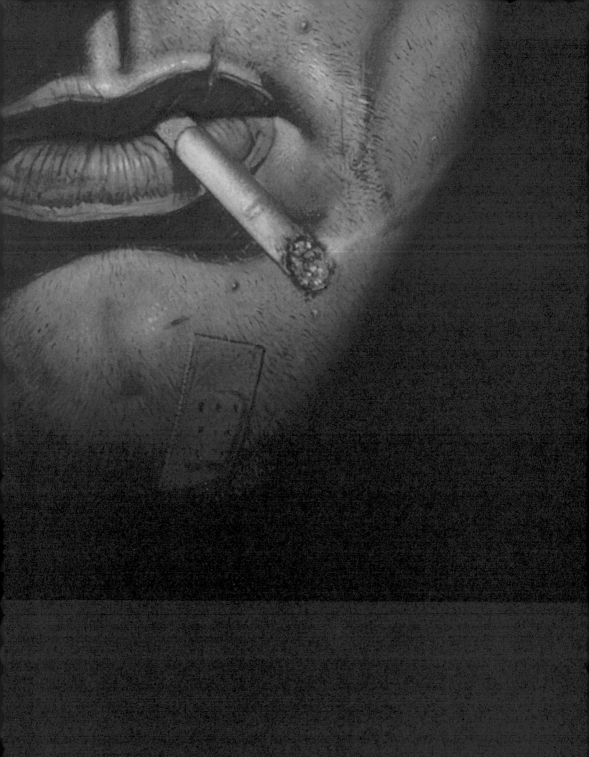

Hooked, **Part Three**
Epiphany

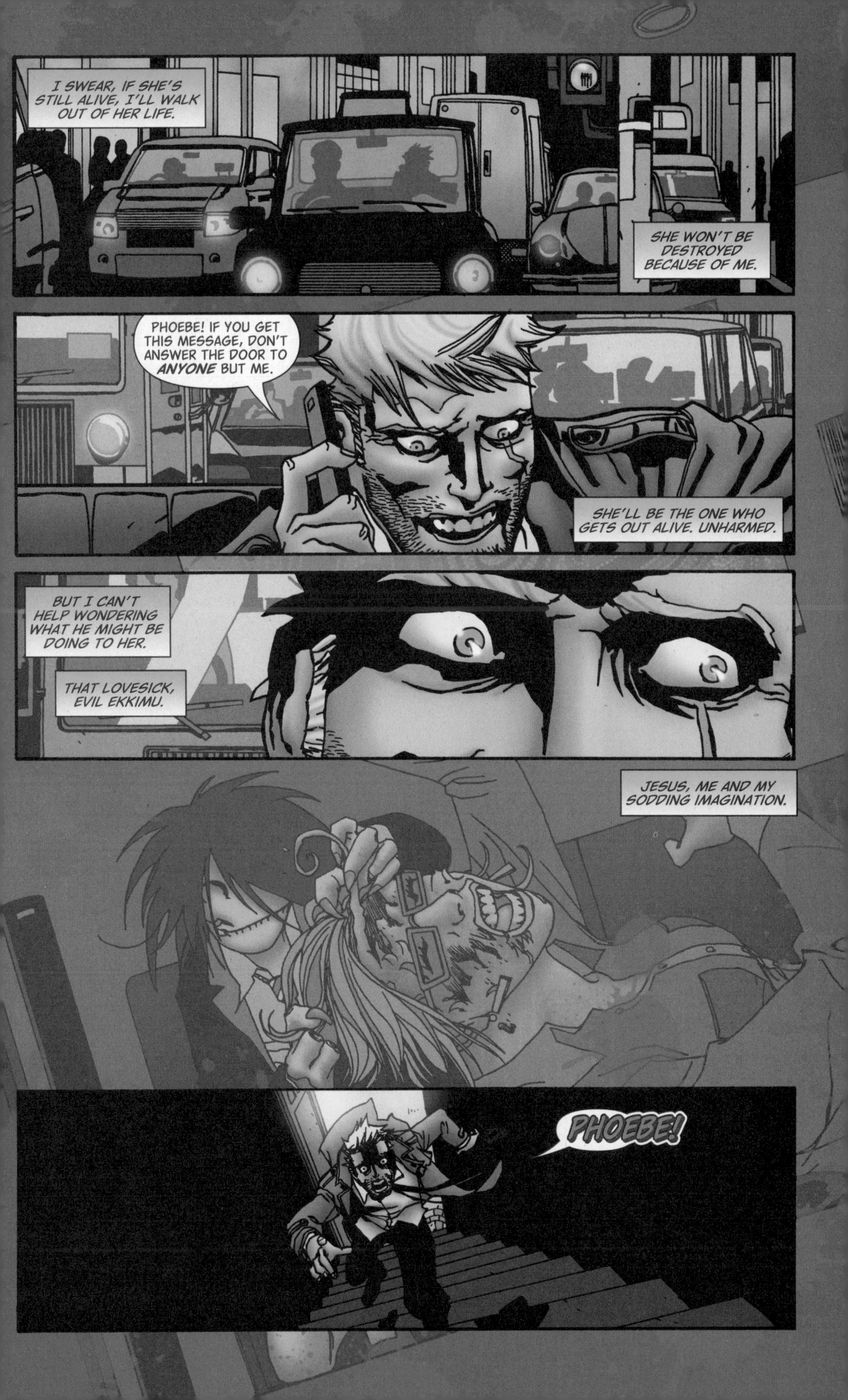

I SWEAR, IF SHE'S STILL ALIVE, I'LL WALK OUT OF HER LIFE.
SHE WON'T BE DESTROYED BECAUSE OF ME.
PHOEBE! IF YOU GET THIS MESSAGE, DON'T ANSWER THE DOOR TO ANYONE BUT ME.
SHE'LL BE THE ONE WHO GETS OUT ALIVE. UNHARMED.
BUT I CAN'T HELP WONDERING WHAT HE MIGHT BE DOING TO HER.
THAT LOVESICK, EVIL EKKIMU.
JESUS, ME AND MY SODDING IMAGINATION.
PHOEBE!

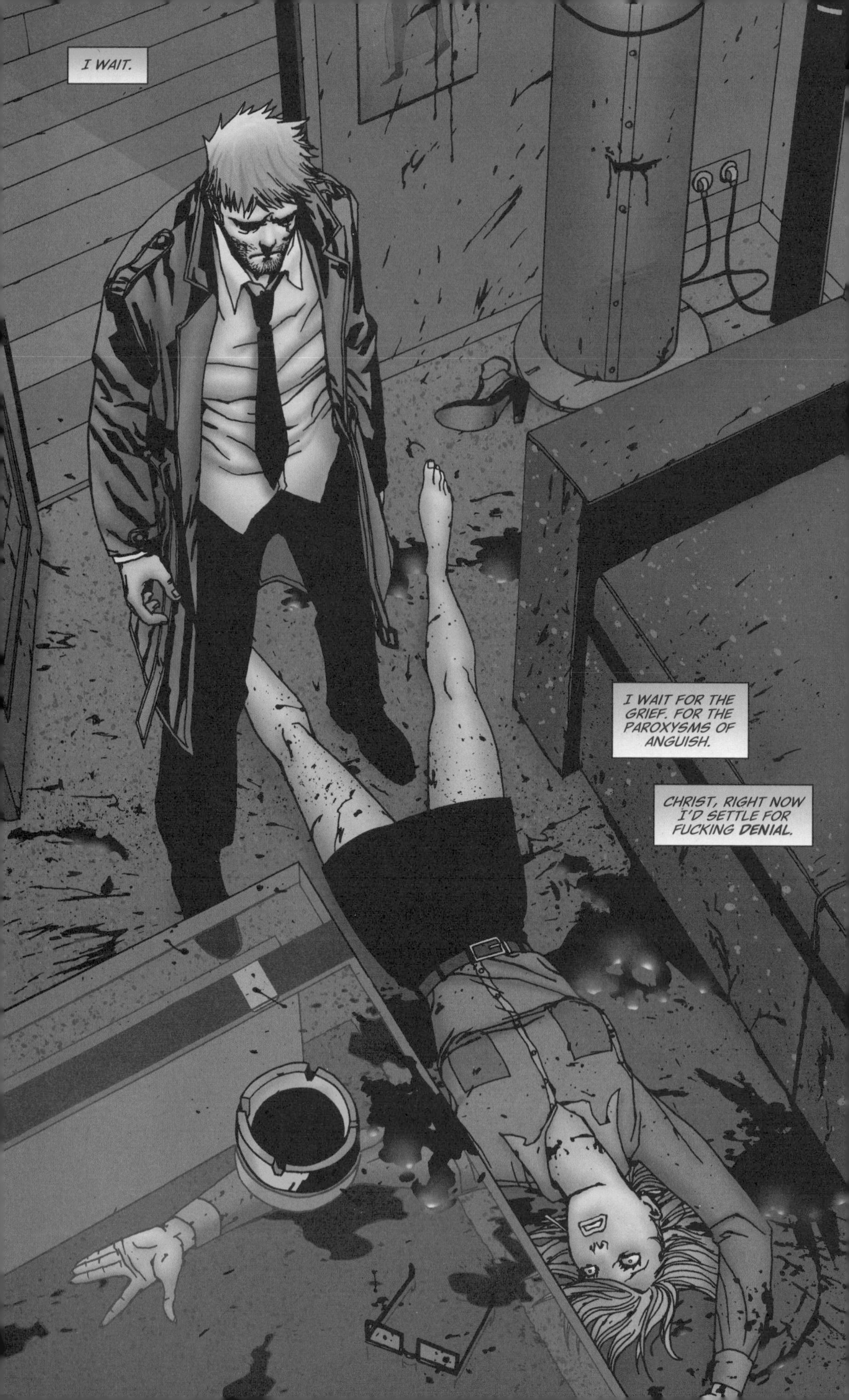
I WAIT.
I WAIT FOR THE GRIEF. FOR THE PAROXYSMS OF ANGUISH.
CHRIST, RIGHT NOW I'D SETTLE FOR FUCKING DENIAL.

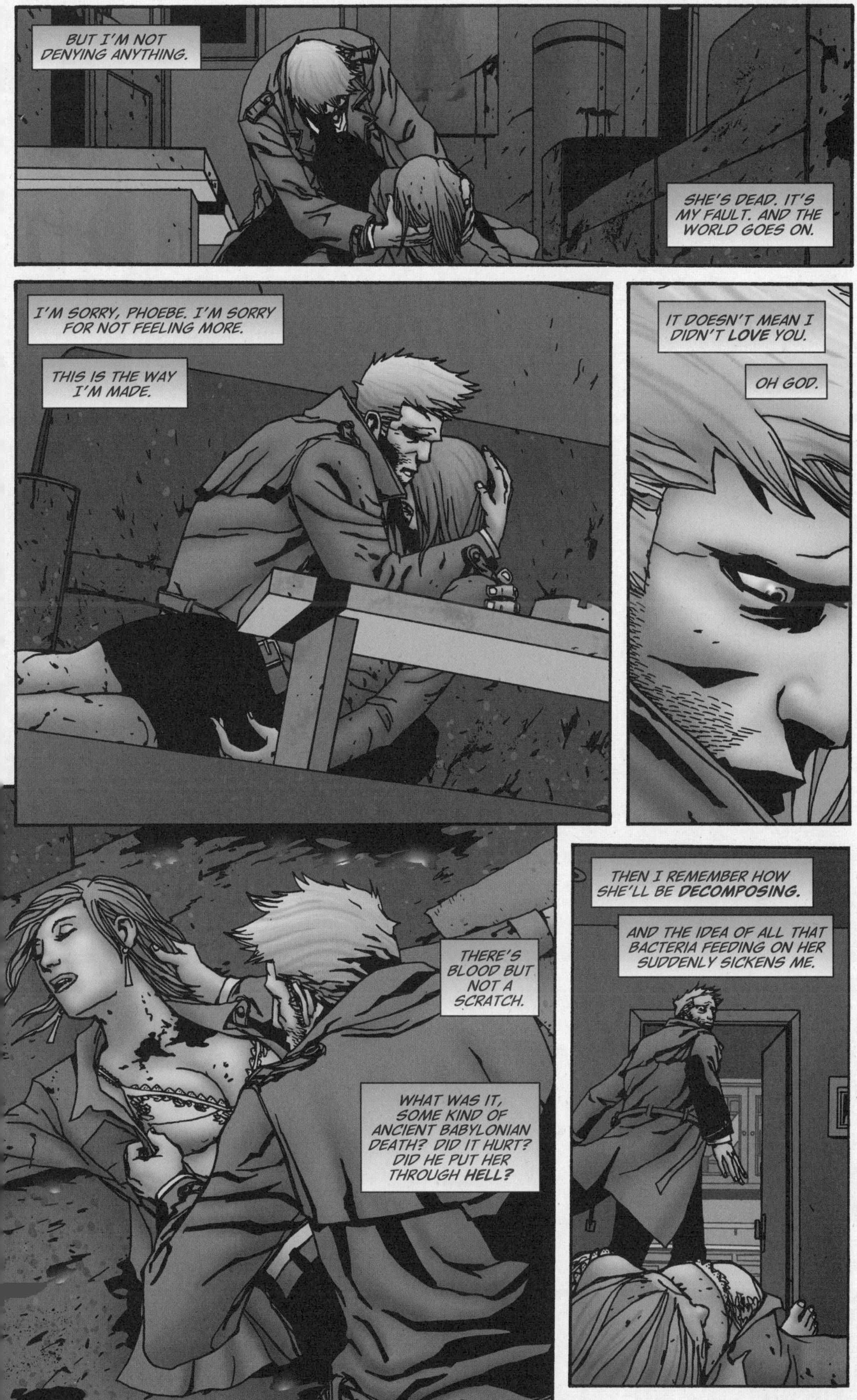
BUT I'M NOT DENYING ANYTHING.
SHE'S DEAD. IT'S MY FAULT. AND THE WORLD GOES ON.
I'M SORRY, PHOEBE. I'M SORRY FOR NOT FEELING MORE.
THIS IS THE WAY I'M MADE.
IT DOESN'T MEAN I DIDN'T LOVE YOU.
OH GOD.
THERE'S BLOOD BUT NOT A SCRATCH.
WHAT WAS IT, SOME KIND OF ANCIENT BABYLONIAN DEATH? DID IT HURT? DID HE PUT HER THROUGH HELL?
THEN I REMEMBER HOW SHE'LL BE DECOMPOSING.
AND THE IDEA OF ALL THAT BACTERIA FEEDING ON HER SUDDENLY SICKENS ME.

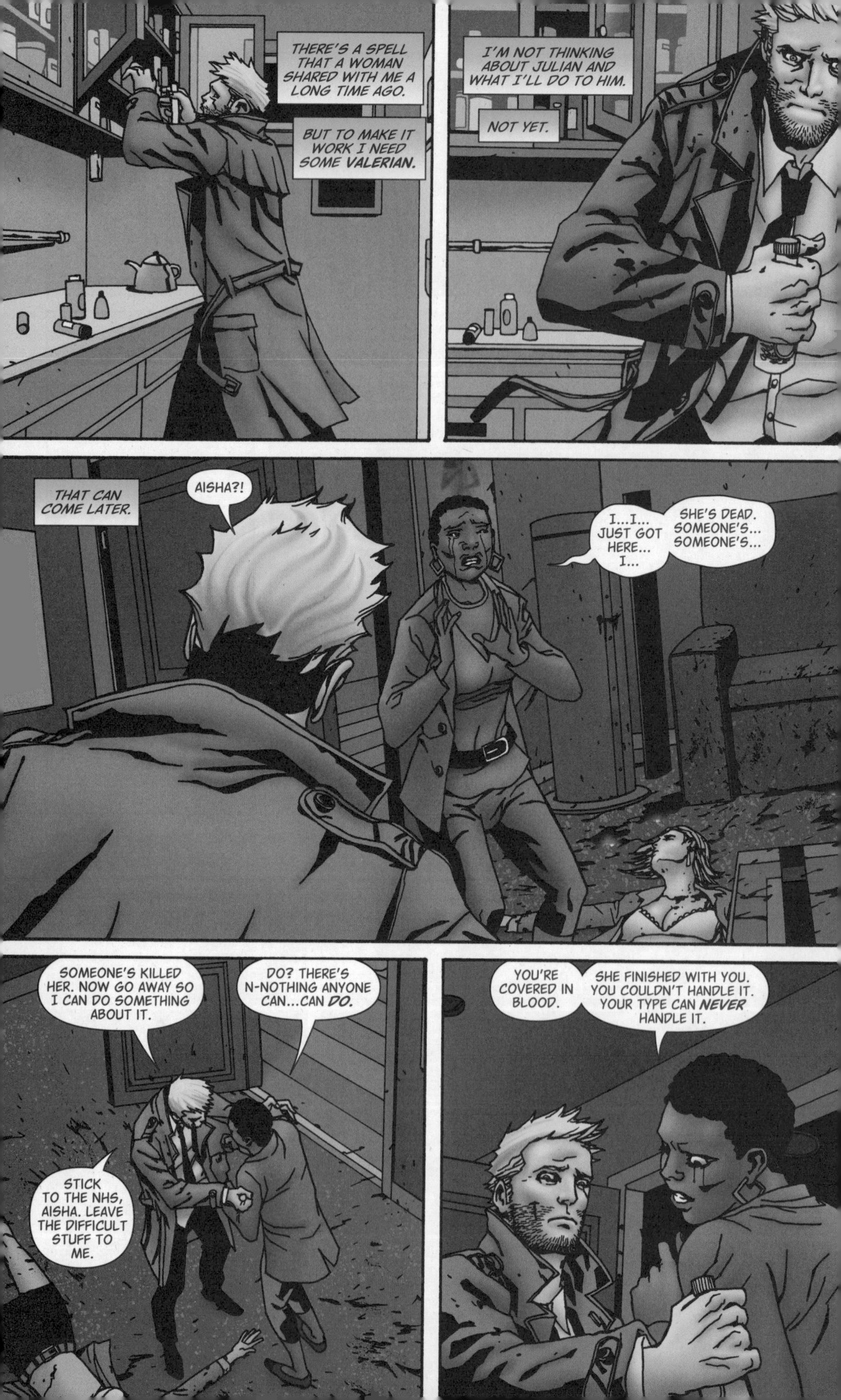
THERE'S A SPELL THAT A WOMAN SHARED WITH ME A LONG TIME AGO.
BUT TO MAKE IT WORK I NEED SOME VALERIAN.
I'M NOT THINKING ABOUT JULIAN AND WHAT I'LL DO TO HIM.
NOT YET.
THAT CAN COME LATER.
AISHA?!
I...I... JUST GOT HERE... I...
SHE'S DEAD. SOMEONE'S... SOMEONE'S...
SOMEONE'S KILLED HER. NOW GO AWAY SO I CAN DO SOMETHING ABOUT IT.
DO? THERE'S N-NOTHING ANYONE CAN...CAN DO.
STICK TO THE NHS, AISHA. LEAVE THE DIFFICULT STUFF TO ME.
YOU'RE COVERED IN BLOOD.
SHE FINISHED WITH YOU. YOU COULDN'T HANDLE IT. YOUR TYPE CAN NEVER HANDLE IT.

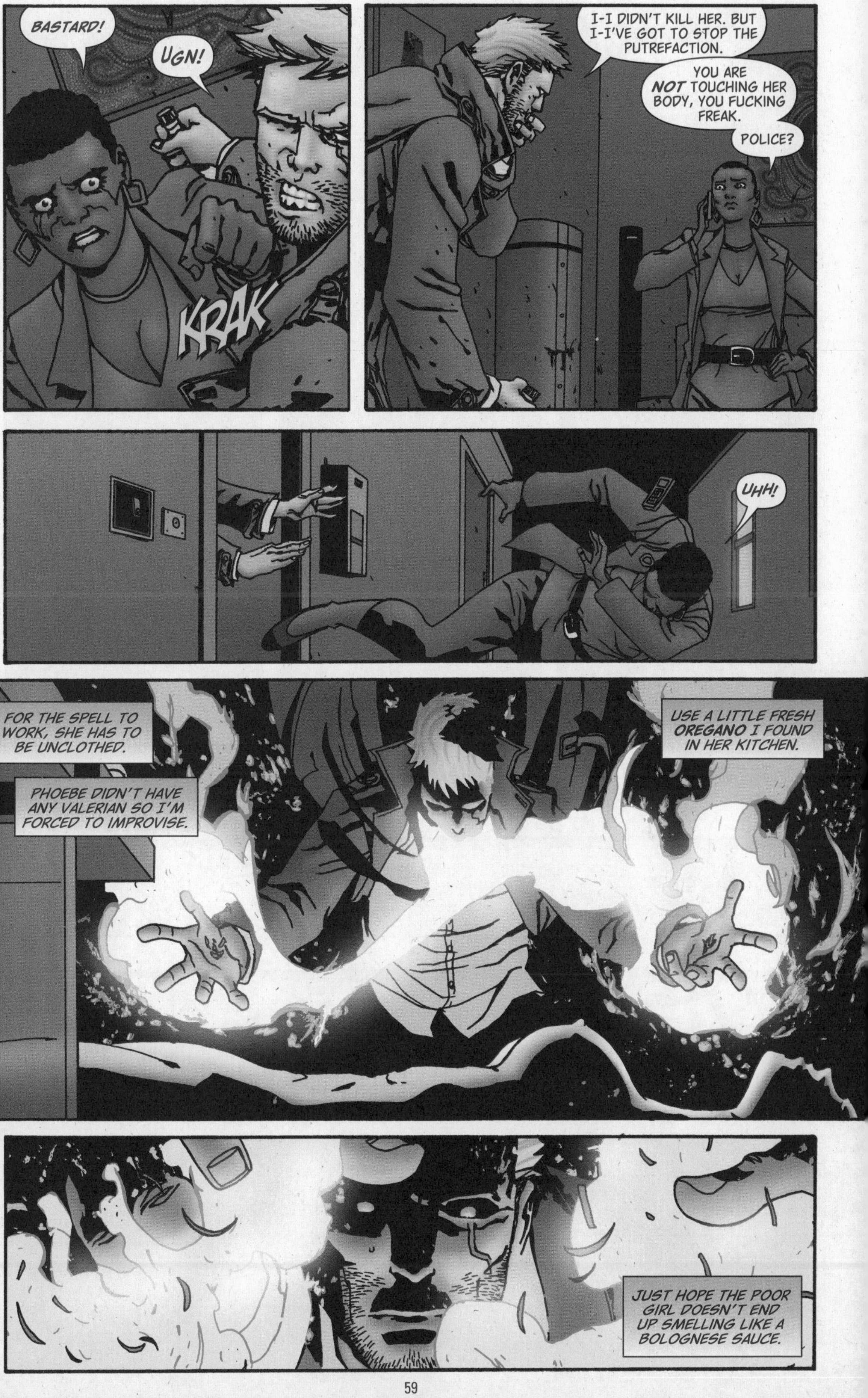
BASTARD!
UGN!
KRAK
I-I DIDN'T KILL HER. BUT I-I'VE GOT TO STOP THE PUTREFACTION.
YOU ARE NOT TOUCHING HER BODY, YOU FUCKING FREAK.
POLICE?
UHH!
FOR THE SPELL TO WORK, SHE HAS TO BE UNCLOTHED.
PHOEBE DIDN'T HAVE ANY VALERIAN SO I'M FORCED TO IMPROVISE.
USE A LITTLE FRESH OREGANO I FOUND IN HER KITCHEN.
JUST HOPE THE POOR GIRL DOESN'T END UP SMELLING LIKE A BOLOGNESE SAUCE.

HURRY UP! HE'S INSIDE. DOING SOMETHING *DEPRAVED* TO HER BODY.

JESUS. NOT ANOTHER ONE.

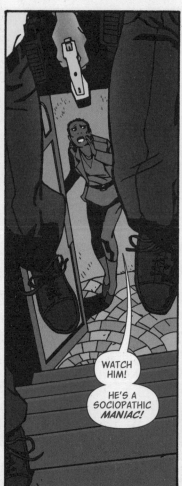

WATCH HIM!

HE'S A SOCIOPATHIC *MANIAC!*

TASER READY, MATTHEWS?

SIR.

"SO, HOW DID YOU GET PAST THEM?"

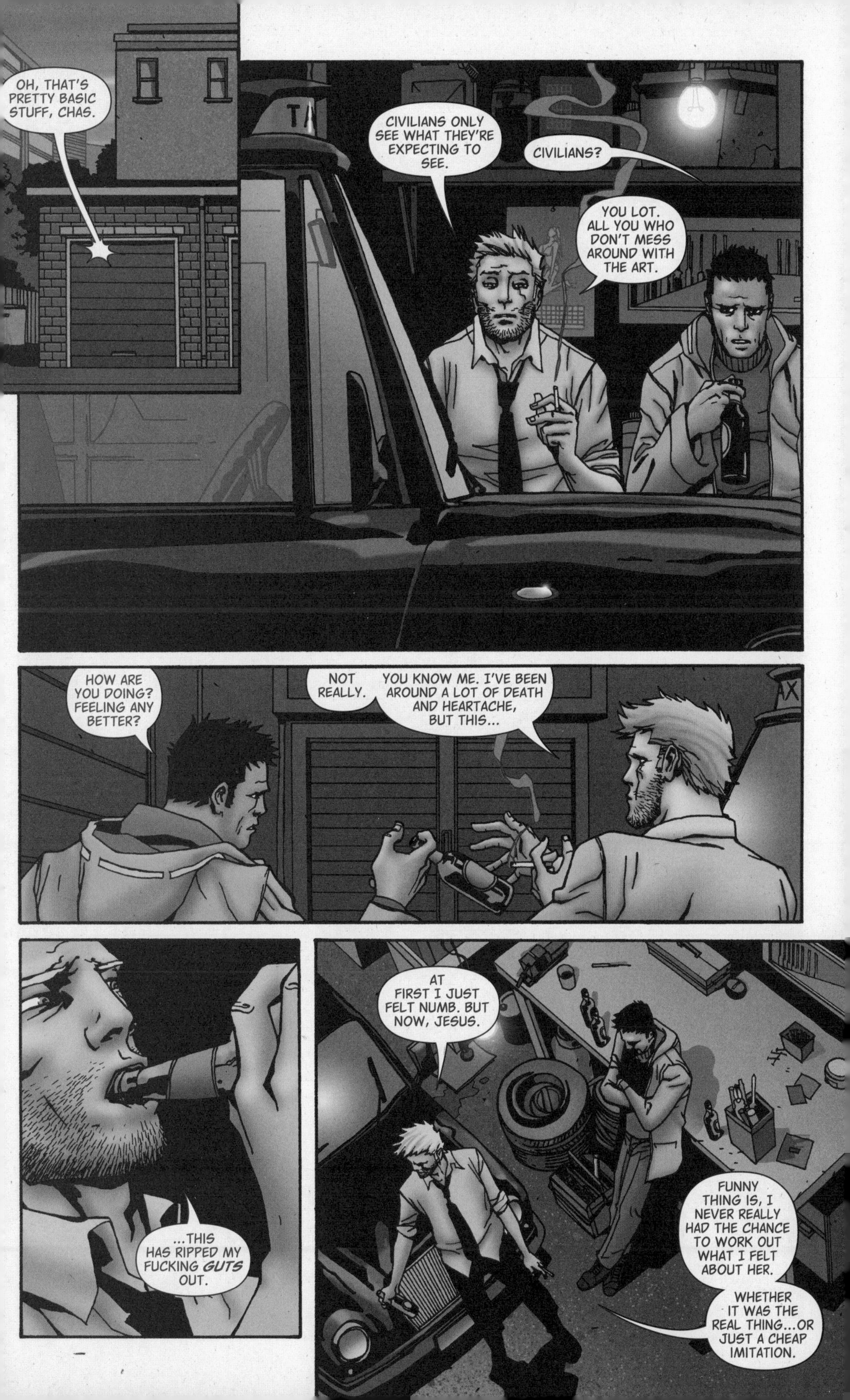

OH, THAT'S PRETTY BASIC STUFF, CHAS.
CIVILIANS ONLY SEE WHAT THEY'RE EXPECTING TO SEE.
CIVILIANS?
YOU LOT. ALL YOU WHO DON'T MESS AROUND WITH THE ART.
HOW ARE YOU DOING? FEELING ANY BETTER?
NOT REALLY.
YOU KNOW ME. I'VE BEEN AROUND A LOT OF DEATH AND HEARTACHE, BUT THIS...
...THIS HAS RIPPED MY FUCKING *GUTS* OUT.
AT FIRST I JUST FELT NUMB. BUT NOW, JESUS.
FUNNY THING IS, I NEVER REALLY HAD THE CHANCE TO WORK OUT WHAT I FELT ABOUT HER.
WHETHER IT WAS THE REAL THING...OR JUST A CHEAP IMITATION.

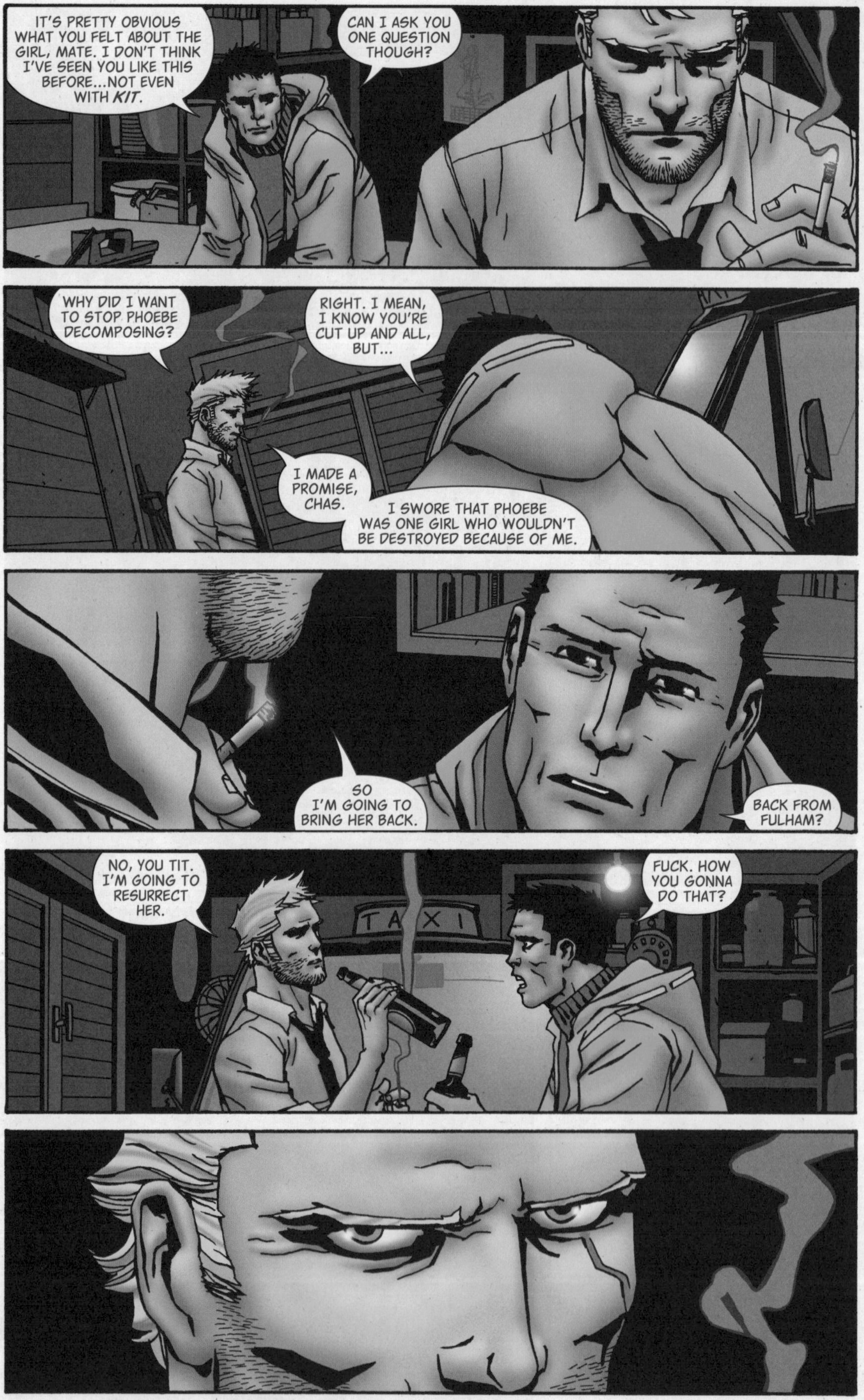
IT'S PRETTY OBVIOUS WHAT YOU FELT ABOUT THE GIRL, MATE. I DON'T THINK I'VE SEEN YOU LIKE THIS BEFORE...NOT EVEN WITH *KIT*.
CAN I ASK YOU ONE QUESTION THOUGH?
WHY DID I WANT TO STOP PHOEBE DECOMPOSING?
RIGHT. I MEAN, I KNOW YOU'RE CUT UP AND ALL, BUT...
I MADE A PROMISE, CHAS.
I SWORE THAT PHOEBE WAS ONE GIRL WHO WOULDN'T BE DESTROYED BECAUSE OF ME.
SO I'M GOING TO BRING HER BACK.
BACK FROM FULHAM?
NO, YOU TIT. I'M GOING TO RESURRECT HER.
FUCK. HOW YOU GONNA DO THAT?
TAXI

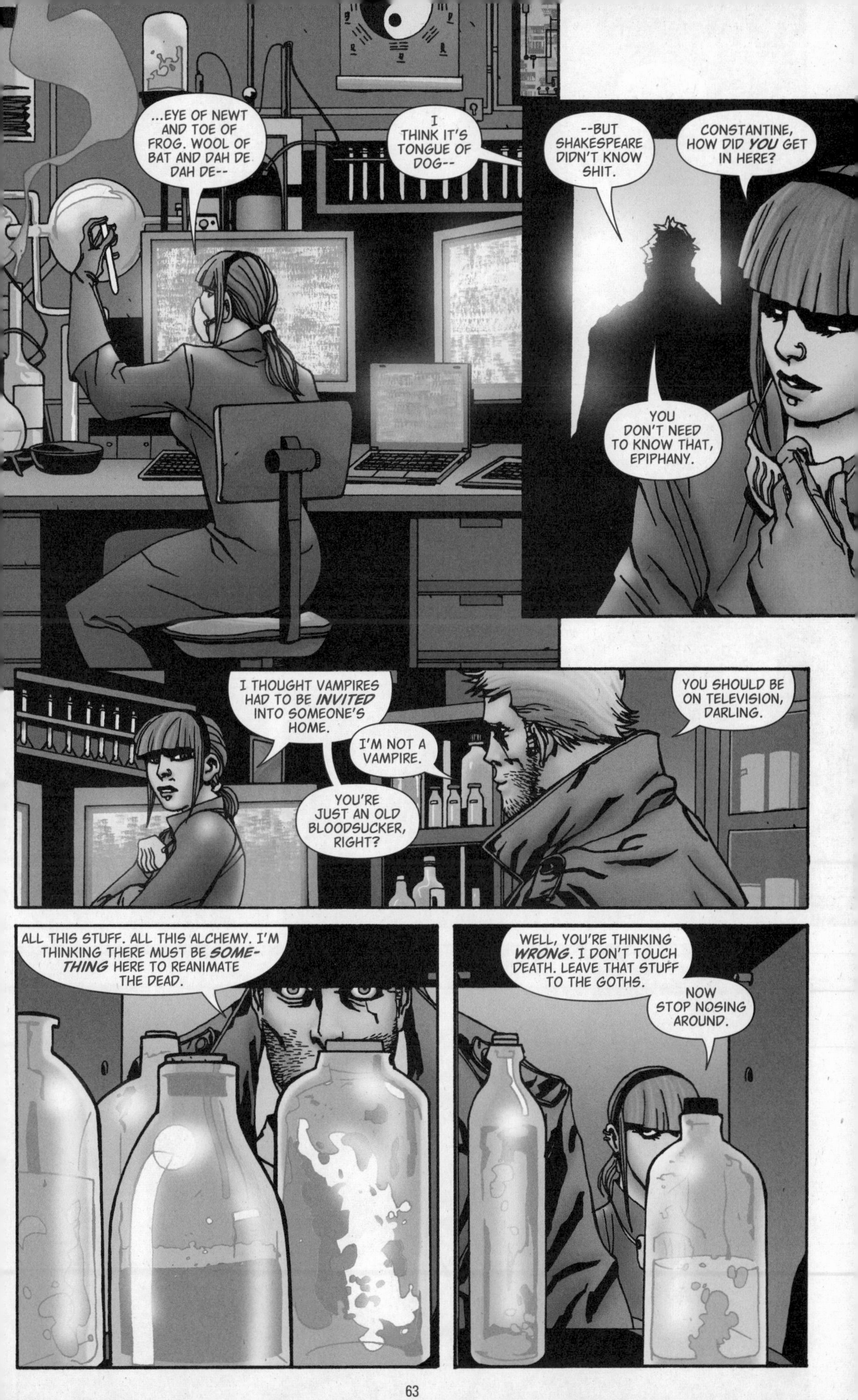
...EYE OF NEWT AND TOE OF FROG. WOOL OF BAT AND DAH DE DAH DE--
I THINK IT'S TONGUE OF DOG--
--BUT SHAKESPEARE DIDN'T KNOW SHIT.
CONSTANTINE, HOW DID *YOU* GET IN HERE?
YOU DON'T NEED TO KNOW THAT, EPIPHANY.
I THOUGHT VAMPIRES HAD TO BE *INVITED* INTO SOMEONE'S HOME.
I'M NOT A VAMPIRE.
YOU'RE JUST AN OLD BLOODSUCKER, RIGHT?
YOU SHOULD BE ON TELEVISION, DARLING.
ALL THIS STUFF. ALL THIS ALCHEMY. I'M THINKING THERE MUST BE *SOMETHING* HERE TO REANIMATE THE DEAD.
WELL, YOU'RE THINKING *WRONG*. I DON'T TOUCH DEATH. LEAVE THAT STUFF TO THE GOTHS.
NOW STOP NOSING AROUND.

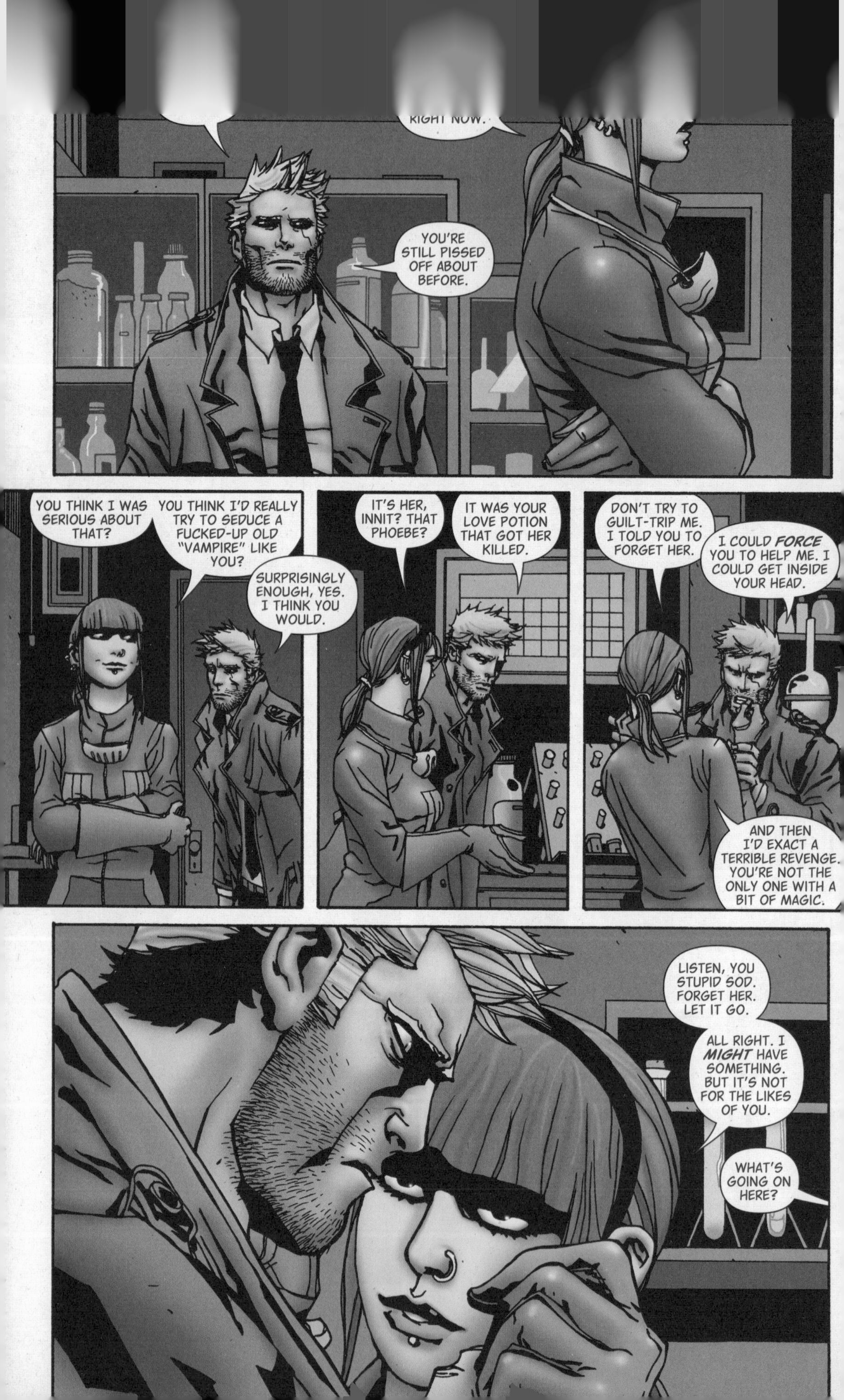
RIGHT NOW.
YOU'RE STILL PISSED OFF ABOUT BEFORE.
YOU THINK I WAS SERIOUS ABOUT THAT?
YOU THINK I'D REALLY TRY TO SEDUCE A FUCKED-UP OLD "VAMPIRE" LIKE YOU?
SURPRISINGLY ENOUGH, YES. I THINK YOU WOULD.
IT'S HER, INNIT? THAT PHOEBE?
IT WAS YOUR LOVE POTION THAT GOT HER KILLED.
DON'T TRY TO GUILT-TRIP ME. I TOLD YOU TO FORGET HER.
I COULD *FORCE* YOU TO HELP ME. I COULD GET INSIDE YOUR HEAD.
AND THEN I'D EXACT A TERRIBLE REVENGE. YOU'RE NOT THE ONLY ONE WITH A BIT OF MAGIC.
LISTEN, YOU STUPID SOD. FORGET HER. LET IT GO.
ALL RIGHT. I *MIGHT* HAVE SOMETHING. BUT IT'S NOT FOR THE LIKES OF YOU.
WHAT'S GOING ON HERE?

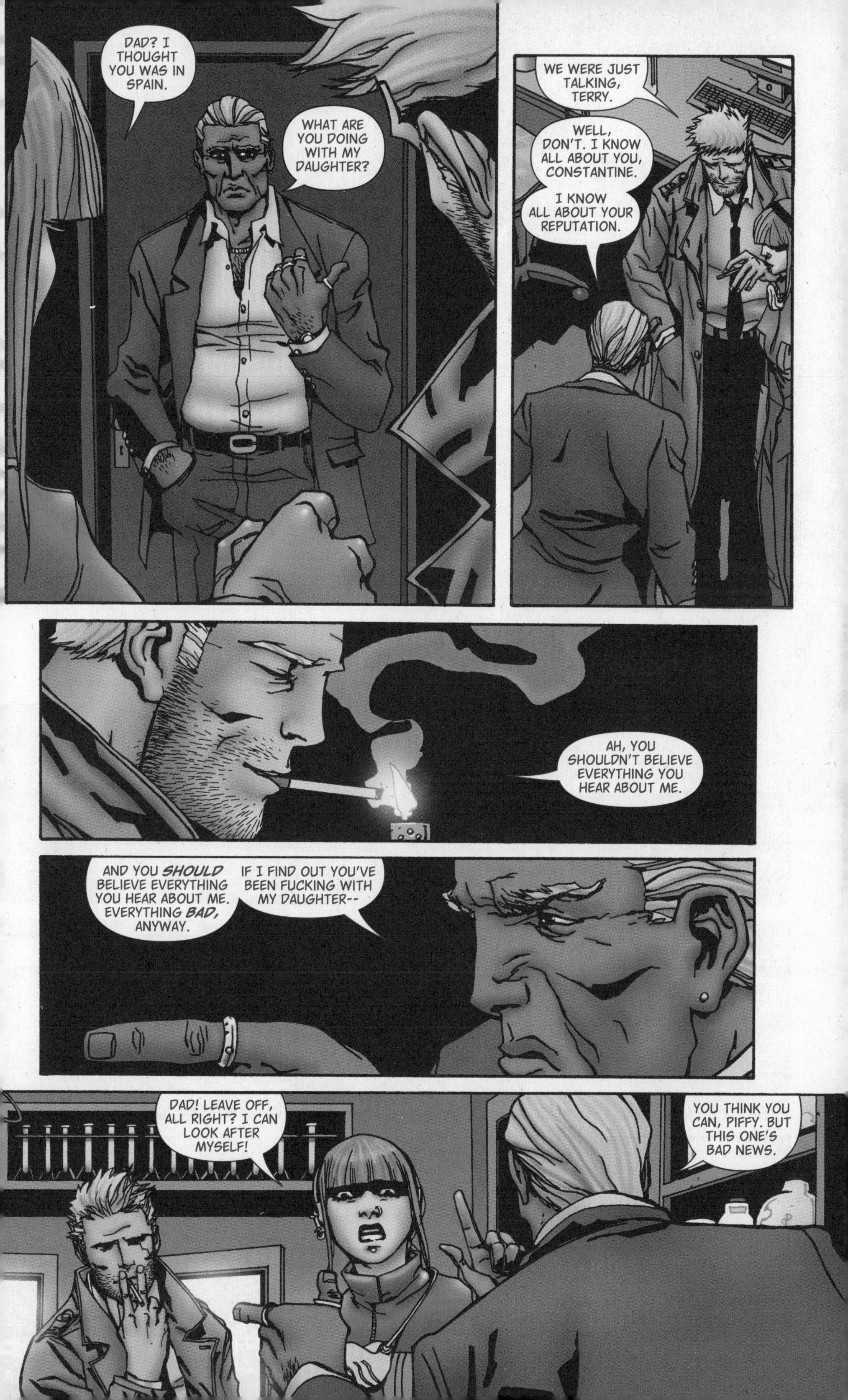
DAD? I THOUGHT YOU WAS IN SPAIN.
WHAT ARE YOU DOING WITH MY DAUGHTER?
WE WERE JUST TALKING, TERRY.
WELL, DON'T. I KNOW ALL ABOUT YOU, CONSTANTINE.
I KNOW ALL ABOUT YOUR REPUTATION.
AH, YOU SHOULDN'T BELIEVE EVERYTHING YOU HEAR ABOUT ME.
AND YOU *SHOULD* BELIEVE EVERYTHING YOU HEAR ABOUT ME. EVERYTHING *BAD,* ANYWAY.
IF I FIND OUT YOU'VE BEEN FUCKING WITH MY DAUGHTER--
DAD! LEAVE OFF, ALL RIGHT? I CAN LOOK AFTER MYSELF!
YOU THINK YOU CAN, PIFFY. BUT THIS ONE'S BAD NEWS.

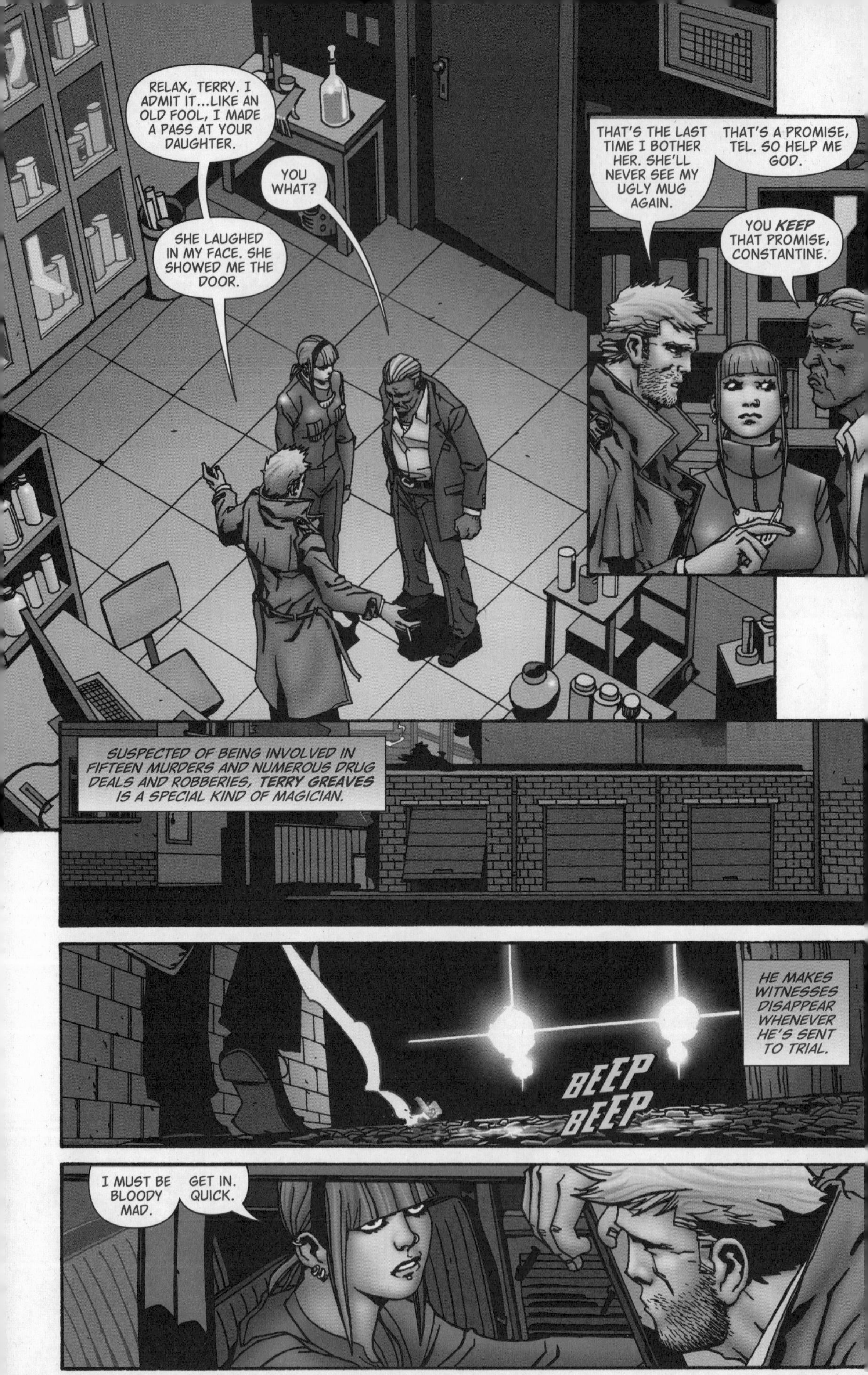
RELAX, TERRY. I ADMIT IT...LIKE AN OLD FOOL, I MADE A PASS AT YOUR DAUGHTER.
YOU WHAT?
SHE LAUGHED IN MY FACE. SHE SHOWED ME THE DOOR.
THAT'S THE LAST TIME I BOTHER HER. SHE'LL NEVER SEE MY UGLY MUG AGAIN.
THAT'S A PROMISE, TEL. SO HELP ME GOD.
YOU KEEP THAT PROMISE, CONSTANTINE.
SUSPECTED OF BEING INVOLVED IN FIFTEEN MURDERS AND NUMEROUS DRUG DEALS AND ROBBERIES, TERRY GREAVES IS A SPECIAL KIND OF MAGICIAN.
HE MAKES WITNESSES DISAPPEAR WHENEVER HE'S SENT TO TRIAL.
BEEP BEEP
I MUST BE BLOODY MAD.
GET IN. QUICK.

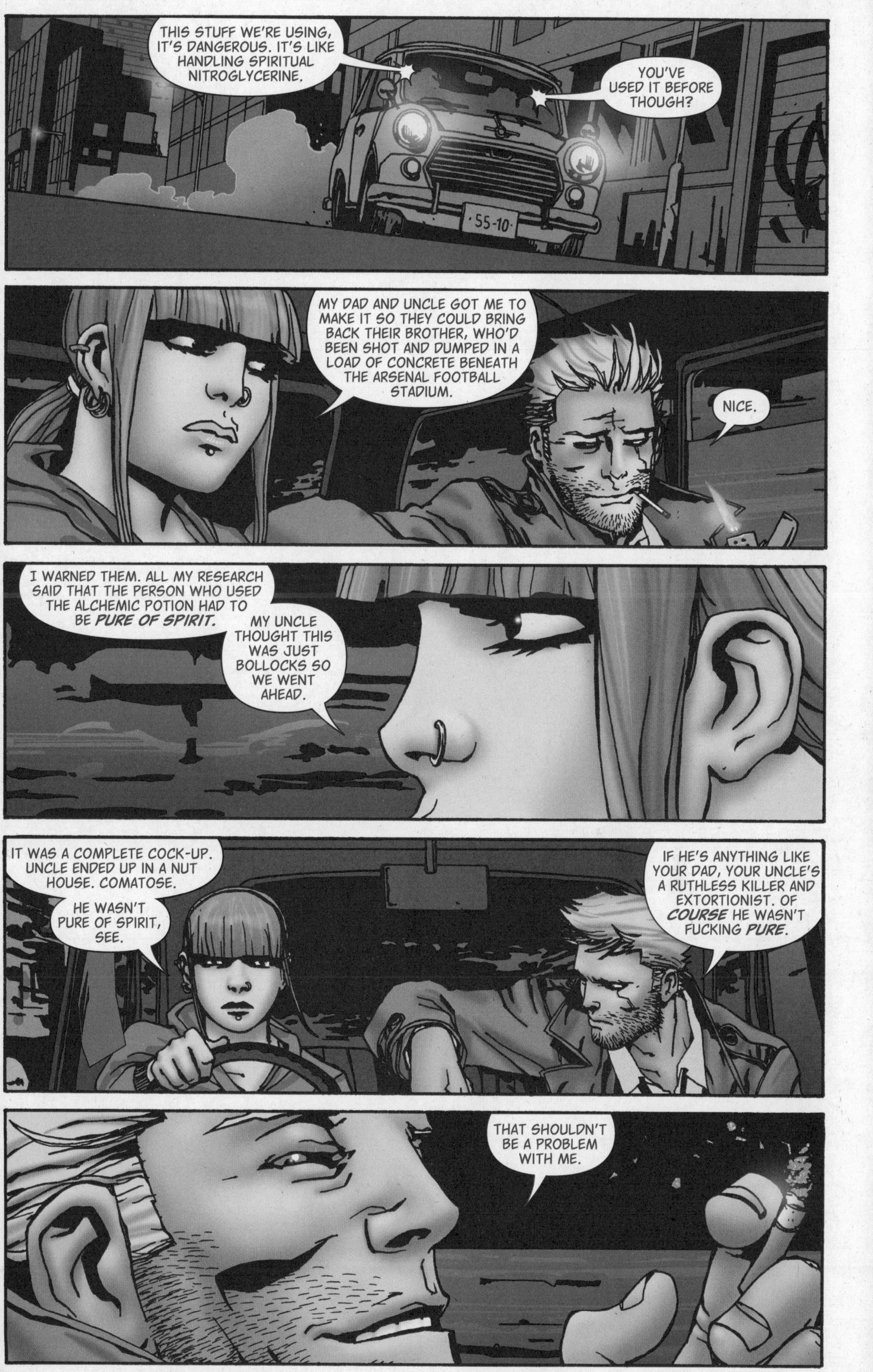
THIS STUFF WE'RE USING, IT'S DANGEROUS. IT'S LIKE HANDLING SPIRITUAL NITROGLYCERINE.
YOU'VE USED IT BEFORE THOUGH?
MY DAD AND UNCLE GOT ME TO MAKE IT SO THEY COULD BRING BACK THEIR BROTHER, WHO'D BEEN SHOT AND DUMPED IN A LOAD OF CONCRETE BENEATH THE ARSENAL FOOTBALL STADIUM.
NICE.
I WARNED THEM. ALL MY RESEARCH SAID THAT THE PERSON WHO USED THE ALCHEMIC POTION HAD TO BE *PURE OF SPIRIT.*
MY UNCLE THOUGHT THIS WAS JUST BOLLOCKS SO WE WENT AHEAD.
IT WAS A COMPLETE COCK-UP. UNCLE ENDED UP IN A NUT HOUSE. COMATOSE.
HE WASN'T PURE OF SPIRIT, SEE.
IF HE'S ANYTHING LIKE YOUR DAD, YOUR UNCLE'S A RUTHLESS KILLER AND EXTORTIONIST. OF ***COURSE*** HE WASN'T FUCKING *PURE*.
THAT SHOULDN'T BE A PROBLEM WITH ME.

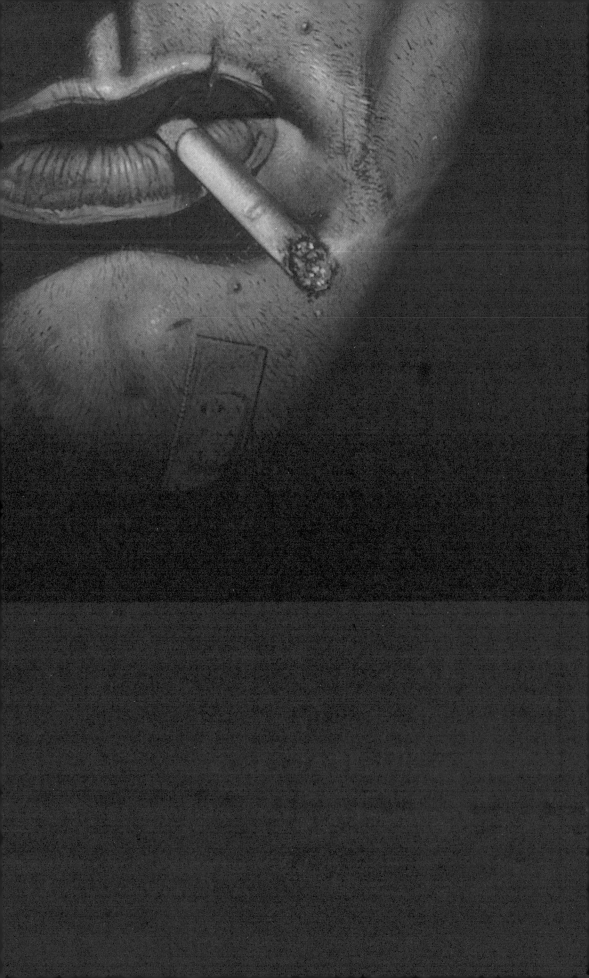

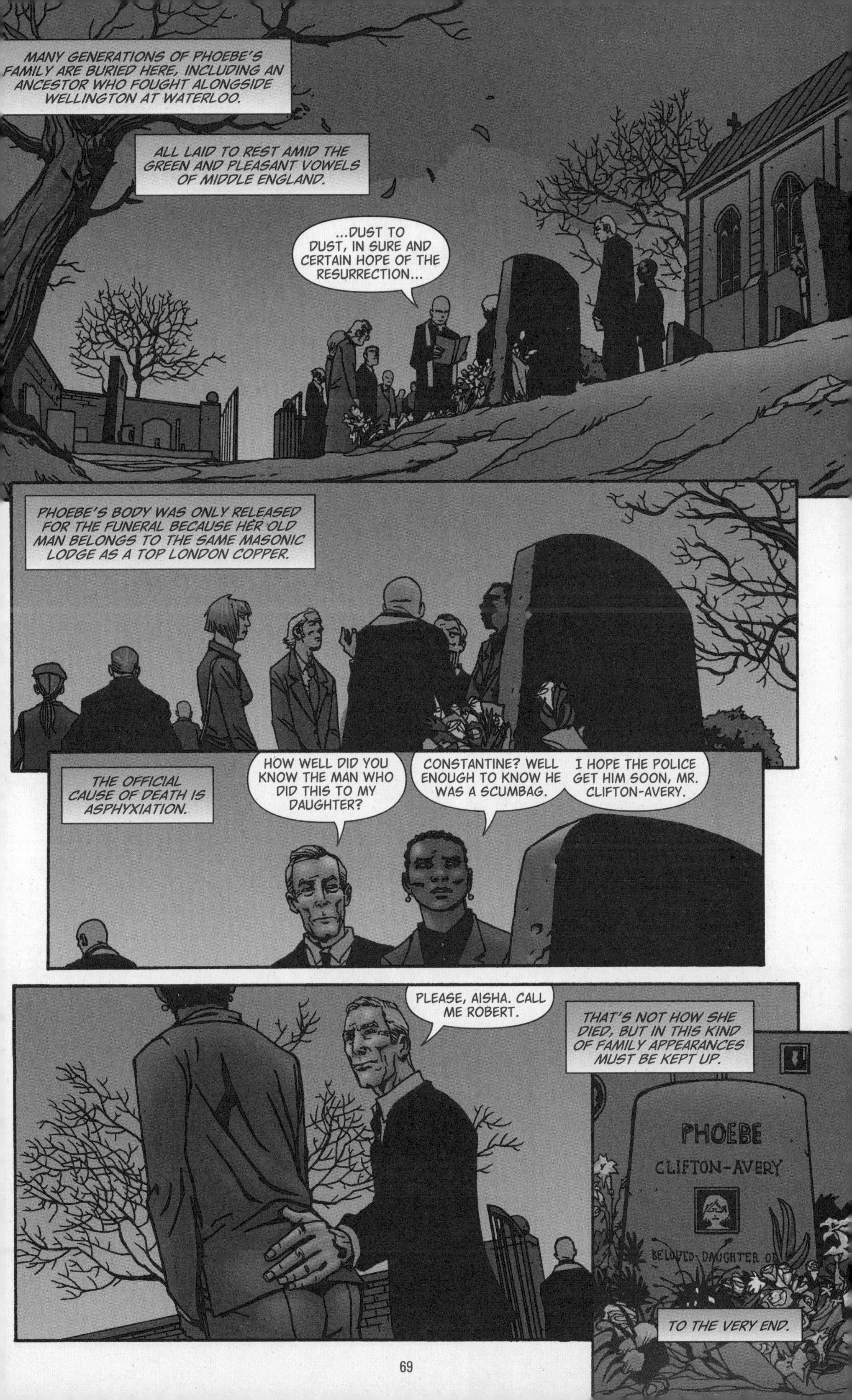
MANY GENERATIONS OF PHOEBE'S FAMILY ARE BURIED HERE, INCLUDING AN ANCESTOR WHO FOUGHT ALONGSIDE WELLINGTON AT WATERLOO.
ALL LAID TO REST AMID THE GREEN AND PLEASANT VOWELS OF MIDDLE ENGLAND.
...DUST TO DUST, IN SURE AND CERTAIN HOPE OF THE RESURRECTION...
PHOEBE'S BODY WAS ONLY RELEASED FOR THE FUNERAL BECAUSE HER OLD MAN BELONGS TO THE SAME MASONIC LODGE AS A TOP LONDON COPPER.
THE OFFICIAL CAUSE OF DEATH IS ASPHYXIATION.
HOW WELL DID YOU KNOW THE MAN WHO DID THIS TO MY DAUGHTER?
CONSTANTINE? WELL ENOUGH TO KNOW HE WAS A SCUMBAG.
I HOPE THE POLICE GET HIM SOON, MR. CLIFTON-AVERY.
PLEASE, AISHA. CALL ME ROBERT.
THAT'S NOT HOW SHE DIED, BUT IN THIS KIND OF FAMILY APPEARANCES MUST BE KEPT UP.
PHOEBE
CLIFTON-AVERY
BELOVED DAUGHTER OF
TO THE VERY END.

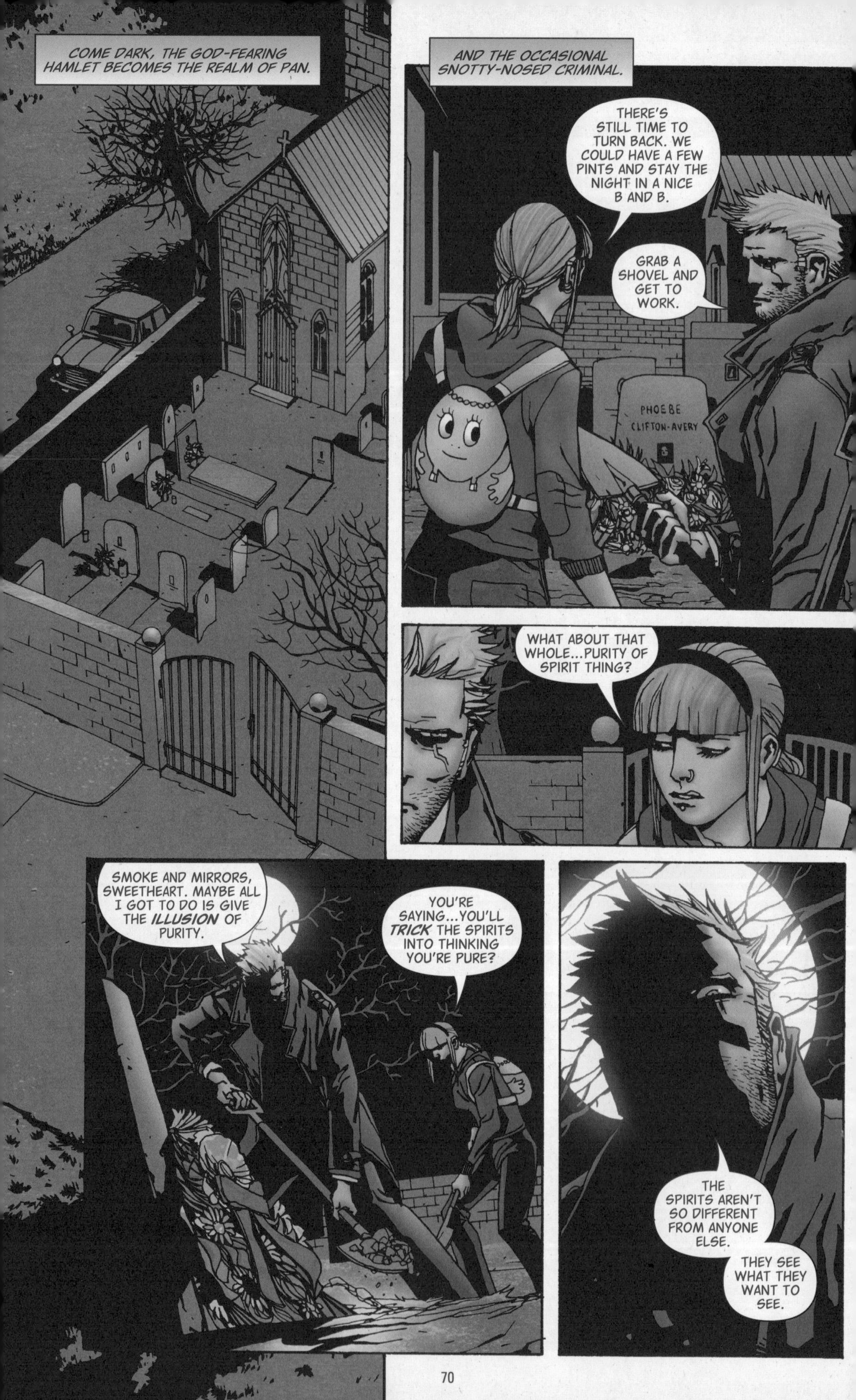
COME DARK, THE GOD-FEARING HAMLET BECOMES THE REALM OF PAN.
AND THE OCCASIONAL SNOTTY-NOSED CRIMINAL.
THERE'S STILL TIME TO TURN BACK. WE COULD HAVE A FEW PINTS AND STAY THE NIGHT IN A NICE B AND B.
GRAB A SHOVEL AND GET TO WORK.
PHOEBE CLIFTON-AVERY
WHAT ABOUT THAT WHOLE...PURITY OF SPIRIT THING?
SMOKE AND MIRRORS, SWEETHEART. MAYBE ALL I GOT TO DO IS GIVE THE *ILLUSION* OF PURITY.
YOU'RE SAYING...YOU'LL *TRICK* THE SPIRITS INTO THINKING YOU'RE PURE?
THE SPIRITS AREN'T SO DIFFERENT FROM ANYONE ELSE.
THEY SEE WHAT THEY WANT TO SEE.

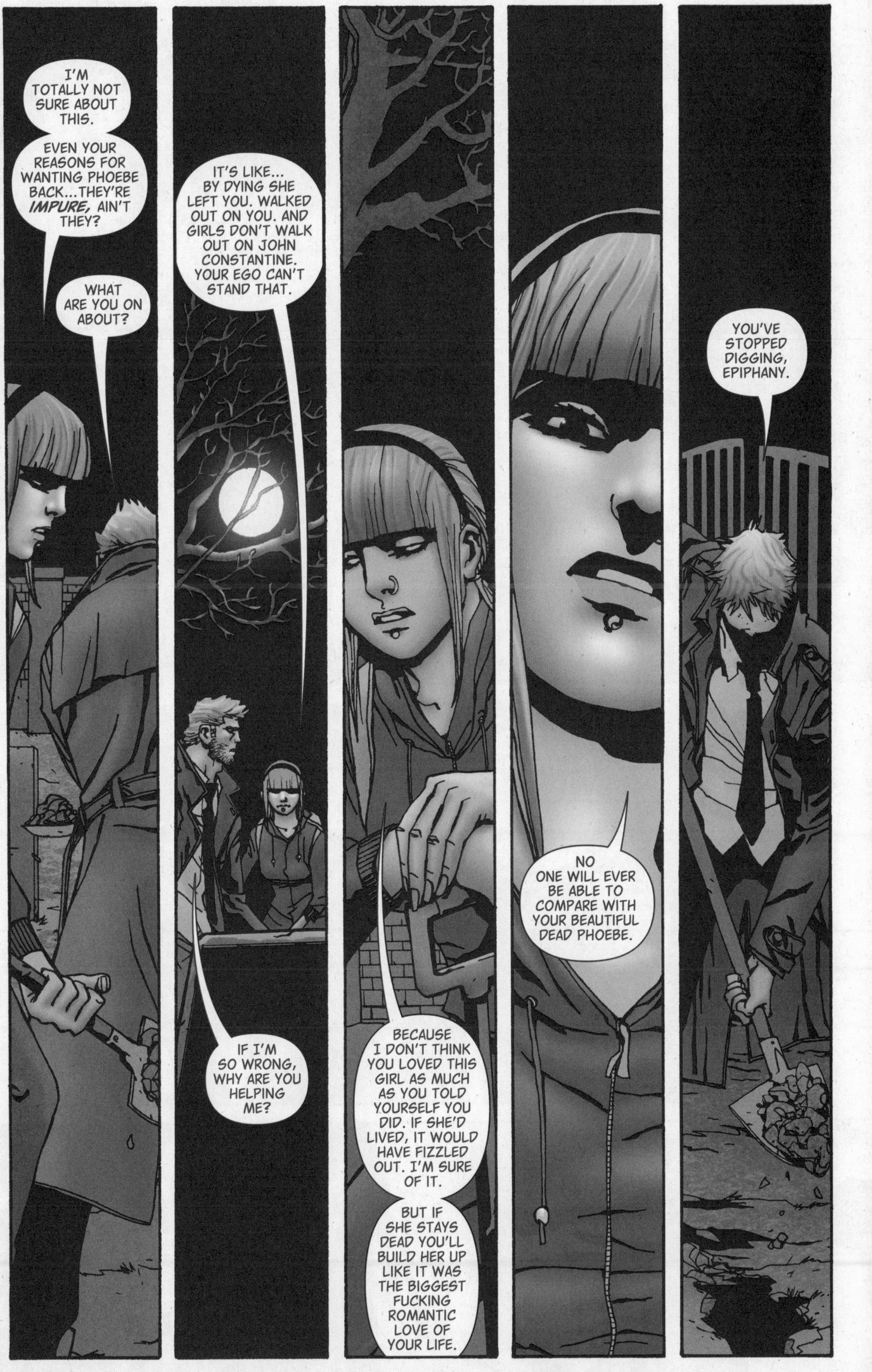
I'M TOTALLY NOT SURE ABOUT THIS.
EVEN YOUR REASONS FOR WANTING PHOEBE BACK...THEY'RE *IMPURE,* AIN'T THEY?
WHAT ARE YOU ON ABOUT?
IT'S LIKE... BY DYING SHE LEFT YOU. WALKED OUT ON YOU. AND GIRLS DON'T WALK OUT ON JOHN CONSTANTINE. YOUR EGO CAN'T STAND THAT.
IF I'M SO WRONG, WHY ARE YOU HELPING ME?
BECAUSE I DON'T THINK YOU LOVED THIS GIRL AS MUCH AS YOU TOLD YOURSELF YOU DID. IF SHE'D LIVED, IT WOULD HAVE FIZZLED OUT. I'M SURE OF IT.
BUT IF SHE STAYS DEAD YOU'LL BUILD HER UP LIKE IT WAS THE BIGGEST FUCKING ROMANTIC LOVE OF YOUR LIFE.
NO ONE WILL EVER BE ABLE TO COMPARE WITH YOUR BEAUTIFUL DEAD PHOEBE.
YOU'VE STOPPED DIGGING, EPIPHANY.

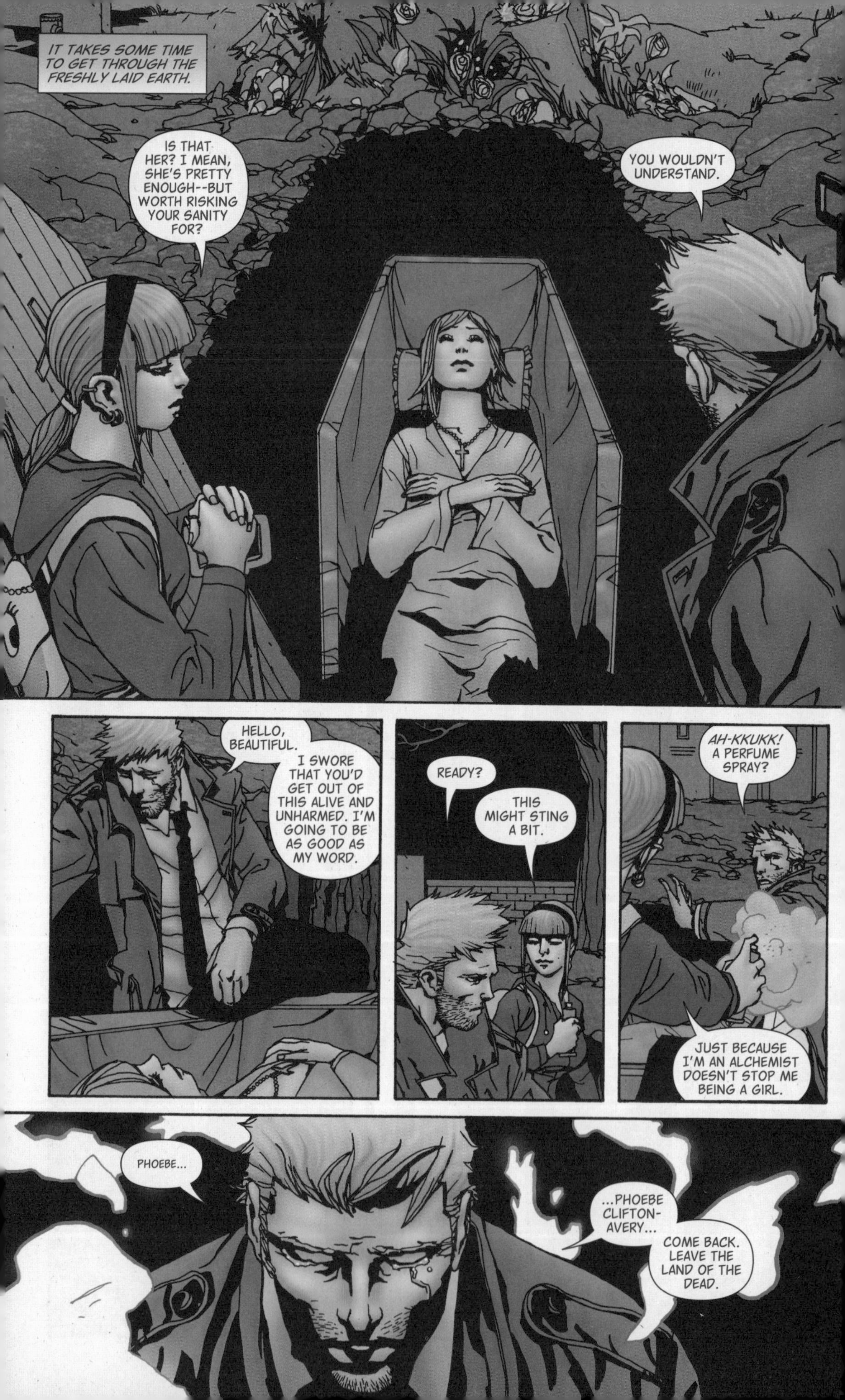

IT TAKES SOME TIME TO GET THROUGH THE FRESHLY LAID EARTH.
IS THAT HER? I MEAN, SHE'S PRETTY ENOUGH--BUT WORTH RISKING YOUR SANITY FOR?
YOU WOULDN'T UNDERSTAND.
HELLO, BEAUTIFUL.
I SWORE THAT YOU'D GET OUT OF THIS ALIVE AND UNHARMED. I'M GOING TO BE AS GOOD AS MY WORD.
READY?
THIS MIGHT STING A BIT.
AH-KKUKK! A PERFUME SPRAY?
JUST BECAUSE I'M AN ALCHEMIST DOESN'T STOP ME BEING A GIRL.
PHOEBE...
...PHOEBE CLIFTON-AVERY...
COME BACK. LEAVE THE LAND OF THE DEAD.

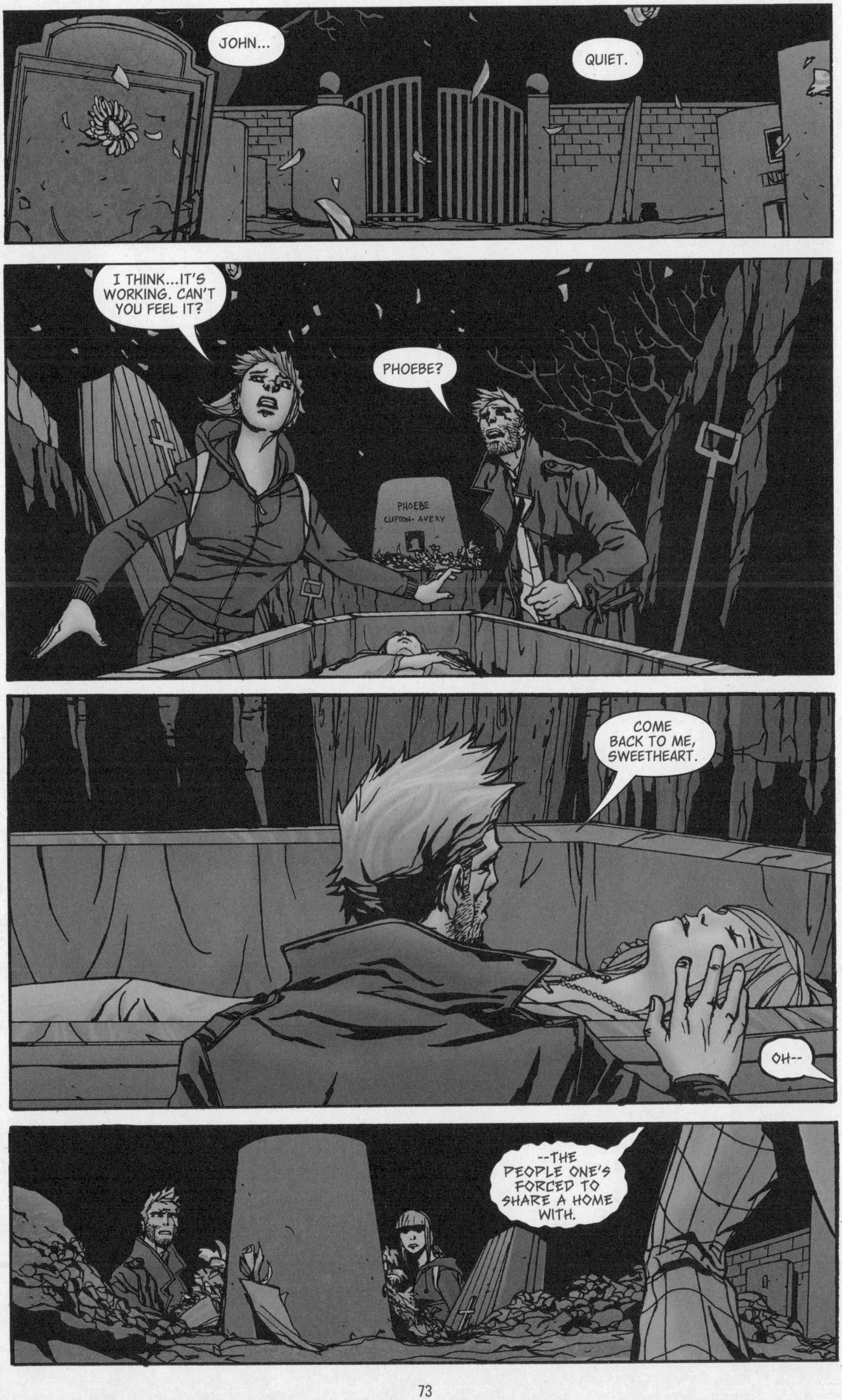
JOHN...
QUIET.
I THINK...IT'S WORKING. CAN'T YOU FEEL IT?
PHOEBE?
PHOEBE CLIFTON-AVERY
COME BACK TO ME, SWEETHEART.
OH--
--THE PEOPLE ONE'S FORCED TO SHARE A HOME WITH.

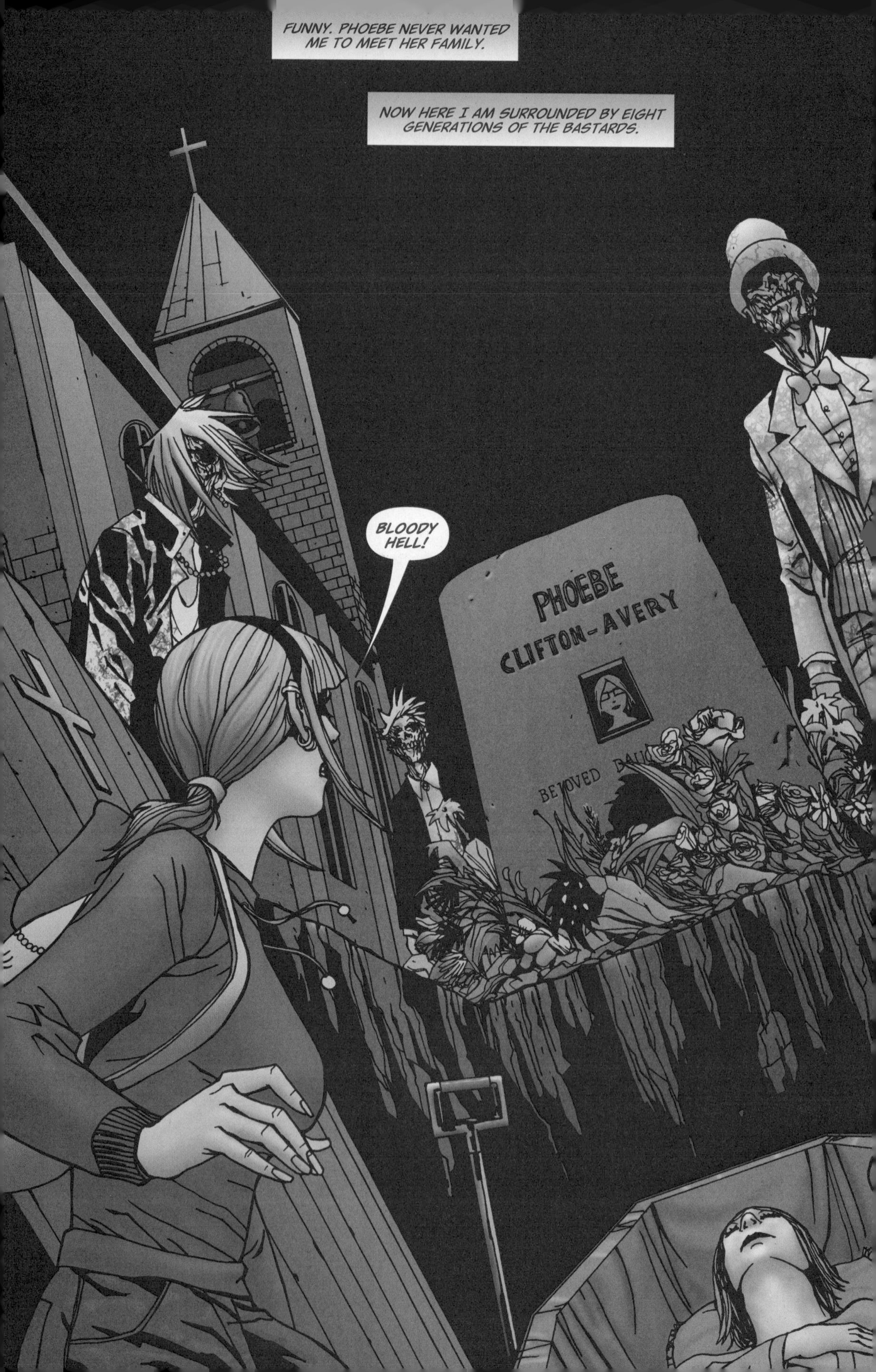
FUNNY. PHOEBE NEVER WANTED ME TO MEET HER FAMILY.
NOW HERE I AM SURROUNDED BY EIGHT GENERATIONS OF THE BASTARDS.
BLOODY HELL!
PHOEBE CLIFTON-AVERY

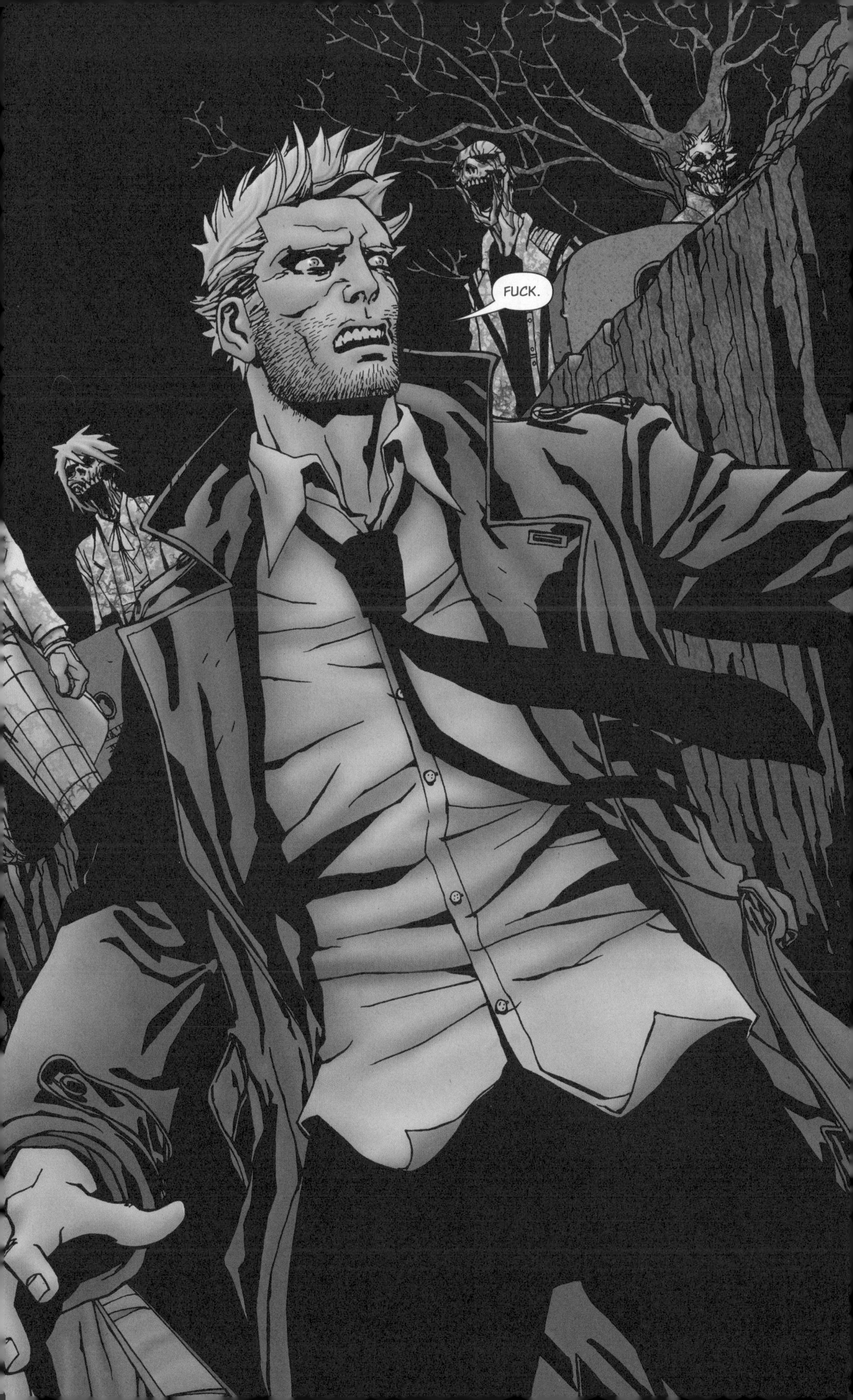
FUCK.

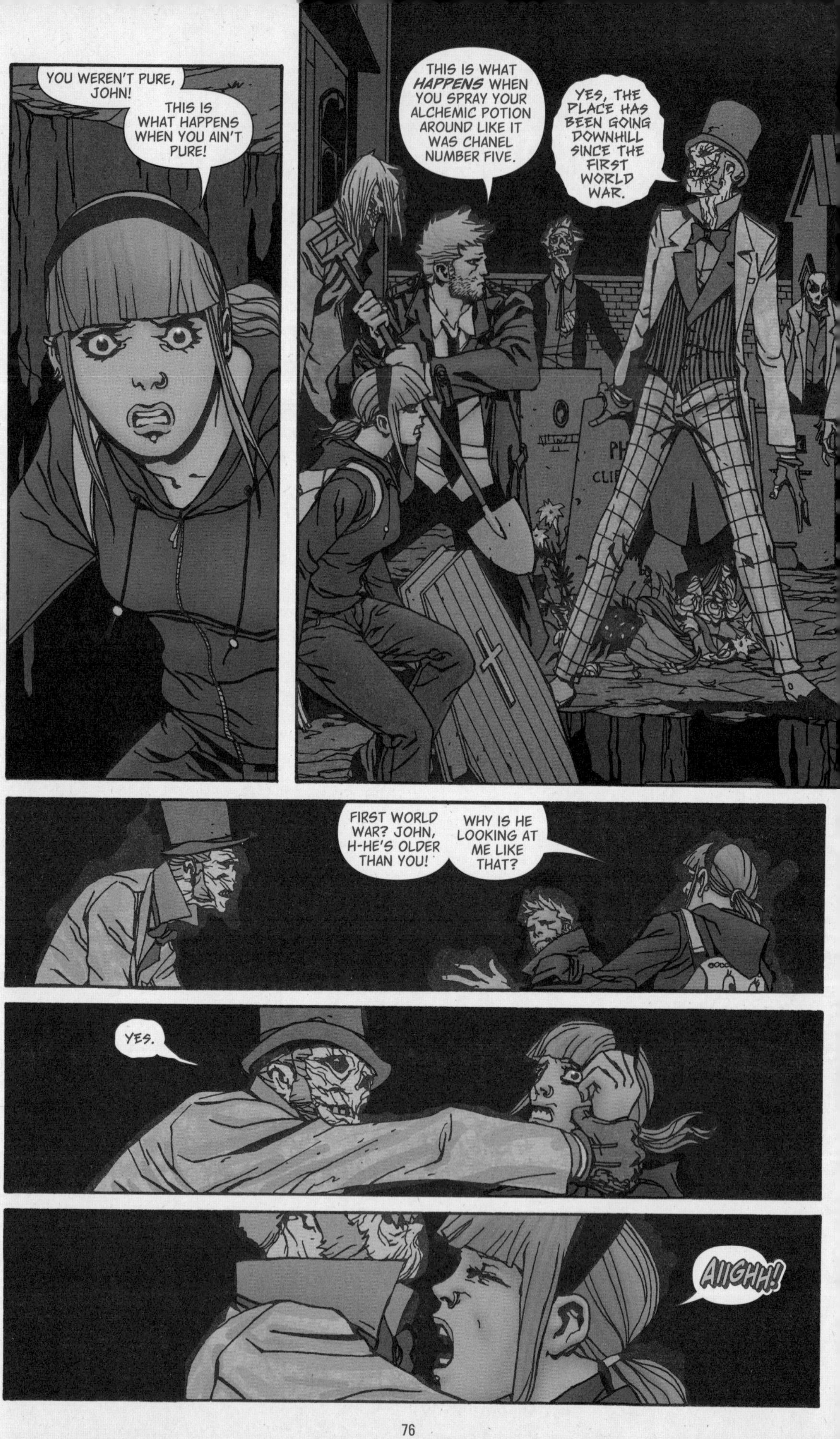
YOU WEREN'T PURE, JOHN!
THIS IS WHAT HAPPENS WHEN YOU AIN'T PURE!
THIS IS WHAT *HAPPENS* WHEN YOU SPRAY YOUR ALCHEMIC POTION AROUND LIKE IT WAS CHANEL NUMBER FIVE.
YES, THE PLACE HAS BEEN GOING DOWNHILL SINCE THE FIRST WORLD WAR.
FIRST WORLD WAR? JOHN, H-HE'S OLDER THAN YOU!
WHY IS HE LOOKING AT ME LIKE THAT?
YES.
AIIGHH!

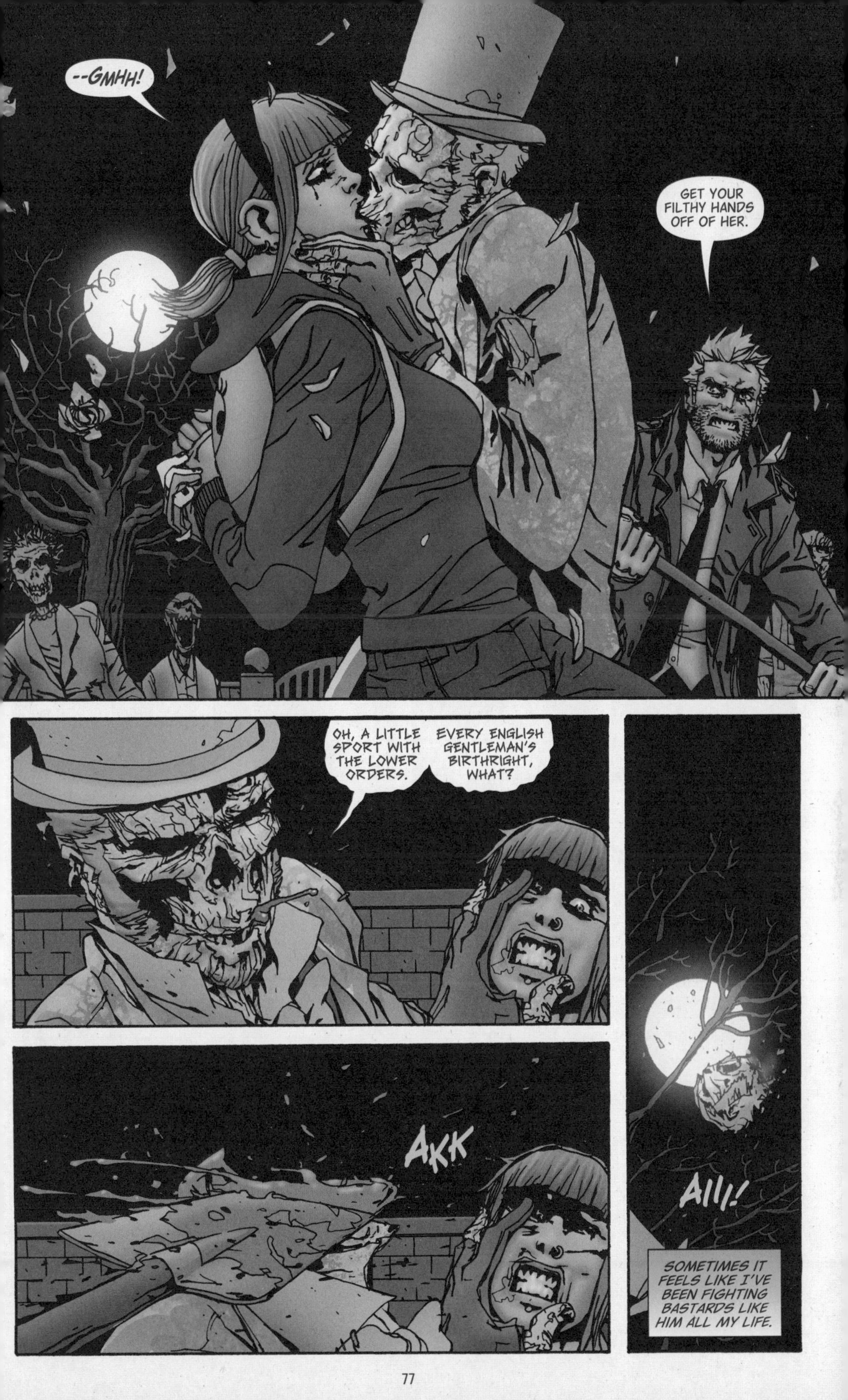
--GMHH!
GET YOUR FILTHY HANDS OFF OF HER.
OH, A LITTLE SPORT WITH THE LOWER ORDERS.
EVERY ENGLISH GENTLEMAN'S BIRTHRIGHT, WHAT?
AKK
AIII!
SOMETIMES IT FEELS LIKE I'VE BEEN FIGHTING BASTARDS LIKE HIM ALL MY LIFE.

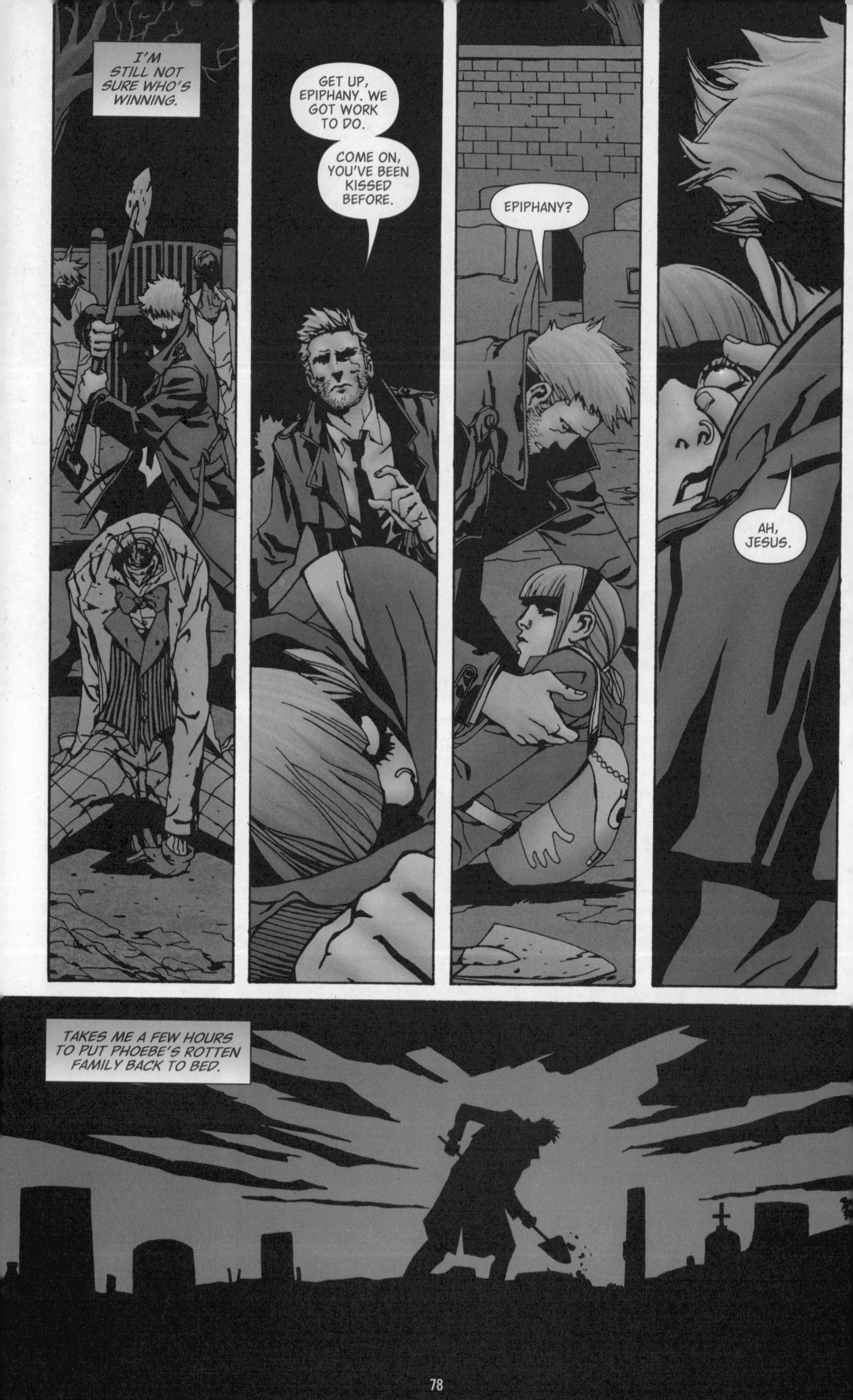
I'M STILL NOT SURE WHO'S WINNING.
GET UP, EPIPHANY. WE GOT WORK TO DO.
COME ON, YOU'VE BEEN KISSED BEFORE.
EPIPHANY?
AH, JESUS.
TAKES ME A FEW HOURS TO PUT PHOEBE'S ROTTEN FAMILY BACK TO BED.

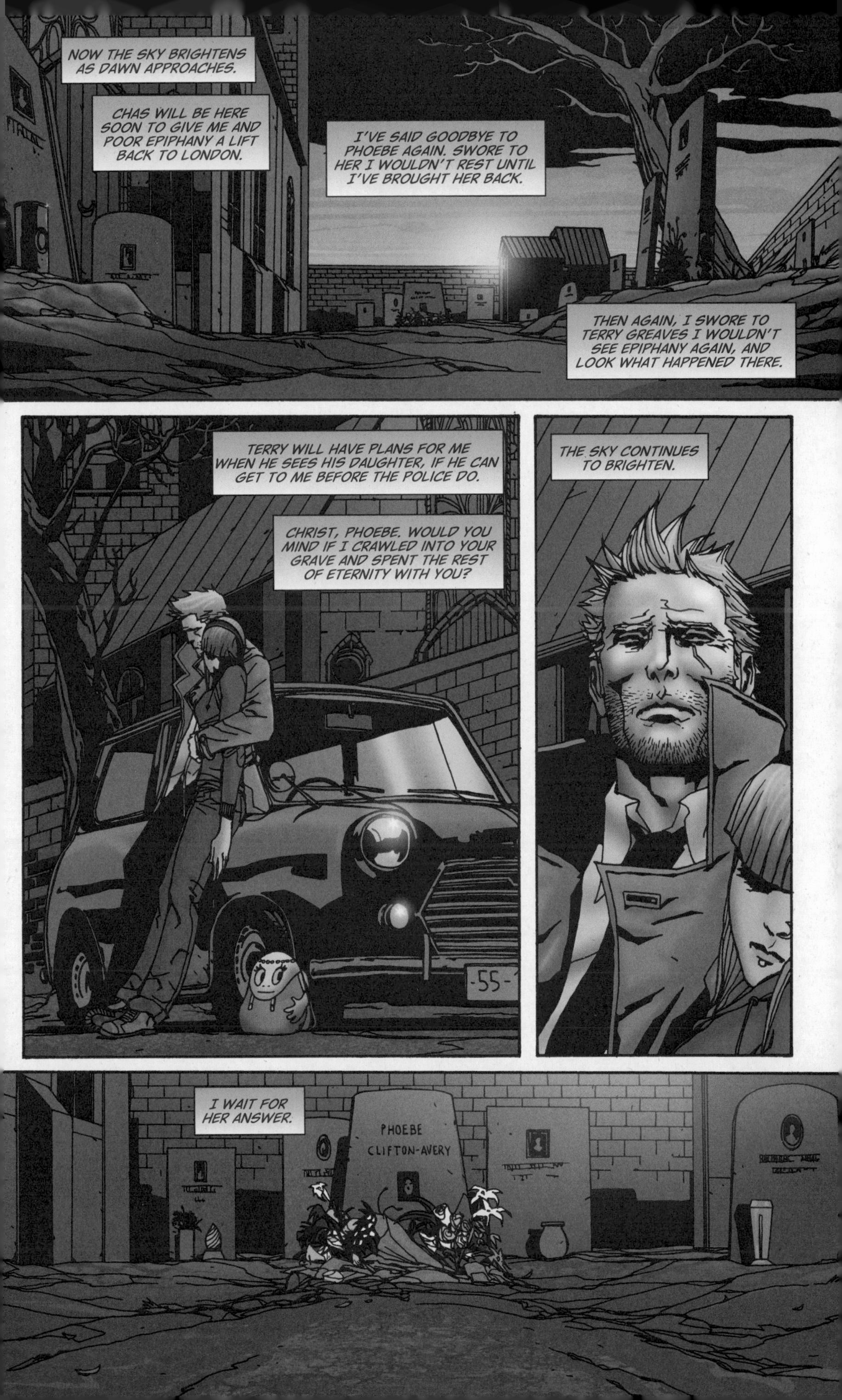
NOW THE SKY BRIGHTENS AS DAWN APPROACHES.
CHAS WILL BE HERE SOON TO GIVE ME AND POOR EPIPHANY A LIFT BACK TO LONDON.
I'VE SAID GOODBYE TO PHOEBE AGAIN. SWORE TO HER I WOULDN'T REST UNTIL I'VE BROUGHT HER BACK.
THEN AGAIN, I SWORE TO TERRY GREAVES I WOULDN'T SEE EPIPHANY AGAIN, AND LOOK WHAT HAPPENED THERE.
TERRY WILL HAVE PLANS FOR ME WHEN HE SEES HIS DAUGHTER, IF HE CAN GET TO ME BEFORE THE POLICE DO.
CHRIST, PHOEBE. WOULD YOU MIND IF I CRAWLED INTO YOUR GRAVE AND SPENT THE REST OF ETERNITY WITH YOU?
-55-
THE SKY CONTINUES TO BRIGHTEN.
I WAIT FOR HER ANSWER.
PHOEBE
CLIFTON-AVERY

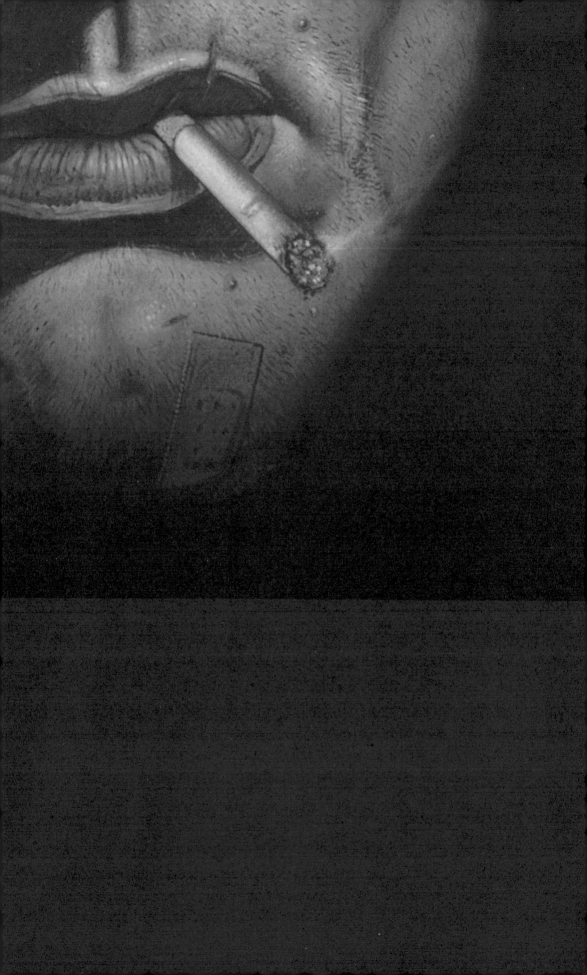

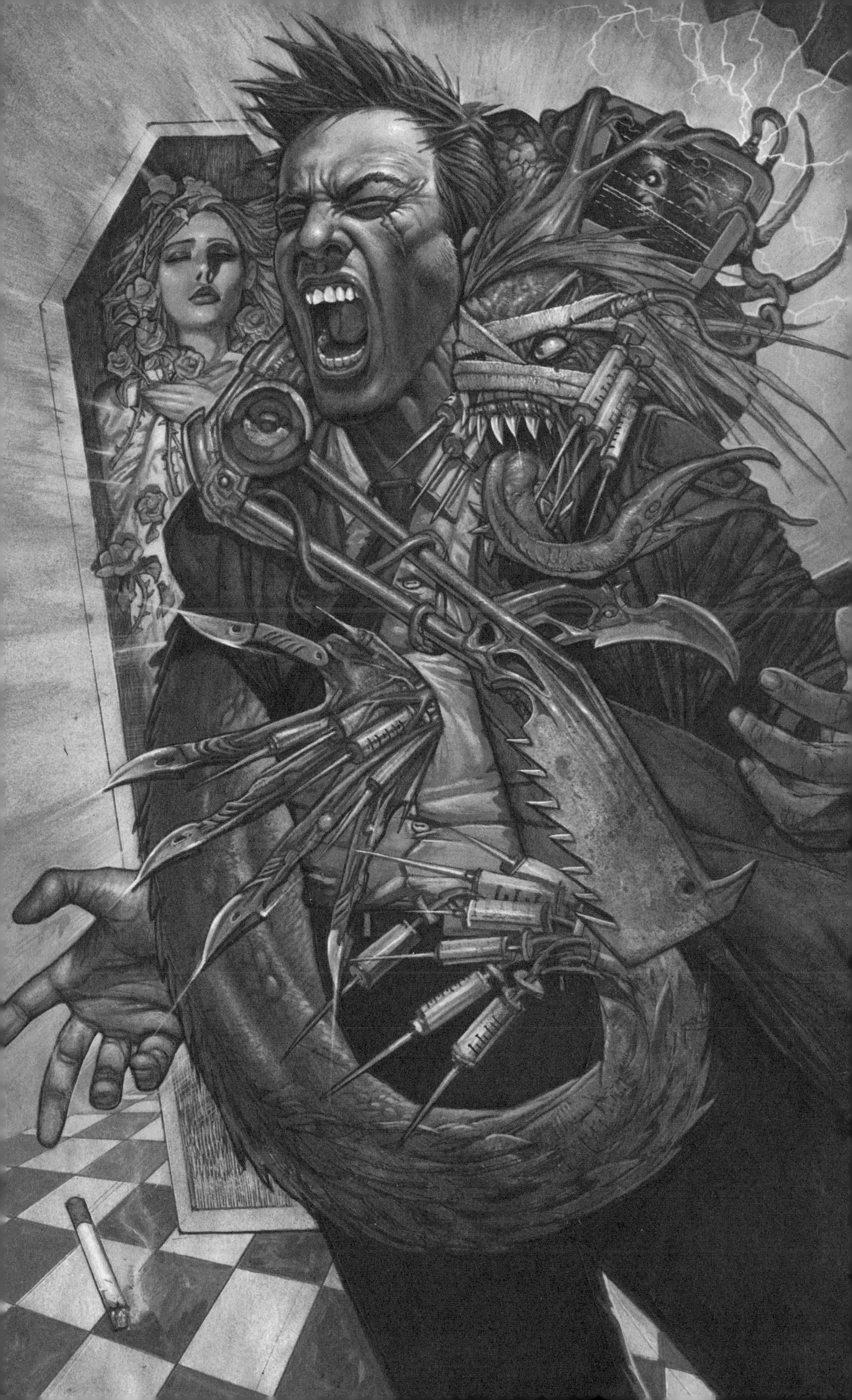

The Cottage

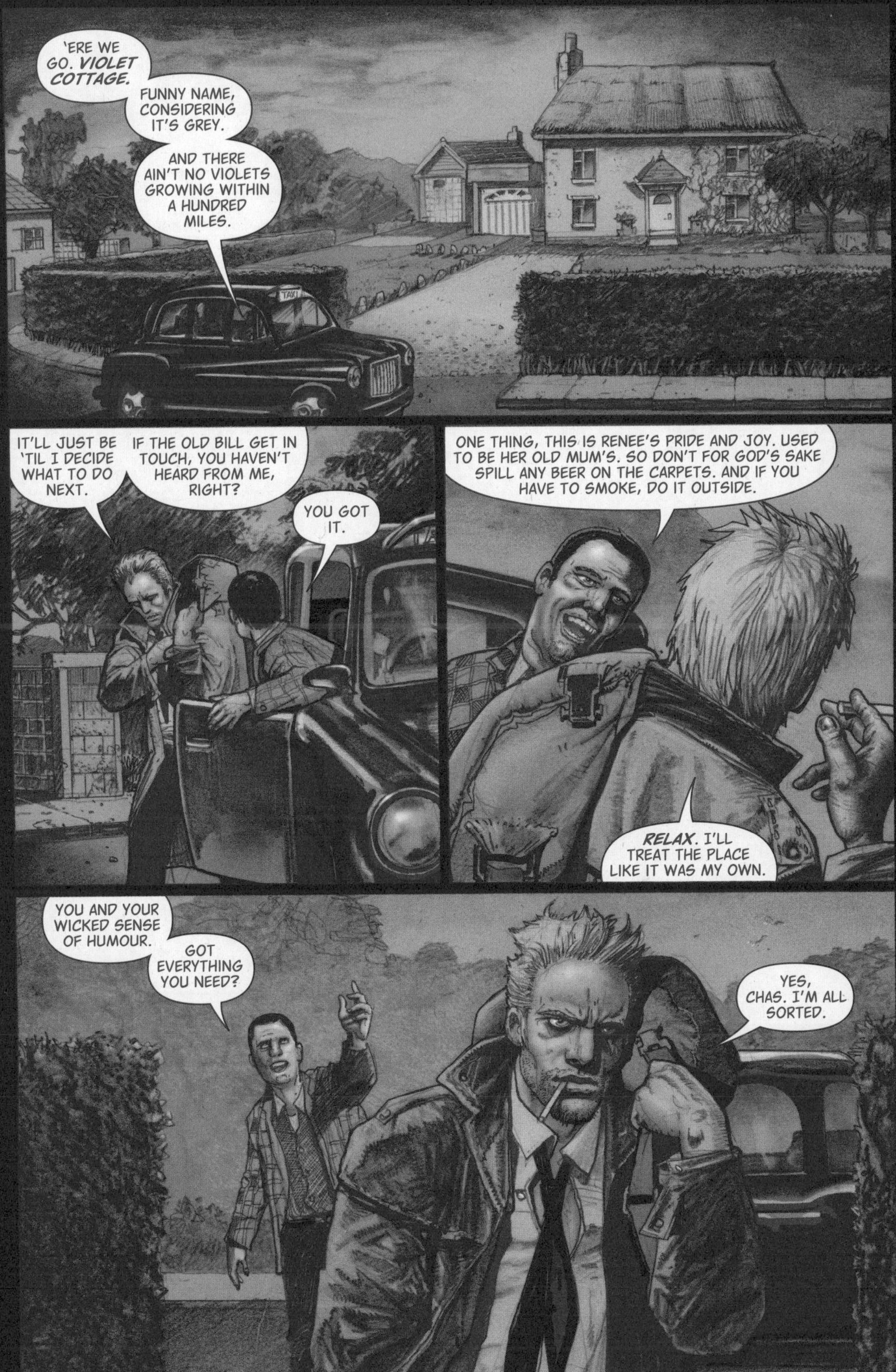
'ERE WE GO. VIOLET COTTAGE.
FUNNY NAME, CONSIDERING IT'S GREY.
AND THERE AIN'T NO VIOLETS GROWING WITHIN A HUNDRED MILES.
IT'LL JUST BE 'TIL I DECIDE WHAT TO DO NEXT.
IF THE OLD BILL GET IN TOUCH, YOU HAVEN'T HEARD FROM ME, RIGHT?
YOU GOT IT.
ONE THING, THIS IS RENEE'S PRIDE AND JOY. USED TO BE HER OLD MUM'S. SO DON'T FOR GOD'S SAKE SPILL ANY BEER ON THE CARPETS. AND IF YOU HAVE TO SMOKE, DO IT OUTSIDE.
RELAX. I'LL TREAT THE PLACE LIKE IT WAS MY OWN.
YOU AND YOUR WICKED SENSE OF HUMOUR.
GOT EVERYTHING YOU NEED?
YES, CHAS. I'M ALL SORTED.

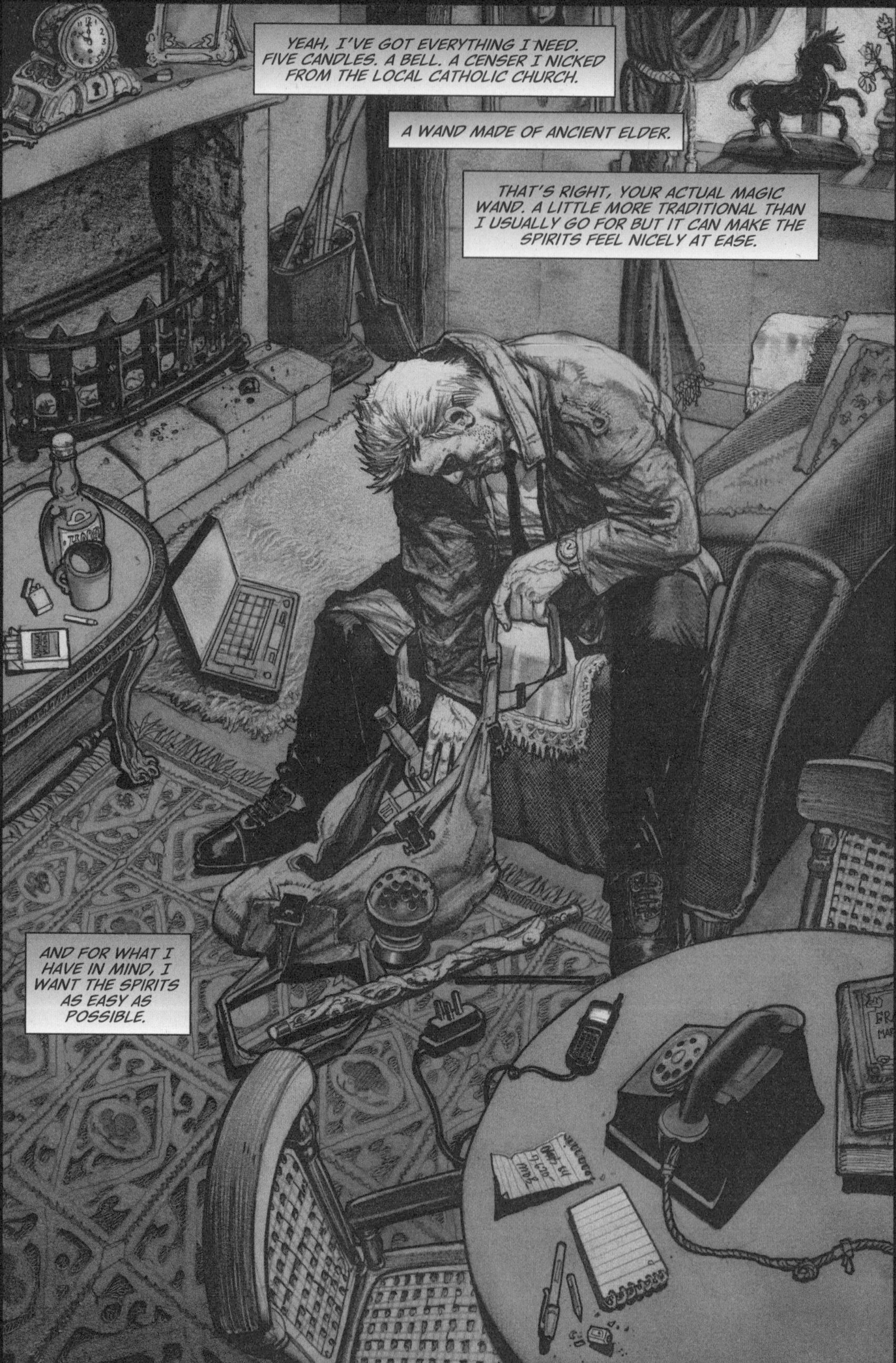
YEAH, I'VE GOT EVERYTHING I NEED. FIVE CANDLES. A BELL. A CENSER I NICKED FROM THE LOCAL CATHOLIC CHURCH.
A WAND MADE OF ANCIENT ELDER.
THAT'S RIGHT, YOUR ACTUAL MAGIC WAND. A LITTLE MORE TRADITIONAL THAN I USUALLY GO FOR BUT IT CAN MAKE THE SPIRITS FEEL NICELY AT EASE.
AND FOR WHAT I HAVE IN MIND, I WANT THE SPIRITS AS EASY AS POSSIBLE.

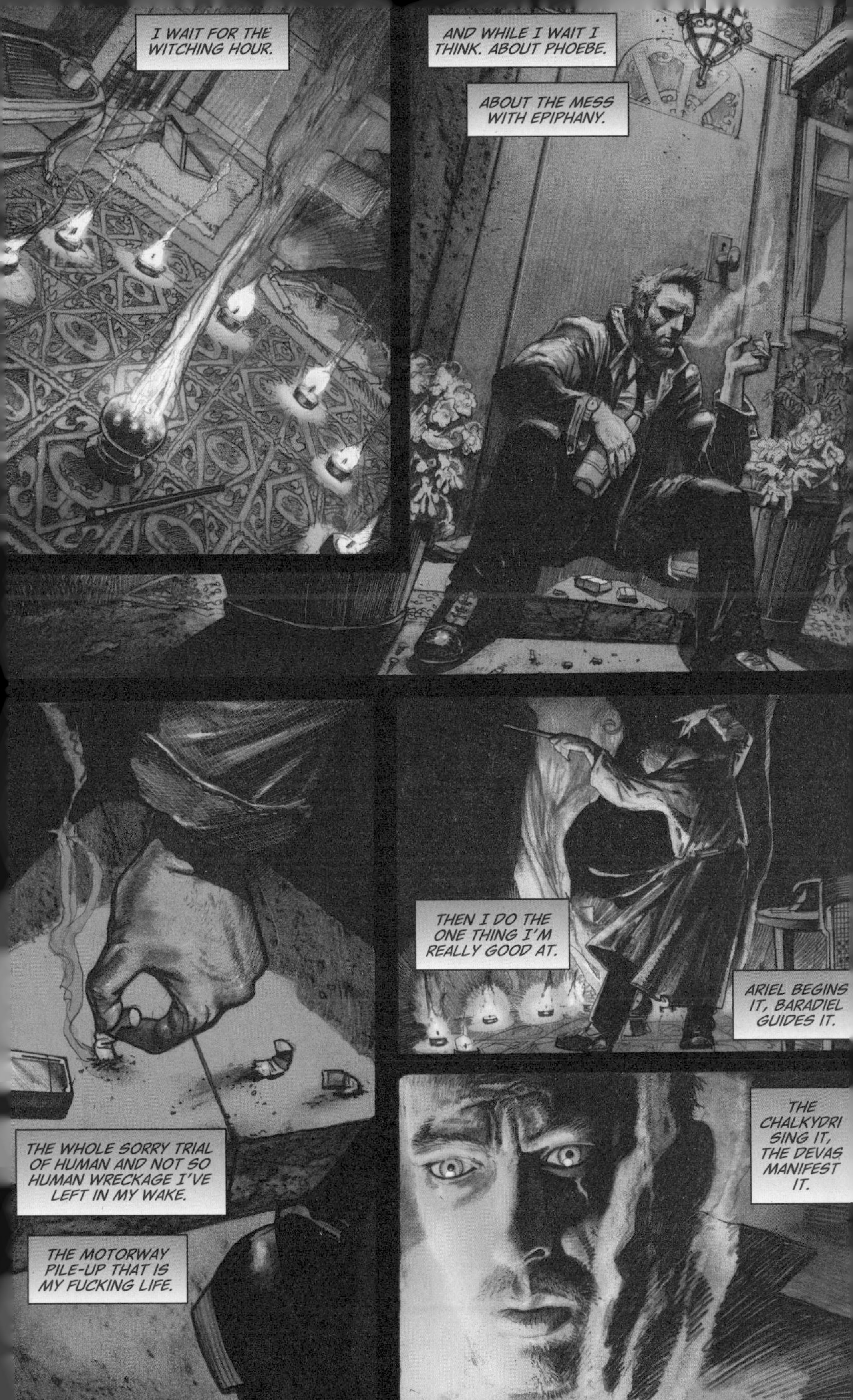
I WAIT FOR THE WITCHING HOUR.
AND WHILE I WAIT I THINK. ABOUT PHOEBE.
ABOUT THE MESS WITH EPIPHANY.
THE WHOLE SORRY TRIAL OF HUMAN AND NOT SO HUMAN WRECKAGE I'VE LEFT IN MY WAKE.
THE MOTORWAY PILE-UP THAT IS MY FUCKING LIFE.
THEN I DO THE ONE THING I'M REALLY GOOD AT.
ARIEL BEGINS IT, BARADIEL GUIDES IT.
THE CHALKYDRI SING IT, THE DEVAS MANIFEST IT.

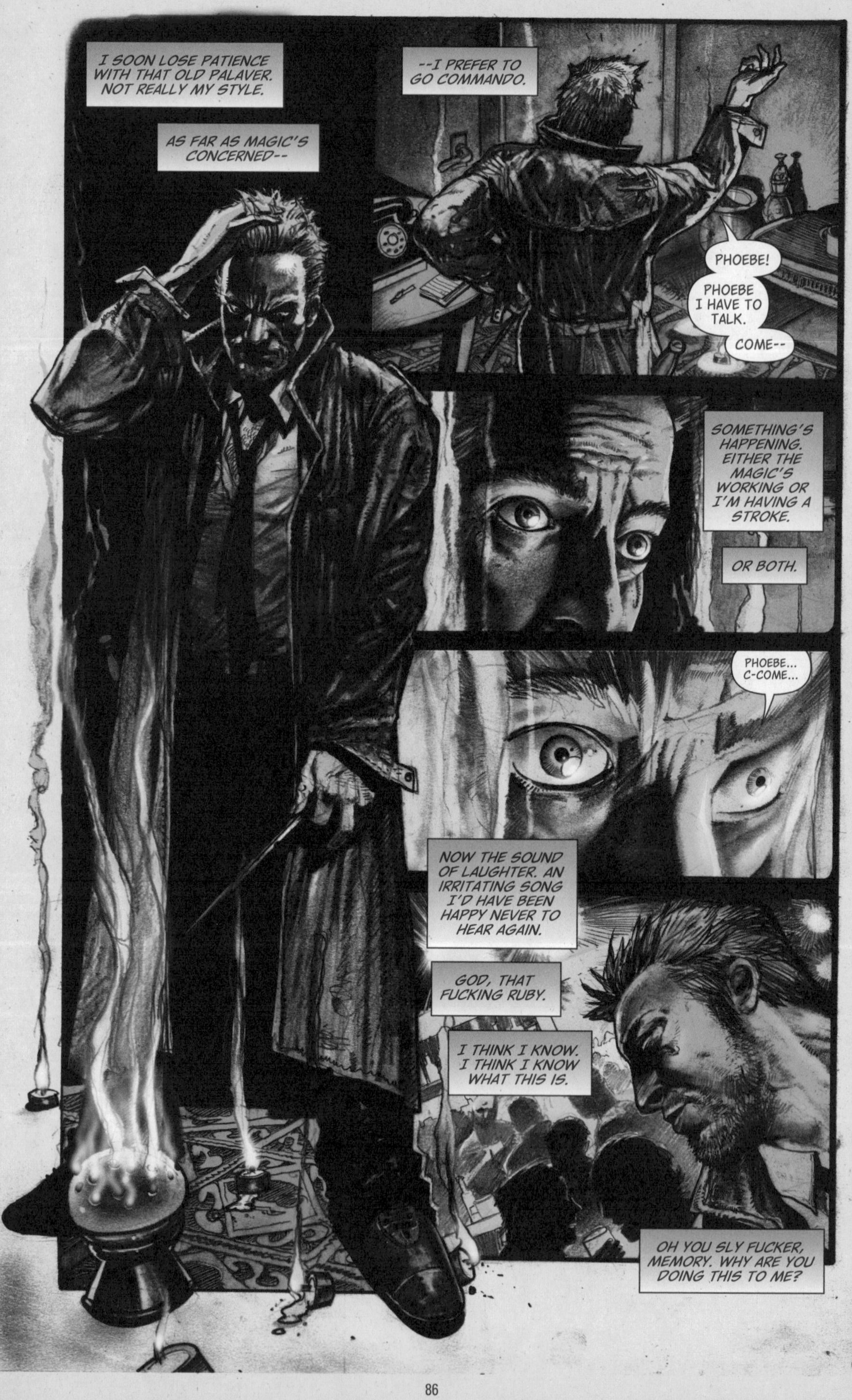

I SOON LOSE PATIENCE WITH THAT OLD PALAVER. NOT REALLY MY STYLE.
AS FAR AS MAGIC'S CONCERNED--
--I PREFER TO GO COMMANDO.
PHOEBE!
PHOEBE I HAVE TO TALK.
COME--
SOMETHING'S HAPPENING. EITHER THE MAGIC'S WORKING OR I'M HAVING A STROKE.
OR BOTH.
PHOEBE... C-COME...
NOW THE SOUND OF LAUGHTER. AN IRRITATING SONG I'D HAVE BEEN HAPPY NEVER TO HEAR AGAIN.
GOD, THAT FUCKING RUBY.
I THINK I KNOW. I THINK I KNOW WHAT THIS IS.
OH YOU SLY FUCKER, MEMORY. WHY ARE YOU DOING THIS TO ME?

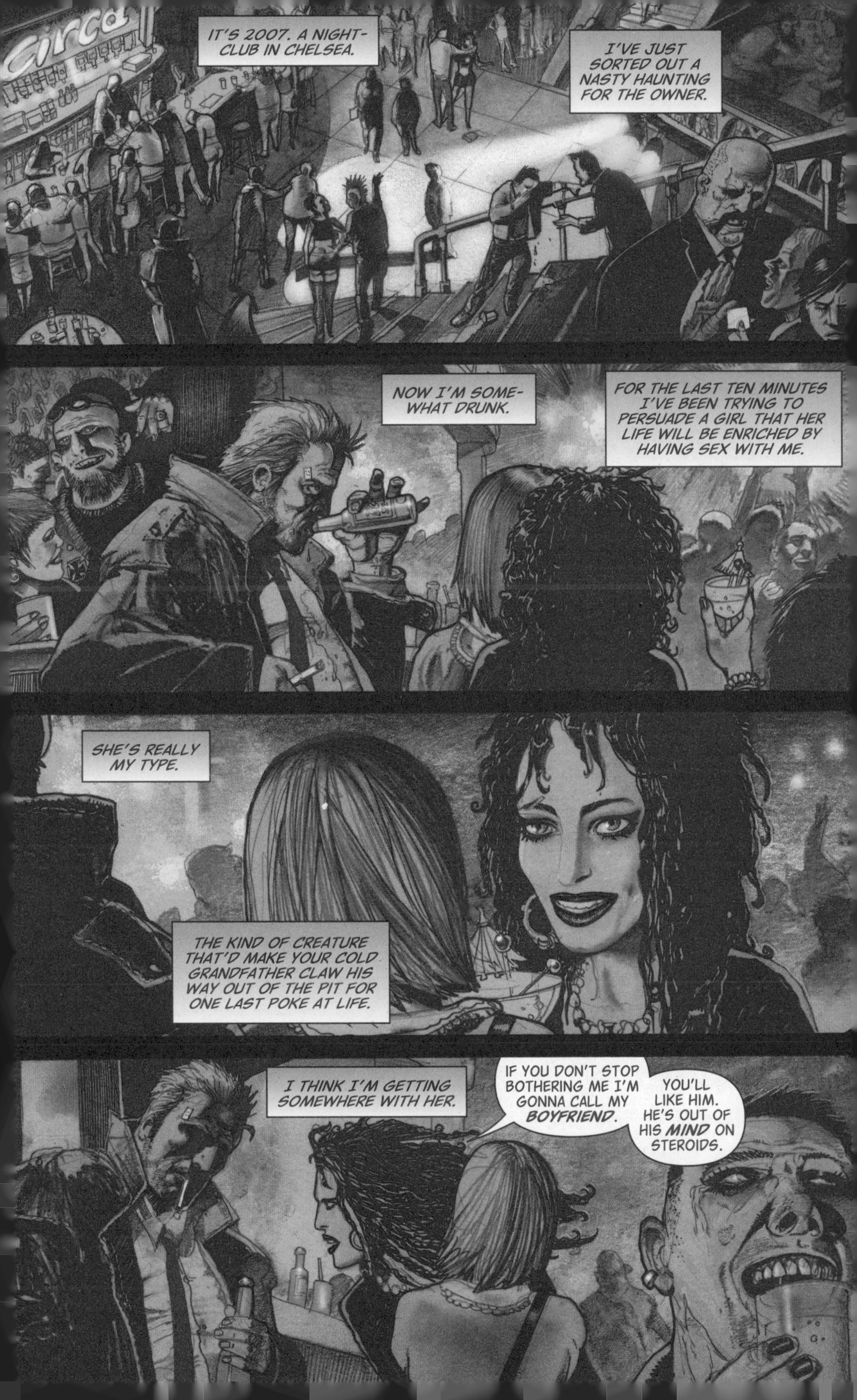

IT'S 2007. A NIGHT-CLUB IN CHELSEA.
I'VE JUST SORTED OUT A NASTY HAUNTING FOR THE OWNER.
NOW I'M SOMEWHAT DRUNK.
FOR THE LAST TEN MINUTES I'VE BEEN TRYING TO PERSUADE A GIRL THAT HER LIFE WILL BE ENRICHED BY HAVING SEX WITH ME.
SHE'S REALLY MY TYPE.
THE KIND OF CREATURE THAT'D MAKE YOUR COLD GRANDFATHER CLAW HIS WAY OUT OF THE PIT FOR ONE LAST POKE AT LIFE.
I THINK I'M GETTING SOMEWHERE WITH HER.
IF YOU DON'T STOP BOTHERING ME I'M GONNA CALL MY **BOYFRIEND**.
YOU'LL LIKE HIM. HE'S OUT OF HIS **MIND** ON STEROIDS.

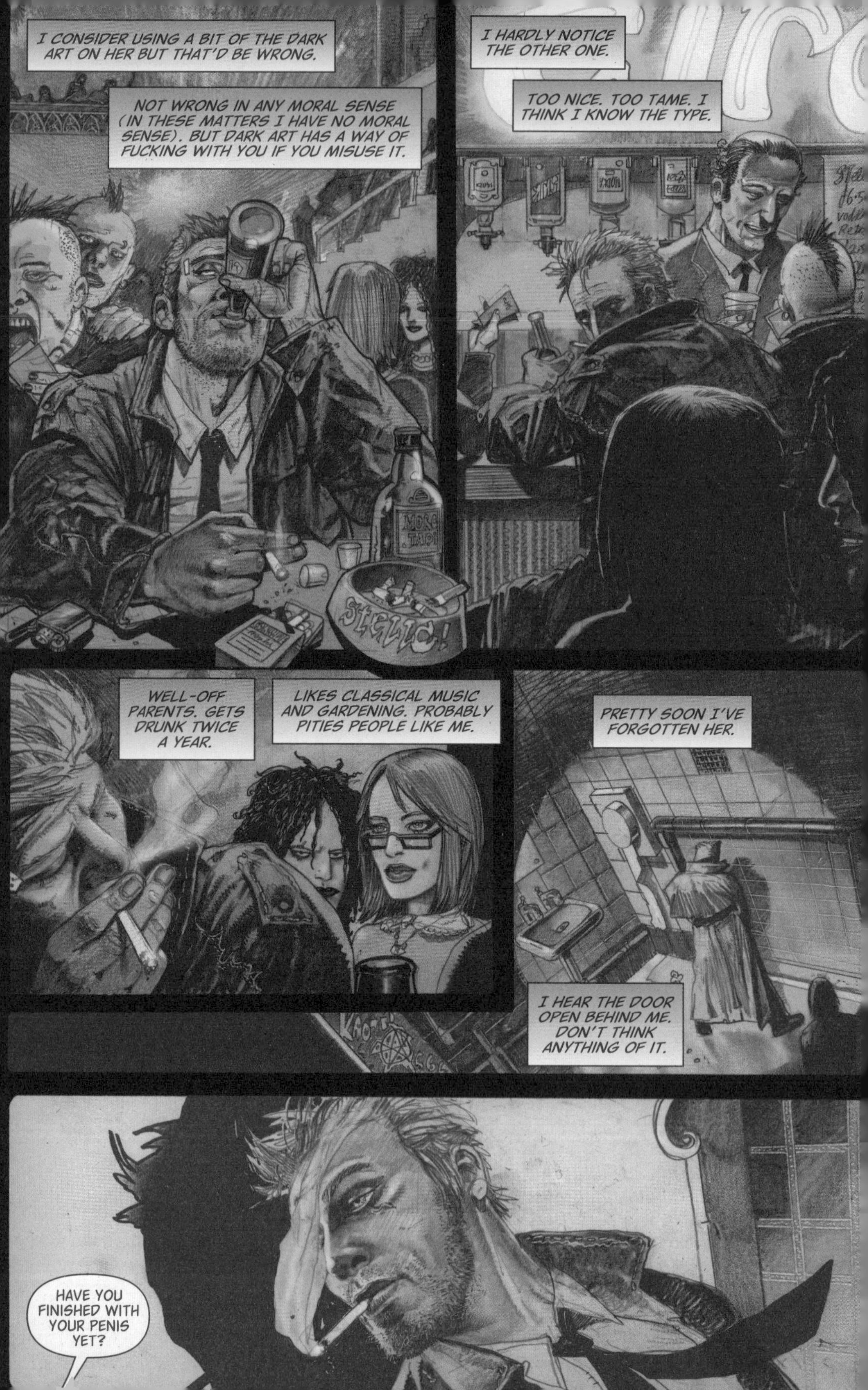
I CONSIDER USING A BIT OF THE DARK ART ON HER BUT THAT'D BE WRONG.
NOT WRONG IN ANY MORAL SENSE (IN THESE MATTERS I HAVE NO MORAL SENSE). BUT DARK ART HAS A WAY OF FUCKING WITH YOU IF YOU MISUSE IT.
I HARDLY NOTICE THE OTHER ONE.
TOO NICE. TOO TAME. I THINK I KNOW THE TYPE.
WELL-OFF PARENTS. GETS DRUNK TWICE A YEAR.
LIKES CLASSICAL MUSIC AND GARDENING. PROBABLY PITIES PEOPLE LIKE ME.
PRETTY SOON I'VE FORGOTTEN HER.
I HEAR THE DOOR OPEN BEHIND ME. DON'T THINK ANYTHING OF IT.
HAVE YOU FINISHED WITH YOUR PENIS YET?

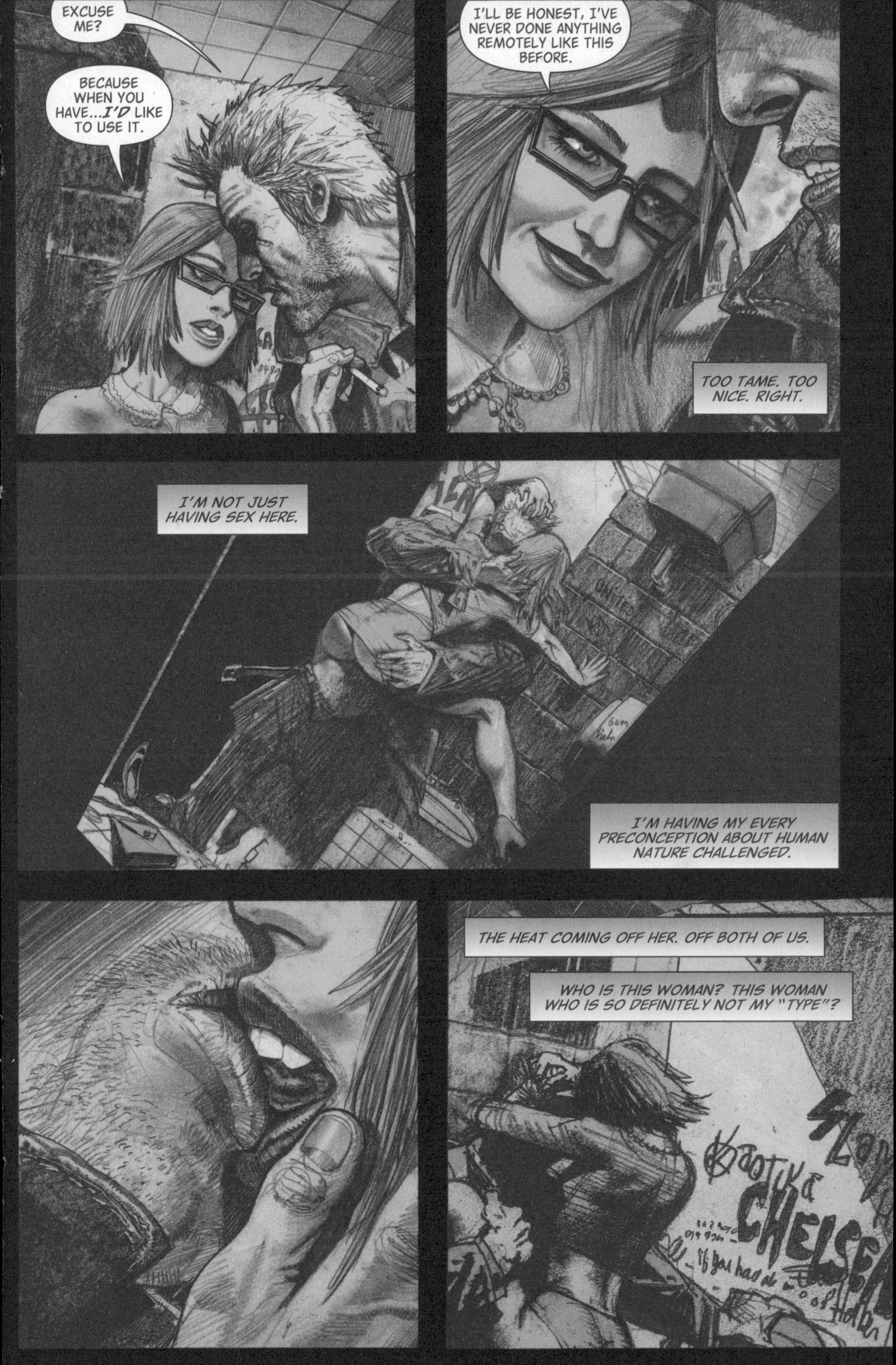
EXCUSE ME?
BECAUSE WHEN YOU HAVE...I'D LIKE TO USE IT.
I'LL BE HONEST, I'VE NEVER DONE ANYTHING REMOTELY LIKE THIS BEFORE.
TOO TAME. TOO NICE. RIGHT.
I'M NOT JUST HAVING SEX HERE.
I'M HAVING MY EVERY PRECONCEPTION ABOUT HUMAN NATURE CHALLENGED.
THE HEAT COMING OFF HER. OFF BOTH OF US.
WHO IS THIS WOMAN? THIS WOMAN WHO IS SO DEFINITELY NOT MY "TYPE"?
CHELSEA

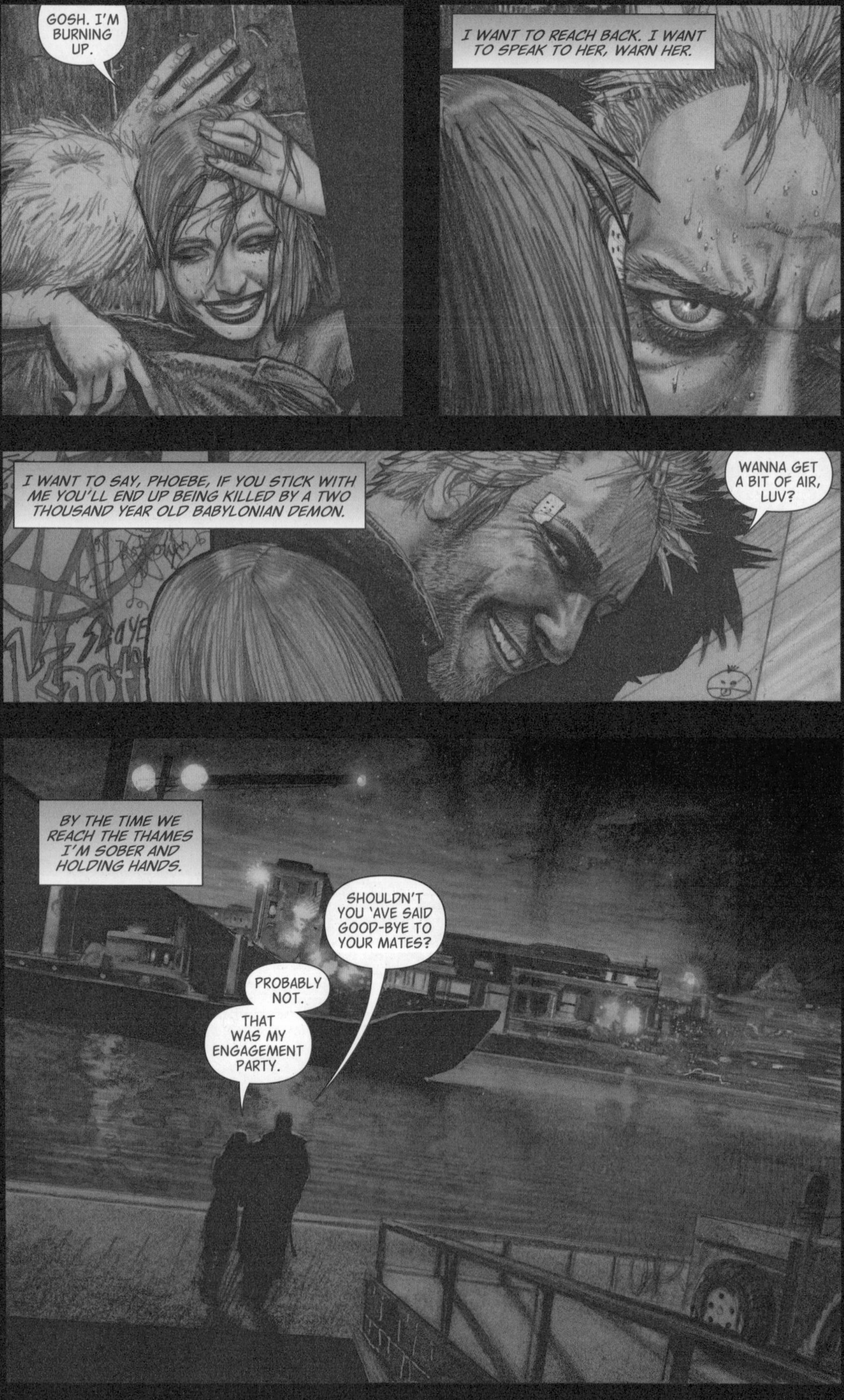
GOSH. I'M BURNING UP.
I WANT TO REACH BACK. I WANT TO SPEAK TO HER, WARN HER.
I WANT TO SAY, PHOEBE, IF YOU STICK WITH ME YOU'LL END UP BEING KILLED BY A TWO THOUSAND YEAR OLD BABYLONIAN DEMON.
WANNA GET A BIT OF AIR, LUV?
BY THE TIME WE REACH THE THAMES I'M SOBER AND HOLDING HANDS.
SHOULDN'T YOU 'AVE SAID GOOD-BYE TO YOUR MATES?
PROBABLY NOT.
THAT WAS MY ENGAGEMENT PARTY.

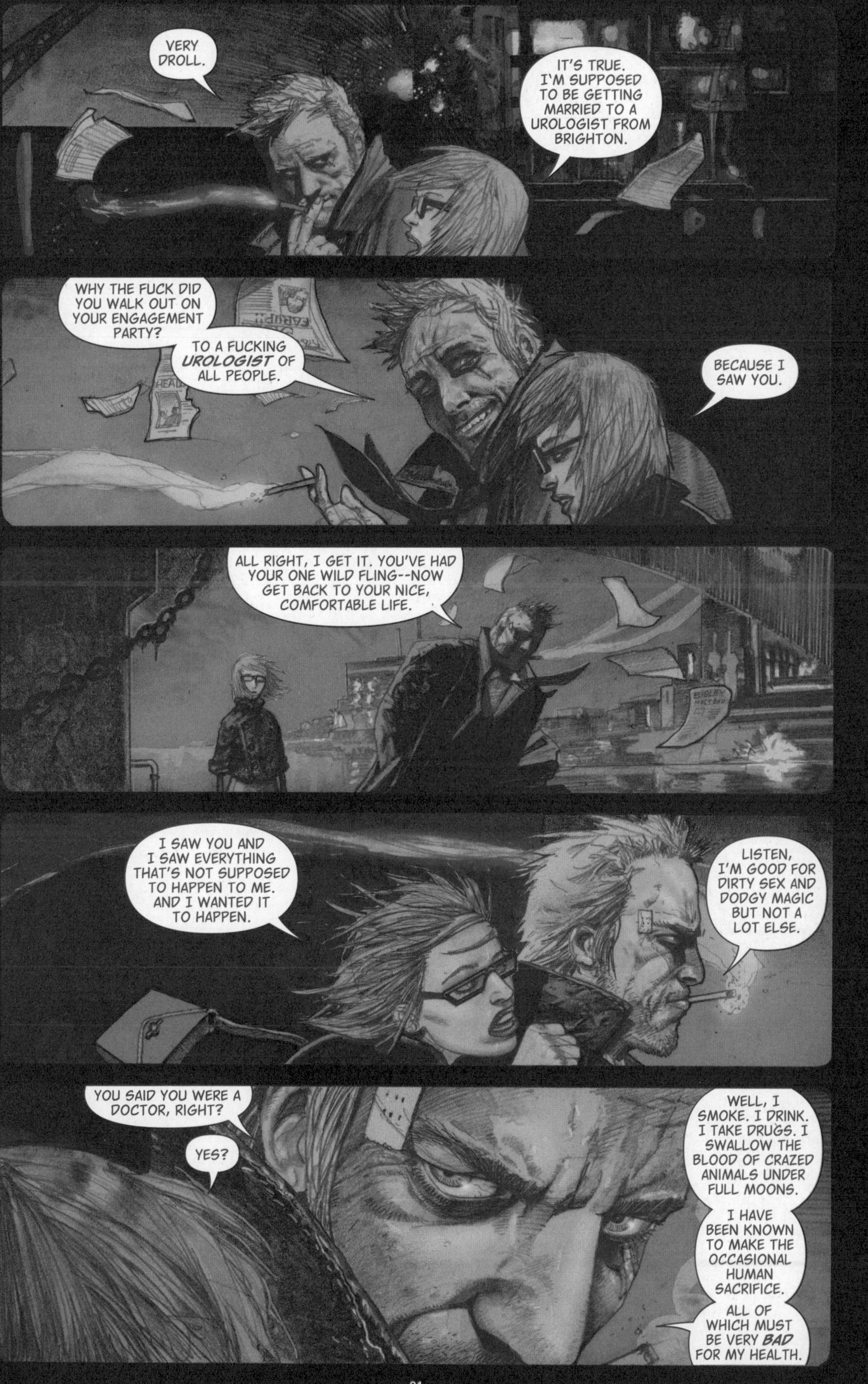
VERY DROLL.
IT'S TRUE. I'M SUPPOSED TO BE GETTING MARRIED TO A UROLOGIST FROM BRIGHTON.
WHY THE FUCK DID YOU WALK OUT ON YOUR ENGAGEMENT PARTY?
TO A FUCKING *UROLOGIST* OF ALL PEOPLE.
BECAUSE I SAW YOU.
ALL RIGHT, I GET IT. YOU'VE HAD YOUR ONE WILD FLING--NOW GET BACK TO YOUR NICE, COMFORTABLE LIFE.
I SAW YOU AND I SAW EVERYTHING THAT'S NOT SUPPOSED TO HAPPEN TO ME. AND I WANTED IT TO HAPPEN.
LISTEN, I'M GOOD FOR DIRTY SEX AND DODGY MAGIC BUT NOT A LOT ELSE.
YOU SAID YOU WERE A DOCTOR, RIGHT?
YES?
WELL, I SMOKE. I DRINK. I TAKE DRUGS. I SWALLOW THE BLOOD OF CRAZED ANIMALS UNDER FULL MOONS.
I HAVE BEEN KNOWN TO MAKE THE OCCASIONAL HUMAN SACRIFICE.
ALL OF WHICH MUST BE VERY *BAD* FOR MY HEALTH.

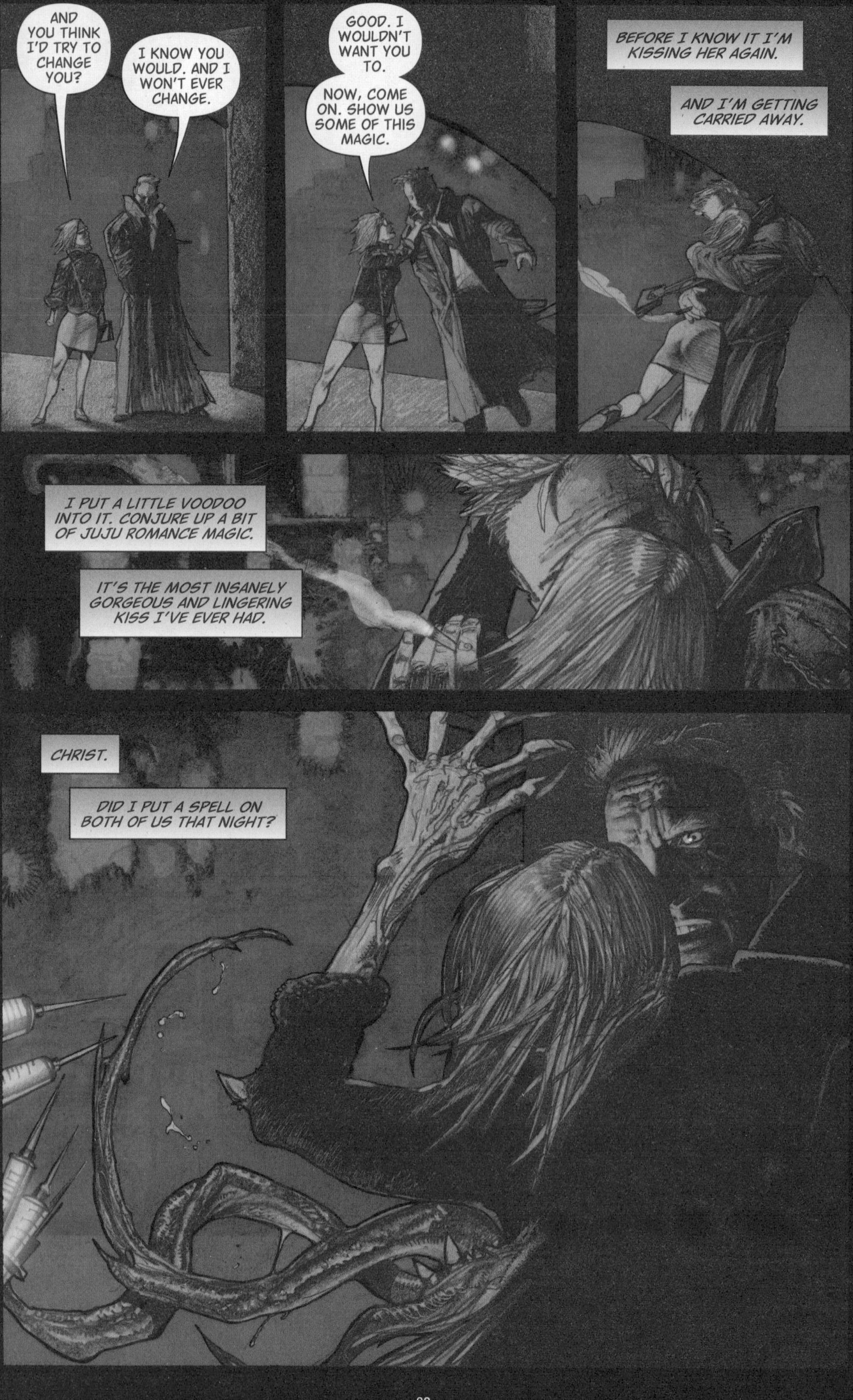
AND YOU THINK I'D TRY TO CHANGE YOU?
I KNOW YOU WOULD. AND I WON'T EVER CHANGE.
GOOD. I WOULDN'T WANT YOU TO.
NOW, COME ON. SHOW US SOME OF THIS MAGIC.
BEFORE I KNOW IT I'M KISSING HER AGAIN.
AND I'M GETTING CARRIED AWAY.
I PUT A LITTLE VOODOO INTO IT. CONJURE UP A BIT OF JUJU ROMANCE MAGIC.
IT'S THE MOST INSANELY GORGEOUS AND LINGERING KISS I'VE EVER HAD.
CHRIST.
DID I PUT A SPELL ON BOTH OF US THAT NIGHT?

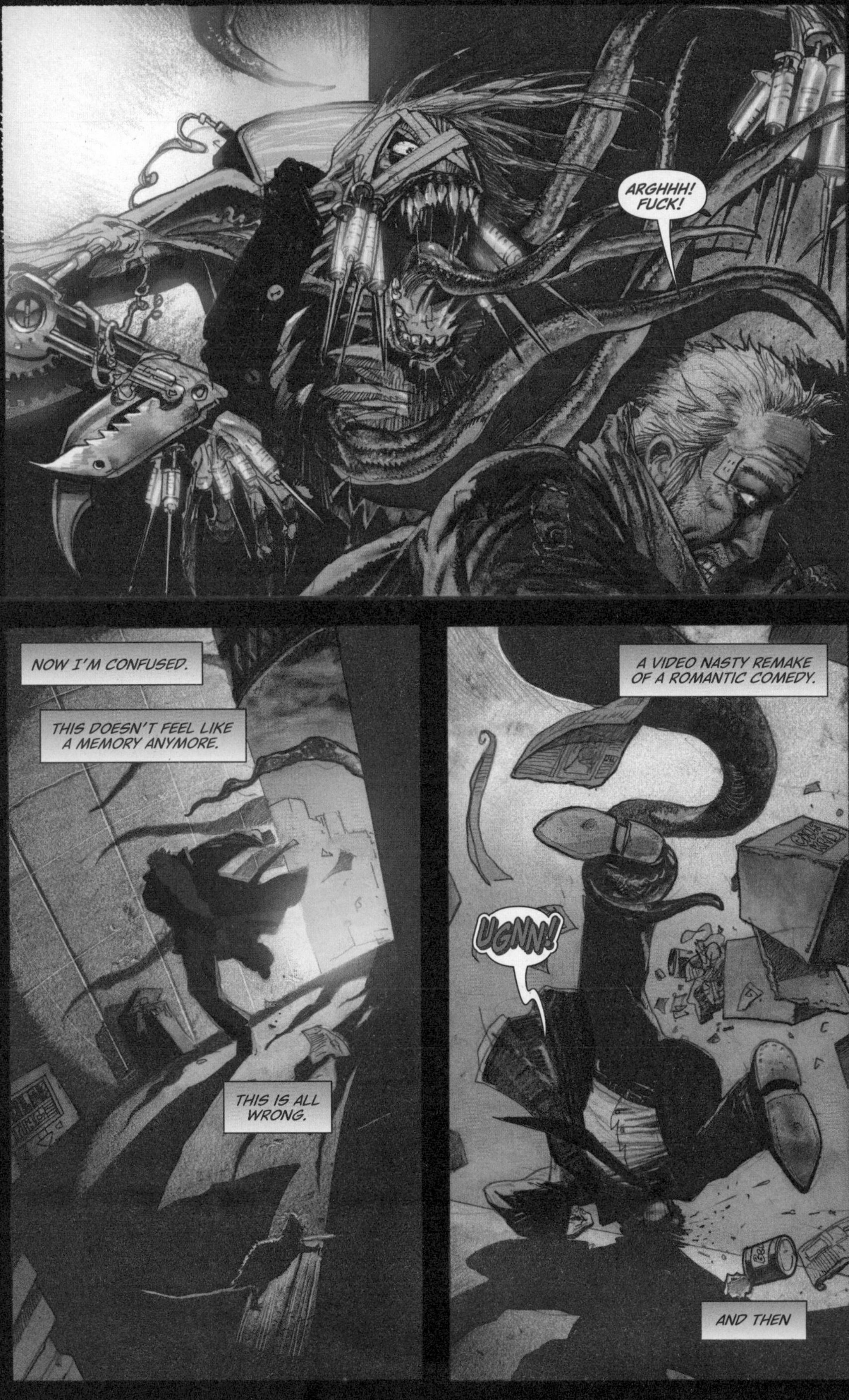
ARGHHH! FUCK!
NOW I'M CONFUSED.
THIS DOESN'T FEEL LIKE A MEMORY ANYMORE.
THIS IS ALL WRONG.
A VIDEO NASTY REMAKE OF A ROMANTIC COMEDY.
UGNN!
AND THEN

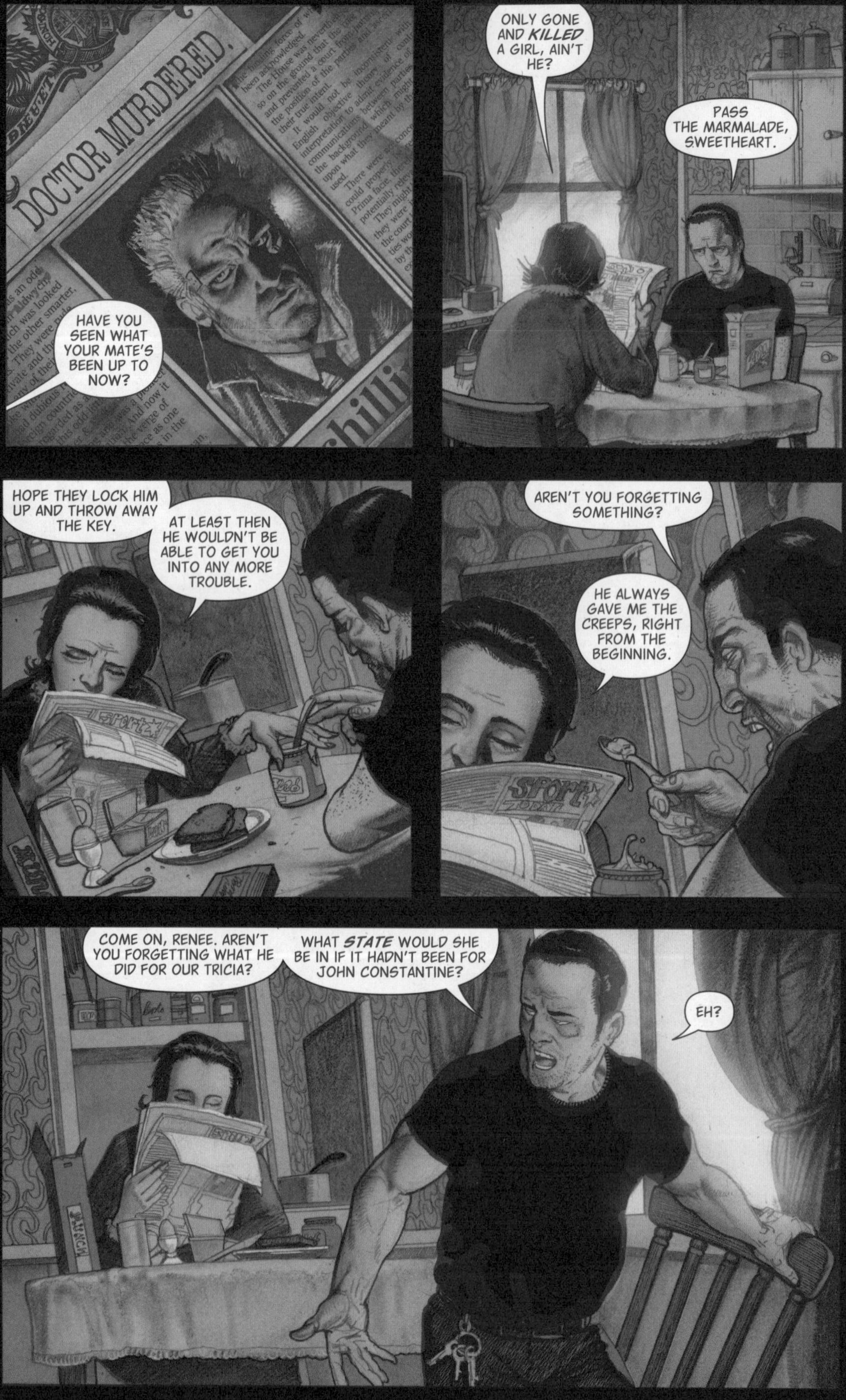
DOCTOR MURDERED.
HAVE YOU SEEN WHAT YOUR MATE'S BEEN UP TO NOW?
ONLY GONE AND *KILLED* A GIRL, AIN'T HE?
PASS THE MARMALADE, SWEETHEART.
HOPE THEY LOCK HIM UP AND THROW AWAY THE KEY.
AT LEAST THEN HE WOULDN'T BE ABLE TO GET YOU INTO ANY MORE TROUBLE.
AREN'T YOU FORGETTING SOMETHING?
HE ALWAYS GAVE ME THE CREEPS, RIGHT FROM THE BEGINNING.
COME ON, RENEE. AREN'T YOU FORGETTING WHAT HE DID FOR OUR TRICIA?
WHAT *STATE* WOULD SHE BE IN IF IT HADN'T BEEN FOR JOHN CONSTANTINE?
EH?

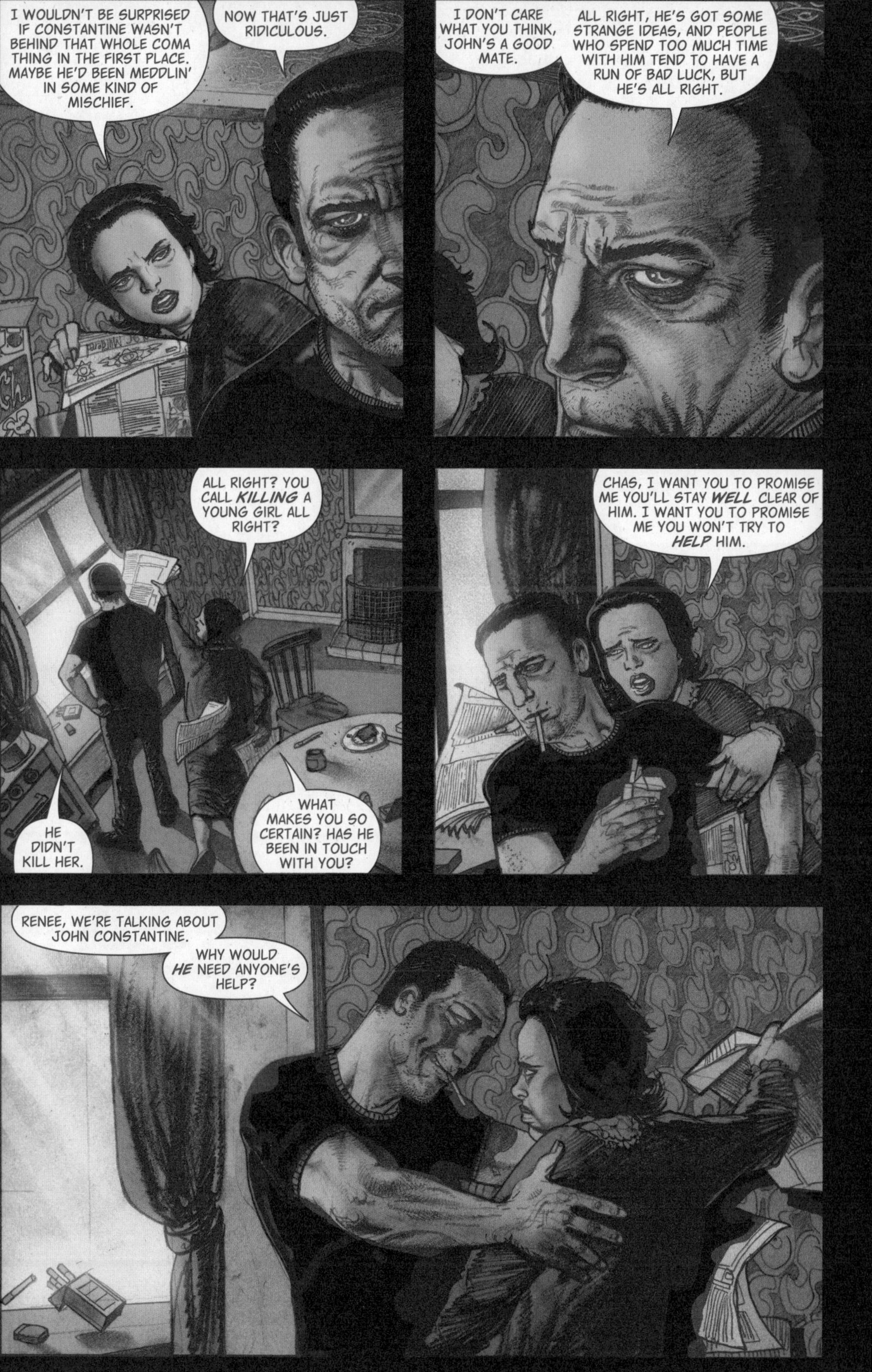
I WOULDN'T BE SURPRISED IF CONSTANTINE WASN'T BEHIND THAT WHOLE COMA THING IN THE FIRST PLACE. MAYBE HE'D BEEN MEDDLIN' IN SOME KIND OF MISCHIEF.
NOW THAT'S JUST RIDICULOUS.
I DON'T CARE WHAT YOU THINK, JOHN'S A GOOD MATE.
ALL RIGHT, HE'S GOT SOME STRANGE IDEAS, AND PEOPLE WHO SPEND TOO MUCH TIME WITH HIM TEND TO HAVE A RUN OF BAD LUCK, BUT HE'S ALL RIGHT.
ALL RIGHT? YOU CALL KILLING A YOUNG GIRL ALL RIGHT?
HE DIDN'T KILL HER.
WHAT MAKES YOU SO CERTAIN? HAS HE BEEN IN TOUCH WITH YOU?
CHAS, I WANT YOU TO PROMISE ME YOU'LL STAY WELL CLEAR OF HIM. I WANT YOU TO PROMISE ME YOU WON'T TRY TO HELP HIM.
RENEE, WE'RE TALKING ABOUT JOHN CONSTANTINE.
WHY WOULD HE NEED ANYONE'S HELP?

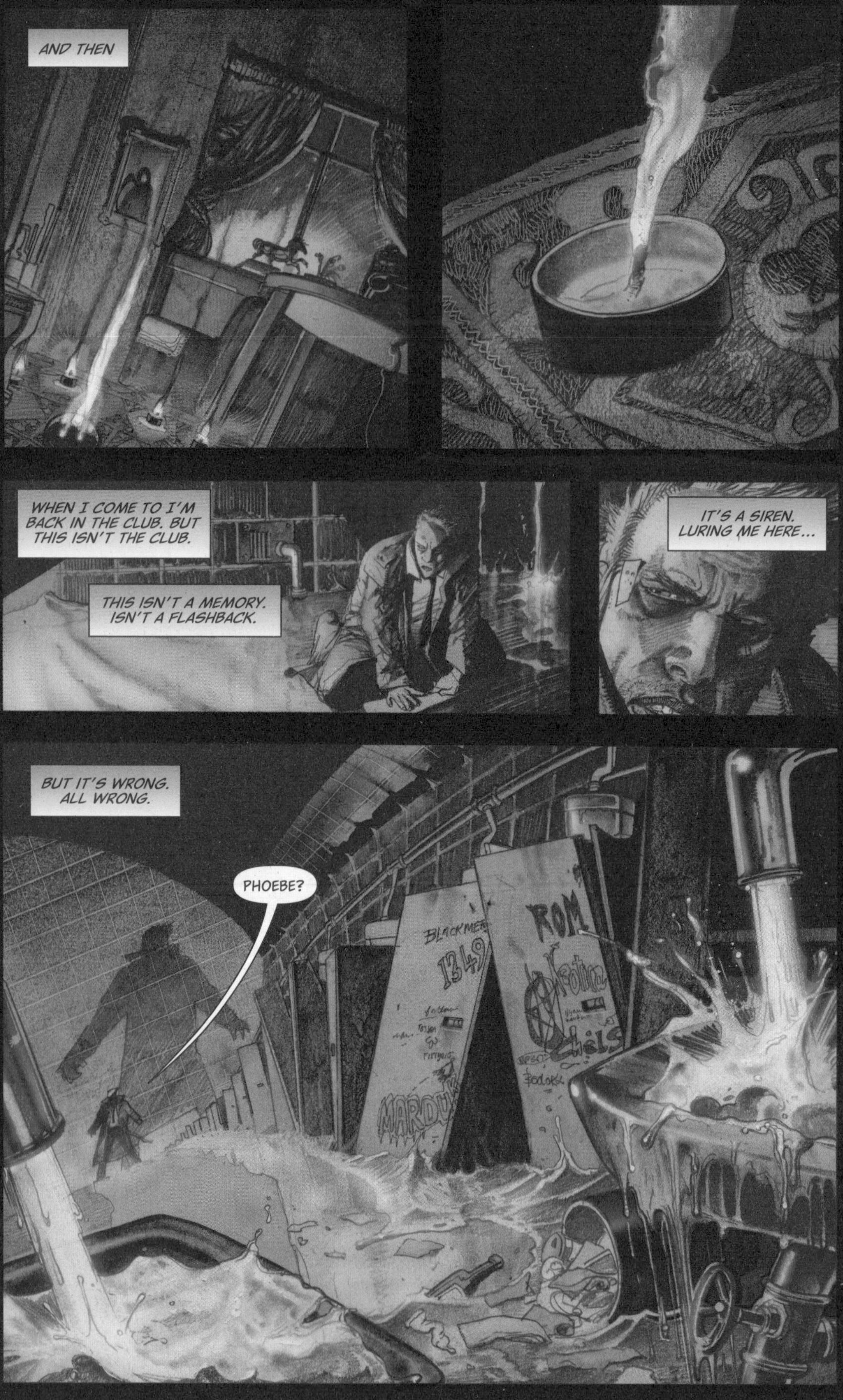
AND THEN
WHEN I COME TO I'M BACK IN THE CLUB. BUT THIS ISN'T THE CLUB.
THIS ISN'T A MEMORY. ISN'T A FLASHBACK.
IT'S A SIREN. LURING ME HERE...
BUT IT'S WRONG. ALL WRONG.
PHOEBE?

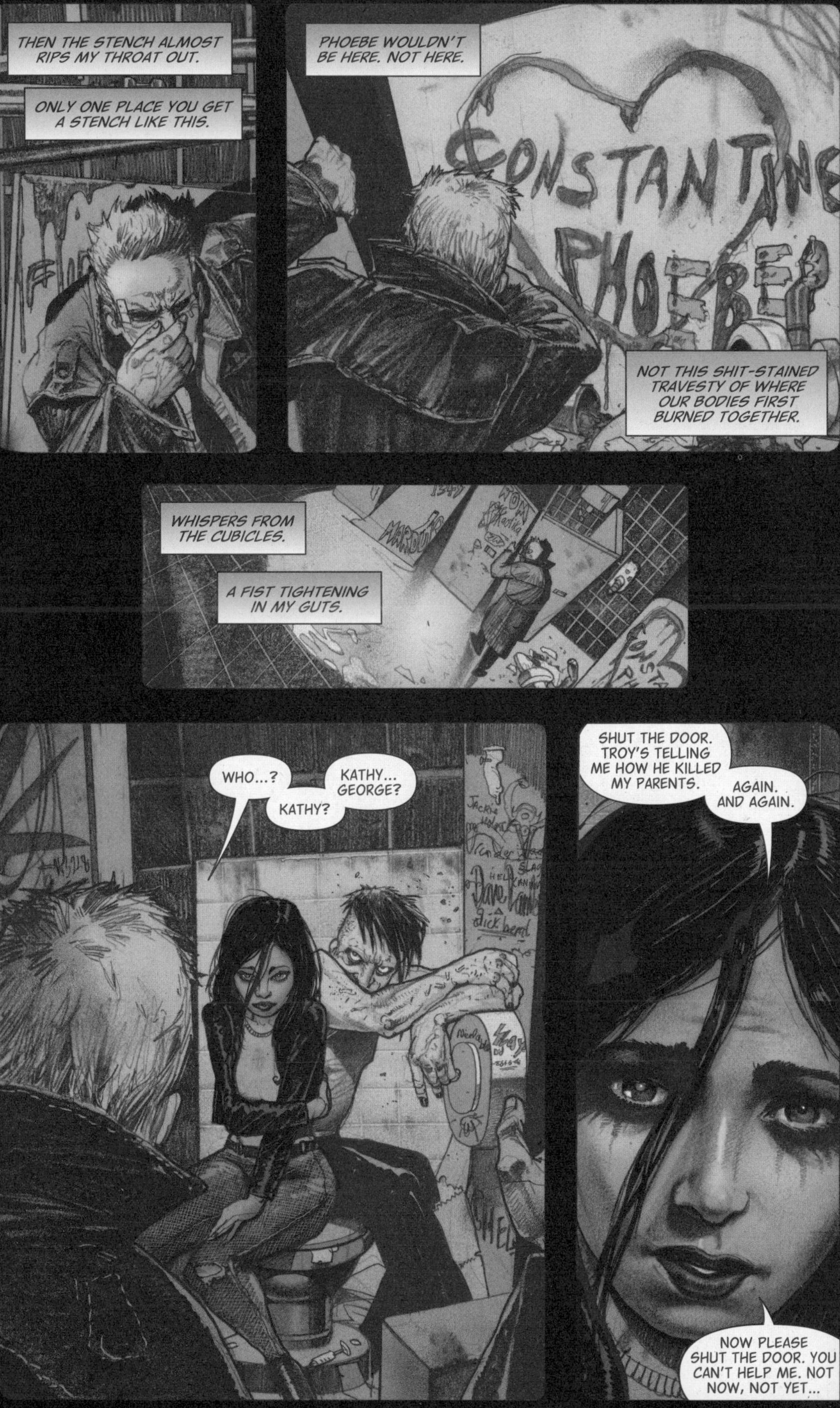
THEN THE STENCH ALMOST RIPS MY THROAT OUT.
ONLY ONE PLACE YOU GET A STENCH LIKE THIS.
PHOEBE WOULDN'T BE HERE. NOT HERE.
CONSTANTINE
PHOEBE
NOT THIS SHIT-STAINED TRAVESTY OF WHERE OUR BODIES FIRST BURNED TOGETHER.
WHISPERS FROM THE CUBICLES.
A FIST TIGHTENING IN MY GUTS.
WHO...?
KATHY?
KATHY... GEORGE?
SHUT THE DOOR. TROY'S TELLING ME HOW HE KILLED MY PARENTS.
AGAIN. AND AGAIN.
NOW PLEASE SHUT THE DOOR. YOU CAN'T HELP ME. NOT NOW, NOT YET...

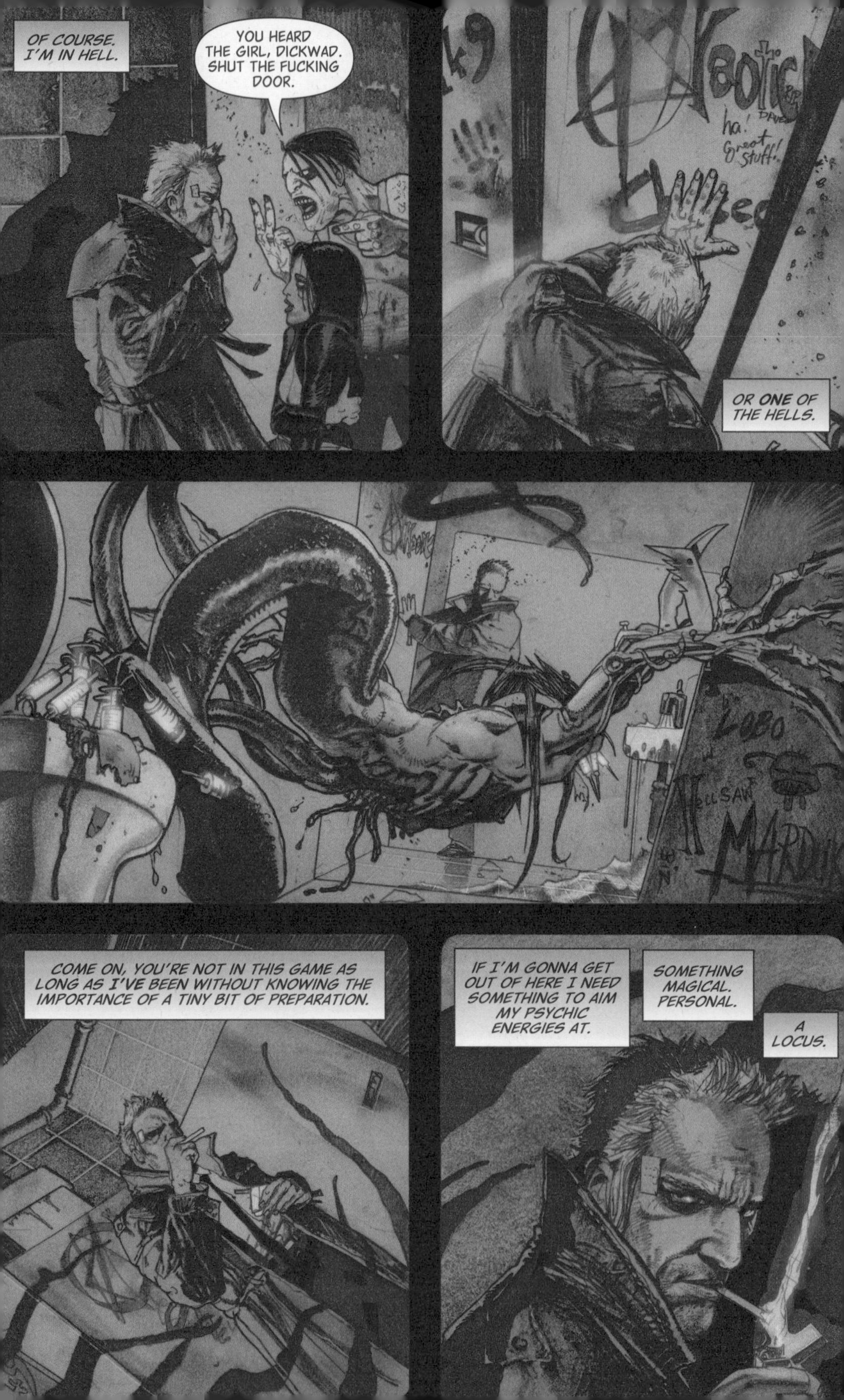
OF COURSE. I'M IN HELL.
YOU HEARD THE GIRL, DICKWAD. SHUT THE FUCKING DOOR.
OR ONE OF THE HELLS.
COME ON, YOU'RE NOT IN THIS GAME AS LONG AS I'VE BEEN WITHOUT KNOWING THE IMPORTANCE OF A TINY BIT OF PREPARATION.
IF I'M GONNA GET OUT OF HERE I NEED SOMETHING TO AIM MY PSYCHIC ENERGIES AT.
SOMETHING MAGICAL. PERSONAL.
A LOCUS.

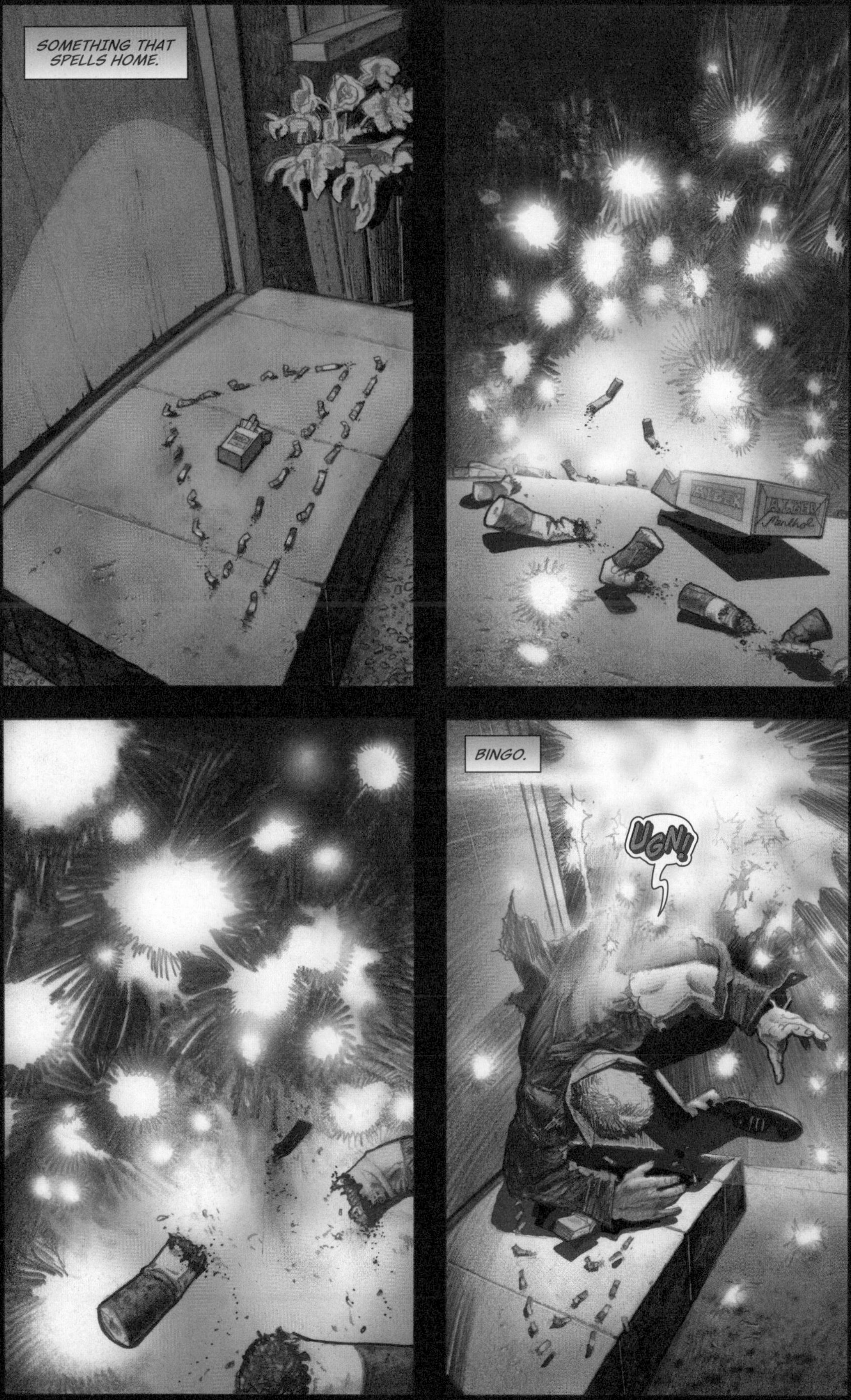
SOMETHING THAT SPELLS HOME.
Menthol
BINGO.
UGN!

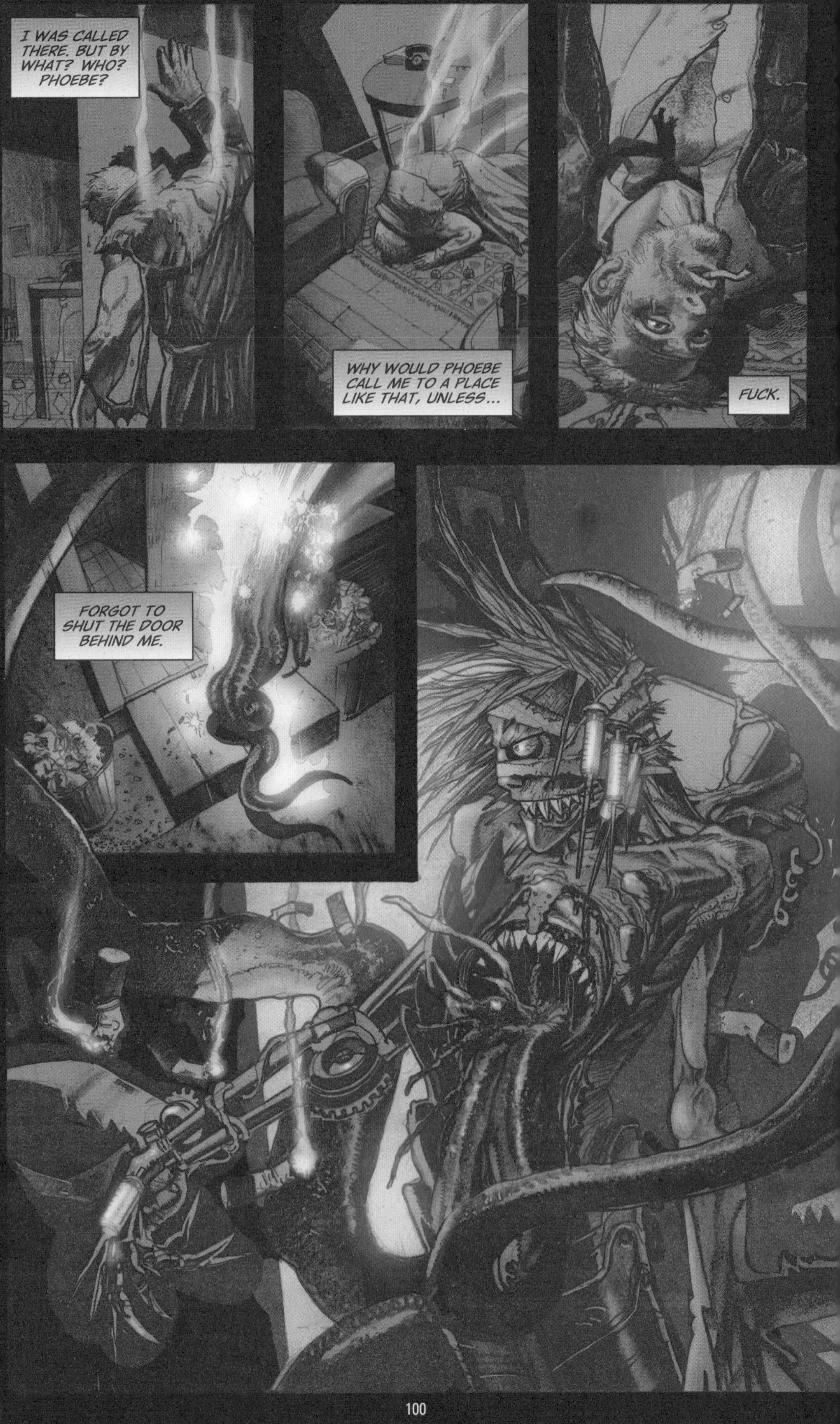
I WAS CALLED THERE. BUT BY WHAT? WHO? PHOEBE?
WHY WOULD PHOEBE CALL ME TO A PLACE LIKE THAT, UNLESS...
FUCK.
FORGOT TO SHUT THE DOOR BEHIND ME.

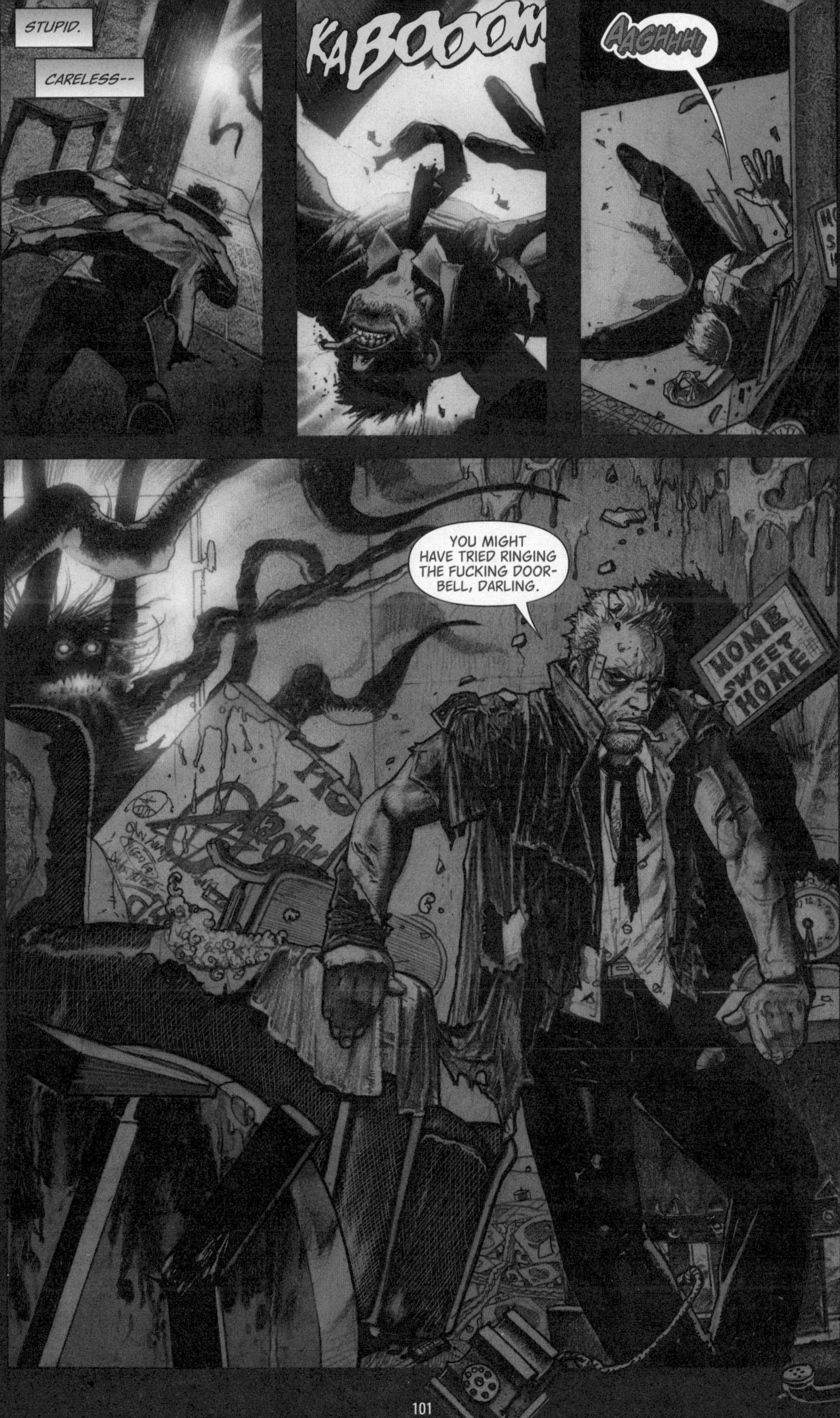
STUPID.
CARELESS--
KABOOOM
AAGHHH!
HOME SWEET HOME
YOU MIGHT HAVE TRIED RINGING THE FUCKING DOOR-BELL, DARLING.

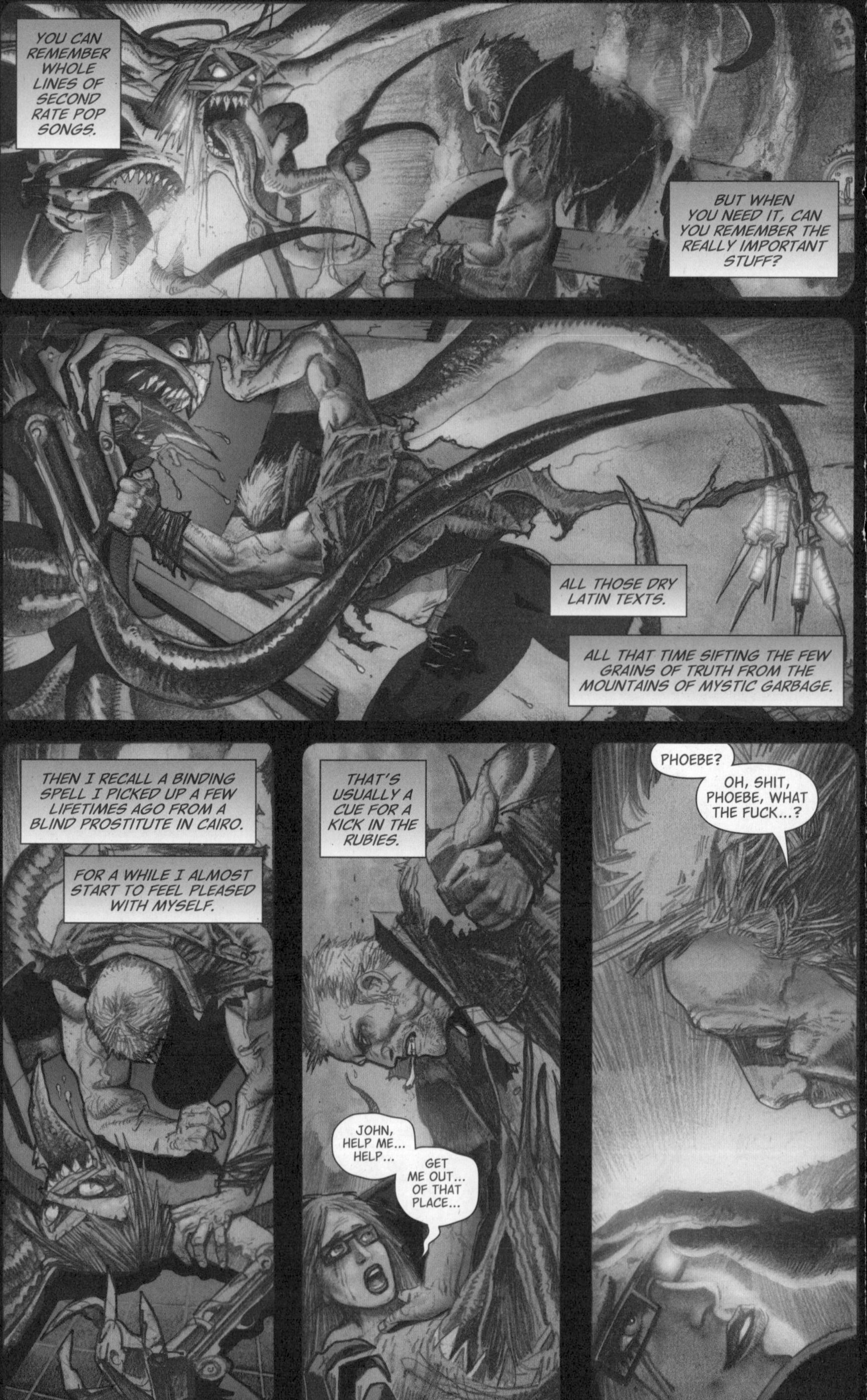
YOU CAN REMEMBER WHOLE LINES OF SECOND RATE POP SONGS.
BUT WHEN YOU NEED IT, CAN YOU REMEMBER THE REALLY IMPORTANT STUFF?
ALL THOSE DRY LATIN TEXTS.
ALL THAT TIME SIFTING THE FEW GRAINS OF TRUTH FROM THE MOUNTAINS OF MYSTIC GARBAGE.
THEN I RECALL A BINDING SPELL I PICKED UP A FEW LIFETIMES AGO FROM A BLIND PROSTITUTE IN CAIRO.
FOR A WHILE I ALMOST START TO FEEL PLEASED WITH MYSELF.
THAT'S USUALLY A CUE FOR A KICK IN THE RUBIES.
JOHN, HELP ME... HELP...
GET ME OUT... OF THAT PLACE...
PHOEBE?
OH, SHIT, PHOEBE, WHAT THE FUCK...?

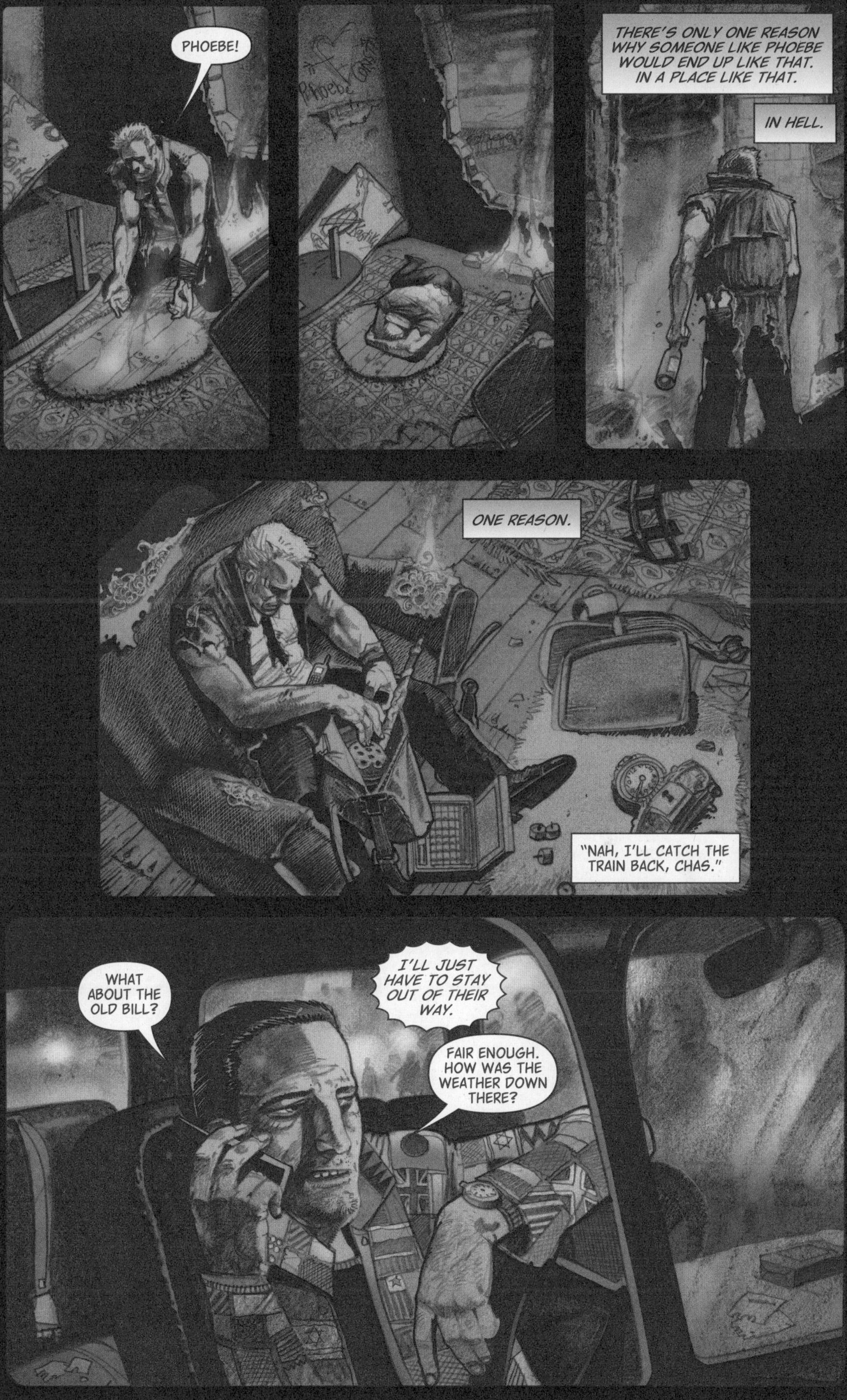
PHOEBE!
THERE'S ONLY ONE REASON WHY SOMEONE LIKE PHOEBE WOULD END UP LIKE THAT. IN A PLACE LIKE THAT.
IN HELL.
ONE REASON.
"NAH, I'LL CATCH THE TRAIN BACK, CHAS."
WHAT ABOUT THE OLD BILL?
I'LL JUST HAVE TO STAY OUT OF THEIR WAY.
FAIR ENOUGH. HOW WAS THE WEATHER DOWN THERE?

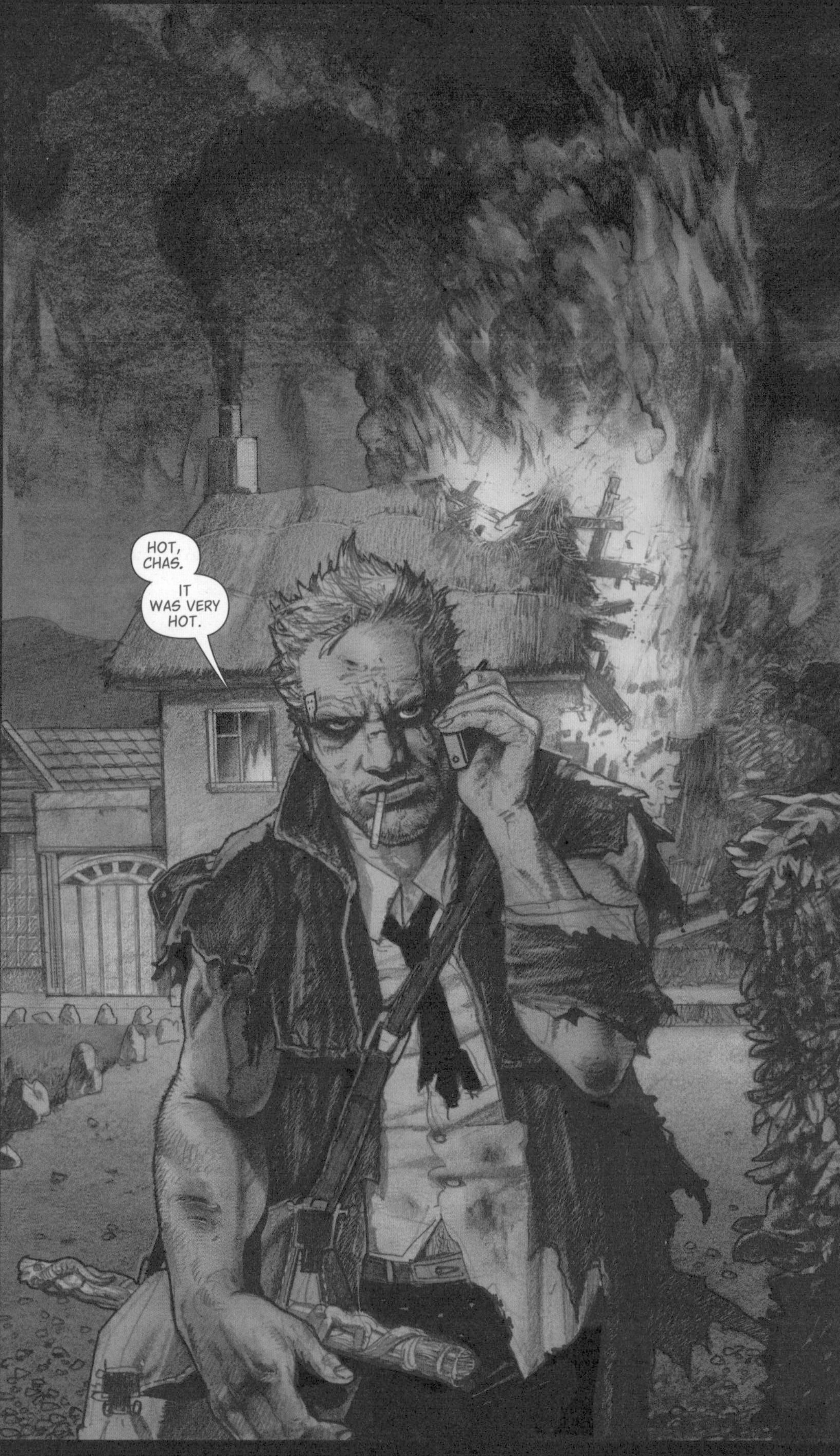
HOT, CHAS.
IT WAS VERY HOT.

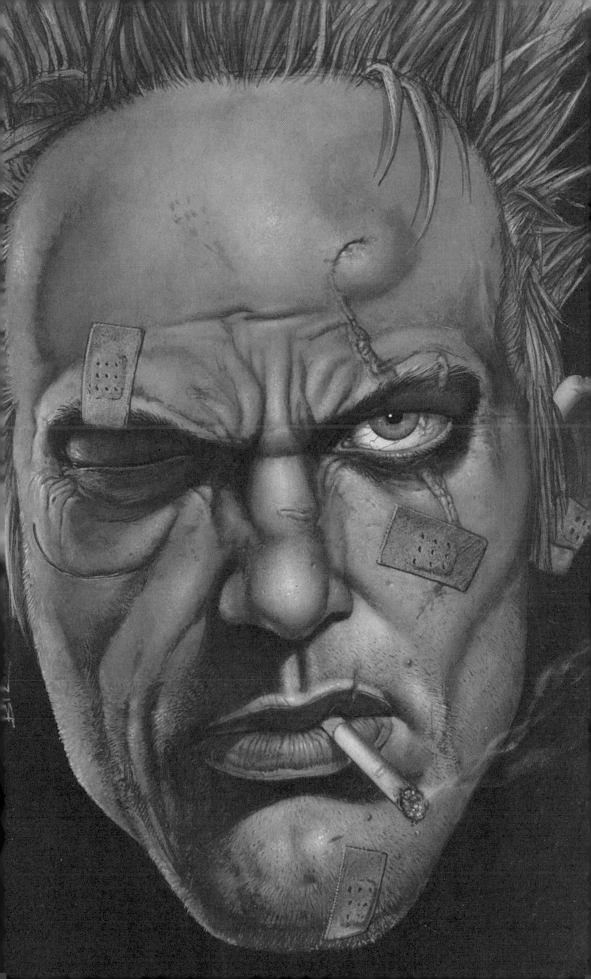

The Long Crap Friday

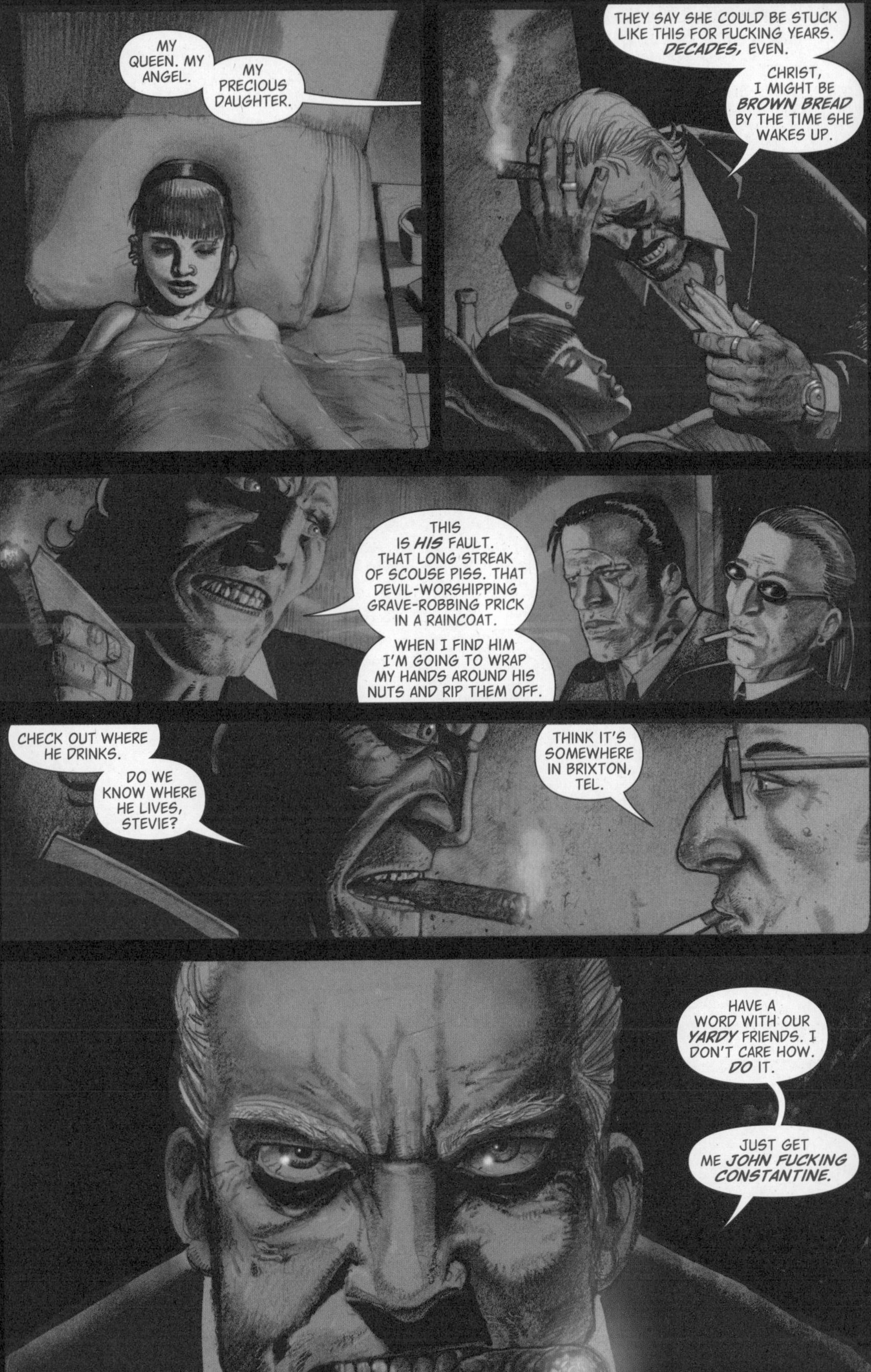
MY QUEEN. MY ANGEL.
MY PRECIOUS DAUGHTER.
THEY SAY SHE COULD BE STUCK LIKE THIS FOR FUCKING YEARS. DECADES, EVEN.
CHRIST, I MIGHT BE BROWN BREAD BY THE TIME SHE WAKES UP.
THIS IS HIS FAULT. THAT LONG STREAK OF SCOUSE PISS. THAT DEVIL-WORSHIPPING GRAVE-ROBBING PRICK IN A RAINCOAT.
WHEN I FIND HIM I'M GOING TO WRAP MY HANDS AROUND HIS NUTS AND RIP THEM OFF.
CHECK OUT WHERE HE DRINKS.
DO WE KNOW WHERE HE LIVES, STEVIE?
THINK IT'S SOMEWHERE IN BRIXTON, TEL.
HAVE A WORD WITH OUR YARDY FRIENDS. I DON'T CARE HOW. DO IT.
JUST GET ME JOHN FUCKING CONSTANTINE.

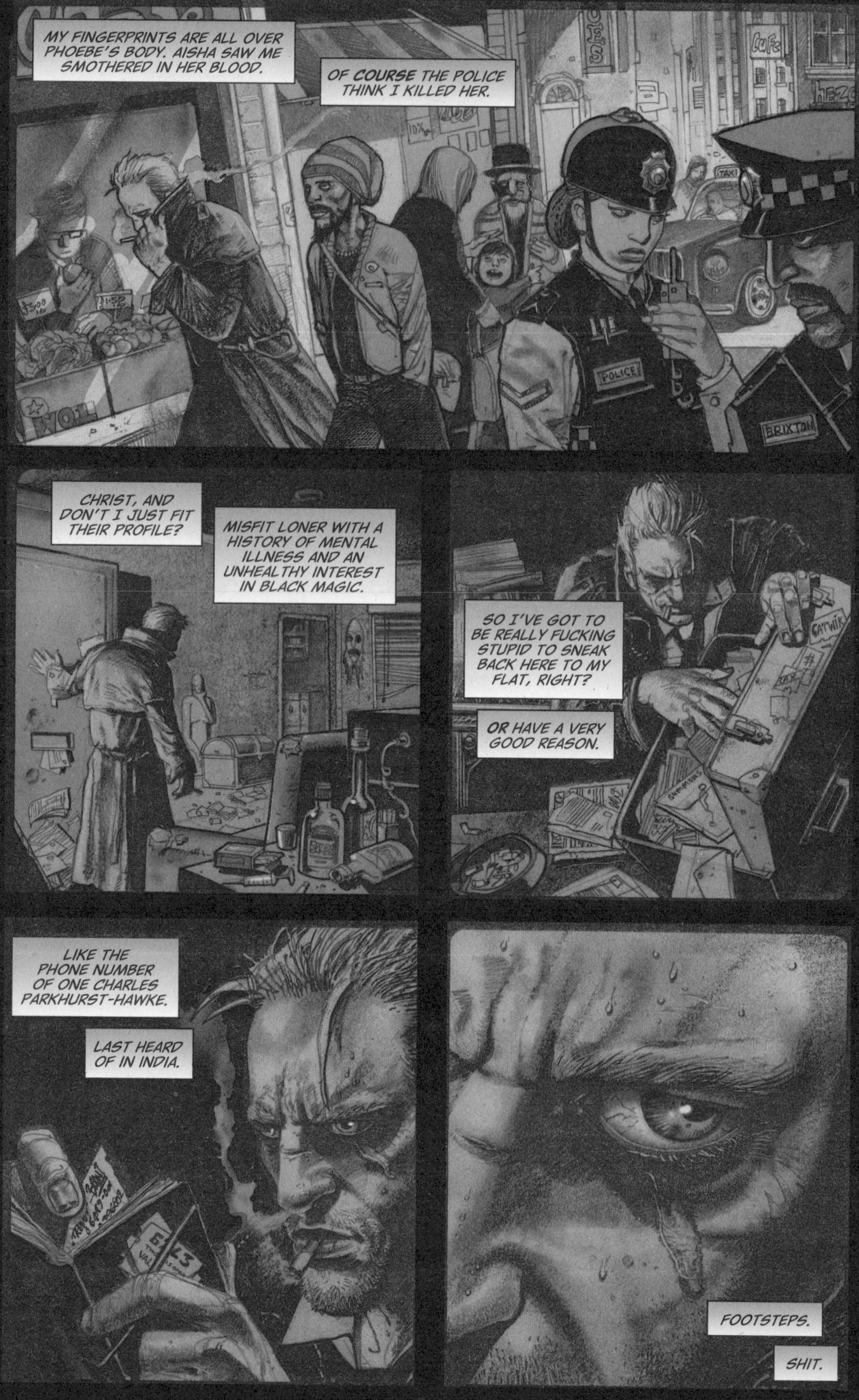
MY FINGERPRINTS ARE ALL OVER PHOEBE'S BODY. AISHA SAW ME SMOTHERED IN HER BLOOD.
OF COURSE THE POLICE THINK I KILLED HER.
POLICE
BRIXTON
CHRIST, AND DON'T I JUST FIT THEIR PROFILE?
MISFIT LONER WITH A HISTORY OF MENTAL ILLNESS AND AN UNHEALTHY INTEREST IN BLACK MAGIC.
SO I'VE GOT TO BE REALLY FUCKING STUPID TO SNEAK BACK HERE TO MY FLAT, RIGHT?
OR HAVE A VERY GOOD REASON.
LIKE THE PHONE NUMBER OF ONE CHARLES PARKHURST-HAWKE.
LAST HEARD OF IN INDIA.
FOOTSTEPS.
SHIT.

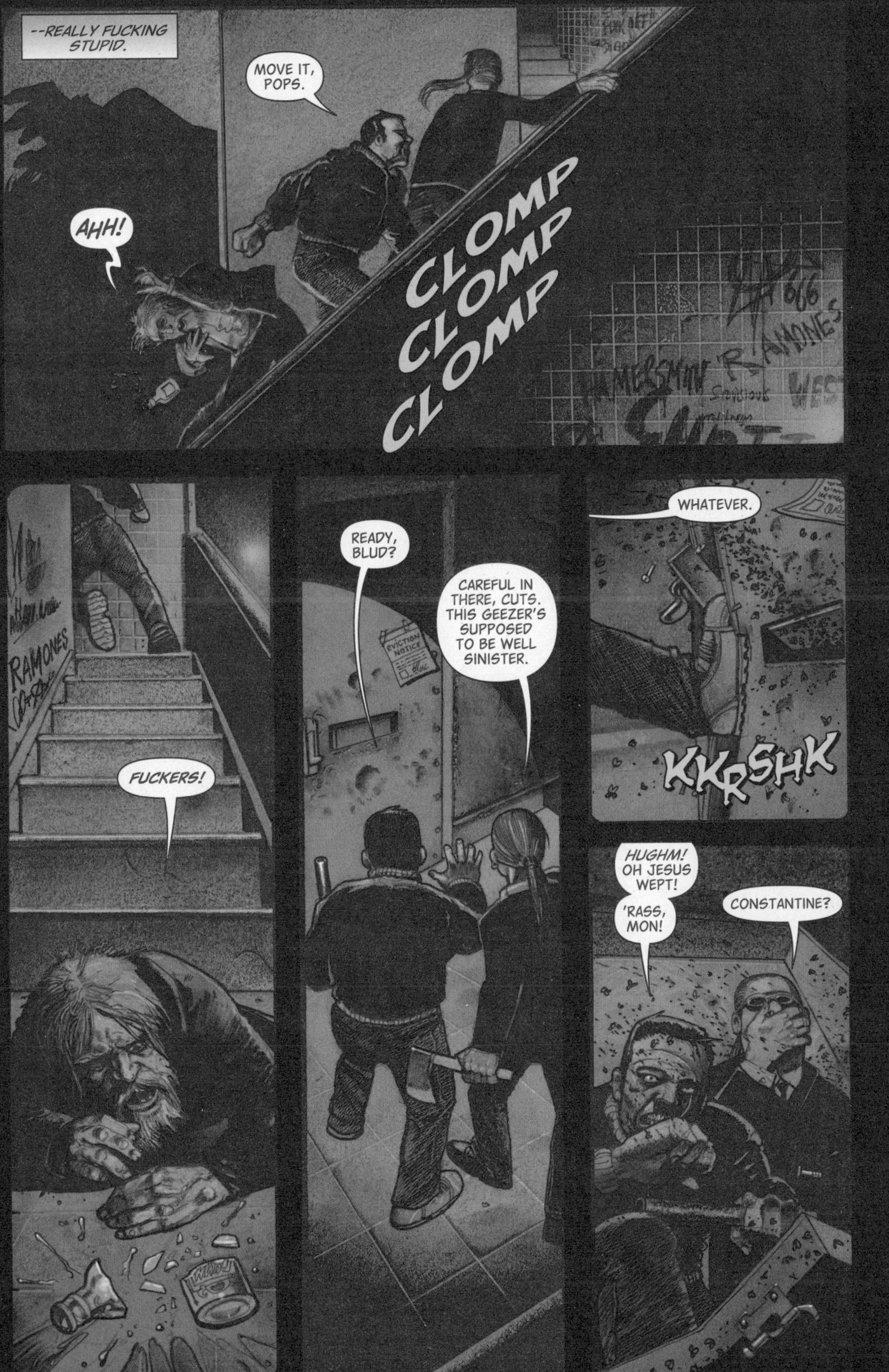
--REALLY FUCKING STUPID.
MOVE IT, POPS.
AHH!
CLOMP
CLOMP
CLOMP
FUCKERS!
READY, BLUD?
CAREFUL IN THERE, CUTS. THIS GEEZER'S SUPPOSED TO BE WELL SINISTER.
EVICTION NOTICE
WHATEVER.
KKRSHK
HUGHM! OH JESUS WEPT!
'RASS, MON!
CONSTANTINE?

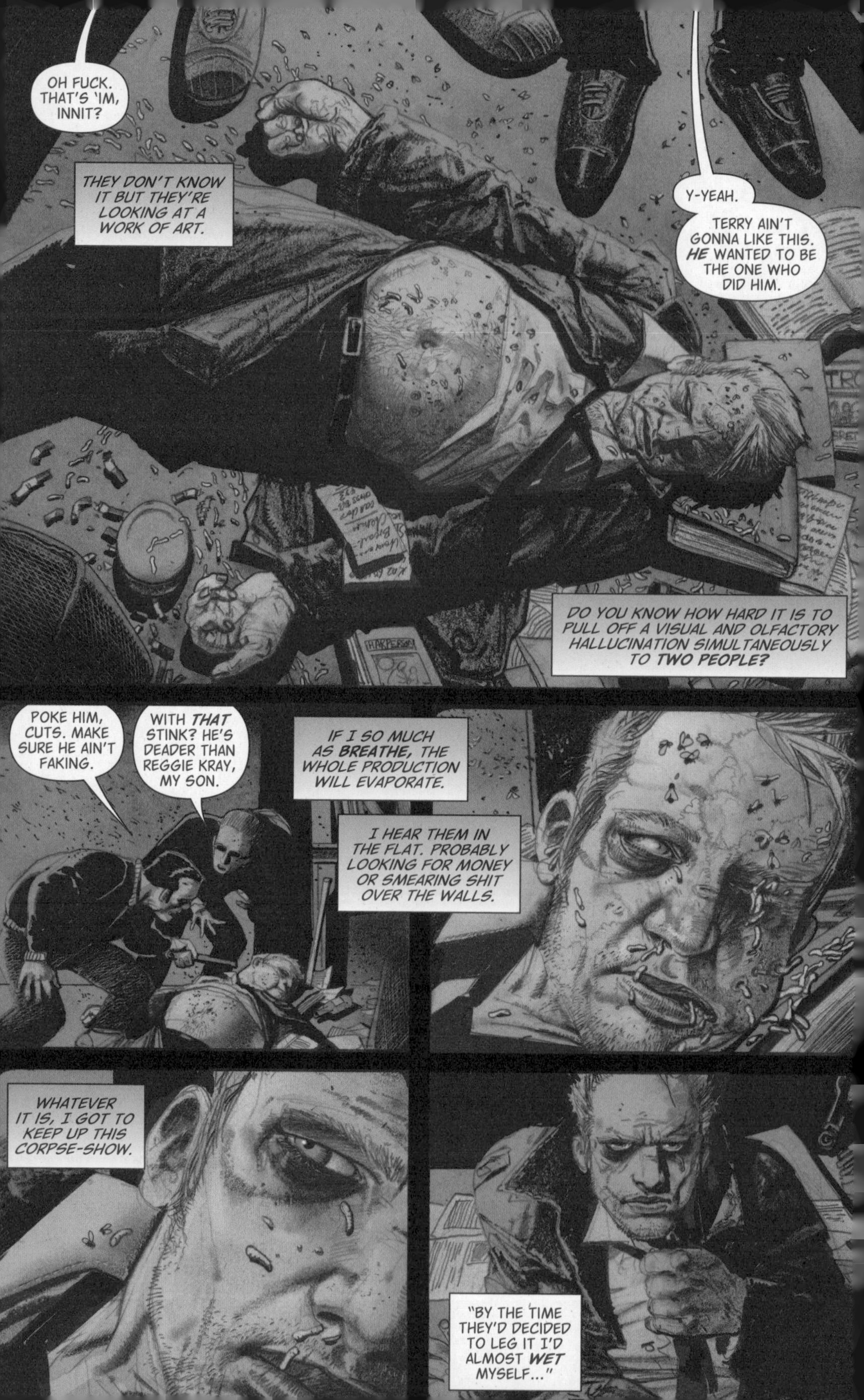
OH FUCK. THAT'S 'IM, INNIT?
THEY DON'T KNOW IT BUT THEY'RE LOOKING AT A WORK OF ART.
Y-YEAH.
TERRY AIN'T GONNA LIKE THIS. HE WANTED TO BE THE ONE WHO DID HIM.
DO YOU KNOW HOW HARD IT IS TO PULL OFF A VISUAL AND OLFACTORY HALLUCINATION SIMULTANEOUSLY TO TWO PEOPLE?
POKE HIM, CUTS. MAKE SURE HE AIN'T FAKING.
WITH THAT STINK? HE'S DEADER THAN REGGIE KRAY, MY SON.
IF I SO MUCH AS BREATHE, THE WHOLE PRODUCTION WILL EVAPORATE.
I HEAR THEM IN THE FLAT. PROBABLY LOOKING FOR MONEY OR SMEARING SHIT OVER THE WALLS.
WHATEVER IT IS, I GOT TO KEEP UP THIS CORPSE-SHOW.
"BY THE TIME THEY'D DECIDED TO LEG IT I'D ALMOST WET MYSELF..."

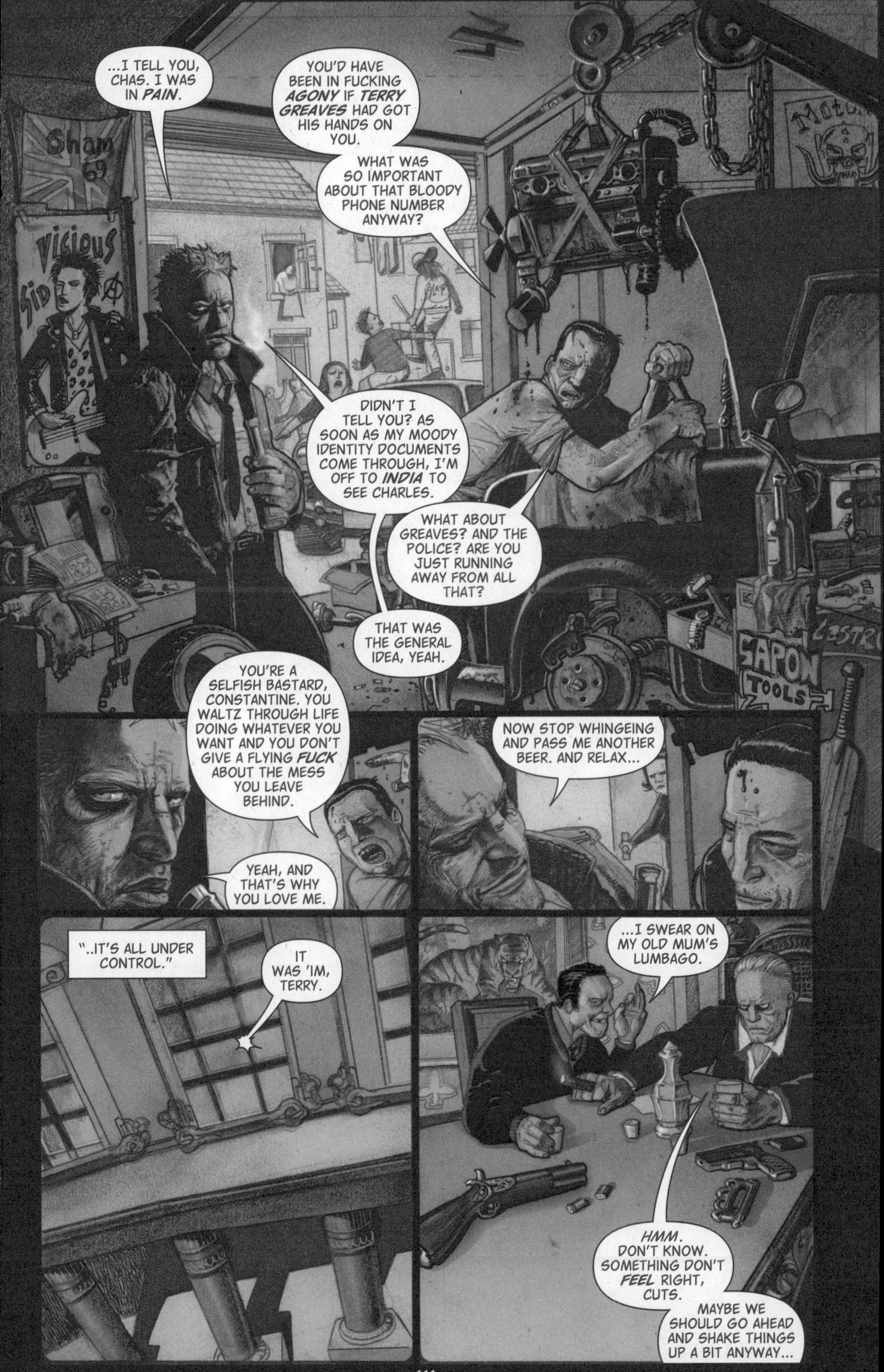
...I TELL YOU, CHAS. I WAS IN PAIN.
YOU'D HAVE BEEN IN FUCKING AGONY IF TERRY GREAVES HAD GOT HIS HANDS ON YOU.
WHAT WAS SO IMPORTANT ABOUT THAT BLOODY PHONE NUMBER ANYWAY?
DIDN'T I TELL YOU? AS SOON AS MY MOODY IDENTITY DOCUMENTS COME THROUGH, I'M OFF TO INDIA TO SEE CHARLES.
WHAT ABOUT GREAVES? AND THE POLICE? ARE YOU JUST RUNNING AWAY FROM ALL THAT?
THAT WAS THE GENERAL IDEA, YEAH.
YOU'RE A SELFISH BASTARD, CONSTANTINE. YOU WALTZ THROUGH LIFE DOING WHATEVER YOU WANT AND YOU DON'T GIVE A FLYING FUCK ABOUT THE MESS YOU LEAVE BEHIND.
YEAH, AND THAT'S WHY YOU LOVE ME.
NOW STOP WHINGEING AND PASS ME ANOTHER BEER. AND RELAX...
"..IT'S ALL UNDER CONTROL."
IT WAS 'IM, TERRY.
...I SWEAR ON MY OLD MUM'S LUMBAGO.
HMM. DON'T KNOW. SOMETHING DON'T FEEL RIGHT, CUTS.
MAYBE WE SHOULD GO AHEAD AND SHAKE THINGS UP A BIT ANYWAY...

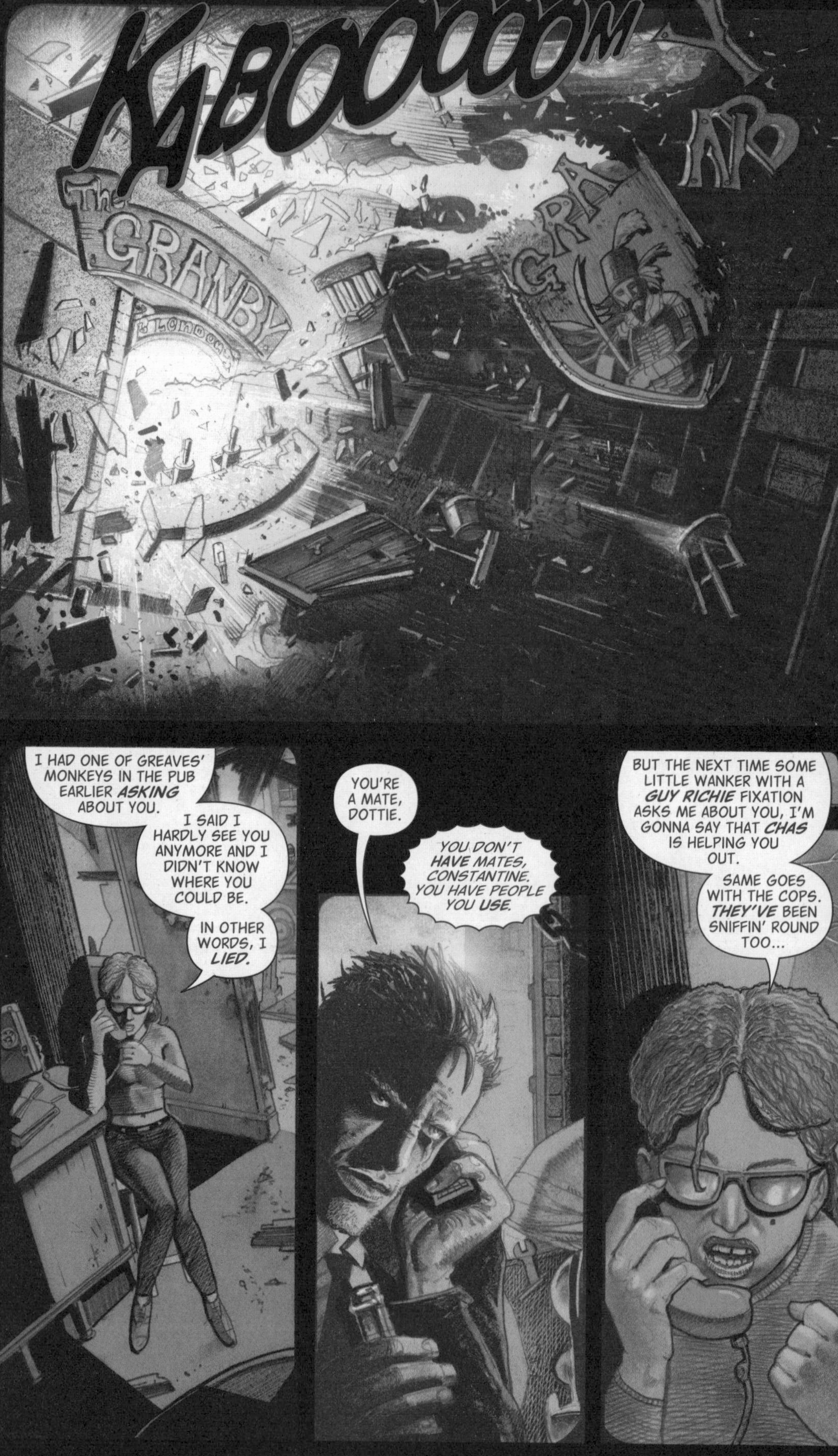
KABOOOOOM
The GRANBY
LONDON
GRA
I HAD ONE OF GREAVES' MONKEYS IN THE PUB EARLIER ASKING ABOUT YOU.
I SAID I HARDLY SEE YOU ANYMORE AND I DIDN'T KNOW WHERE YOU COULD BE.
IN OTHER WORDS, I LIED.
YOU'RE A MATE, DOTTIE.
YOU DON'T HAVE MATES, CONSTANTINE. YOU HAVE PEOPLE YOU USE.
BUT THE NEXT TIME SOME LITTLE WANKER WITH A GUY RICHIE FIXATION ASKS ME ABOUT YOU, I'M GONNA SAY THAT CHAS IS HELPING YOU OUT.
SAME GOES WITH THE COPS. THEY'VE BEEN SNIFFIN' ROUND TOO...

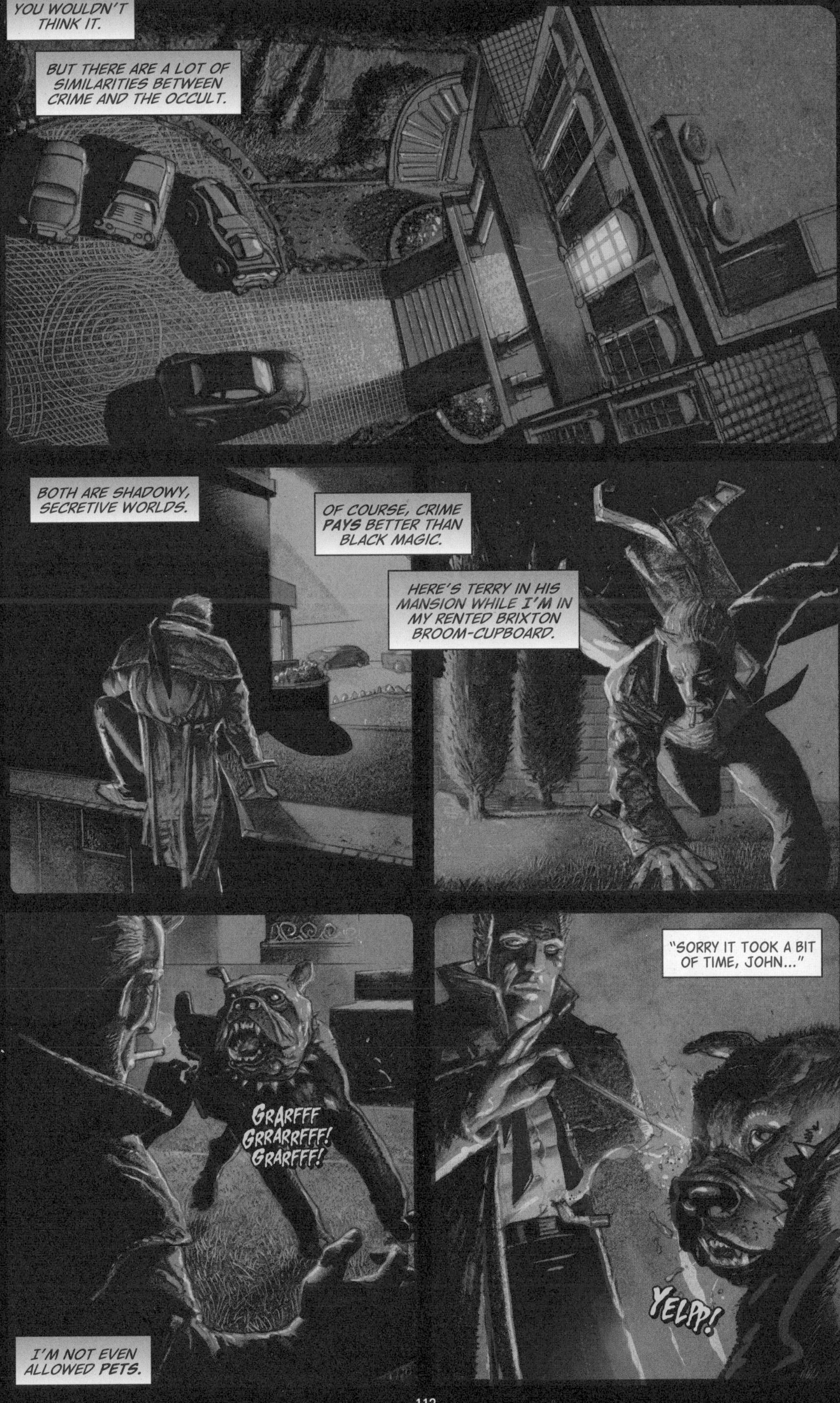
YOU WOULDN'T THINK IT.
BUT THERE ARE A LOT OF SIMILARITIES BETWEEN CRIME AND THE OCCULT.
BOTH ARE SHADOWY, SECRETIVE WORLDS.
OF COURSE, CRIME PAYS BETTER THAN BLACK MAGIC.
HERE'S TERRY IN HIS MANSION WHILE I'M IN MY RENTED BRIXTON BROOM-CUPBOARD.
GRARFFF GRRARRFFF! GRARFFF!
I'M NOT EVEN ALLOWED PETS.
"SORRY IT TOOK A BIT OF TIME, JOHN..."
YELPP!

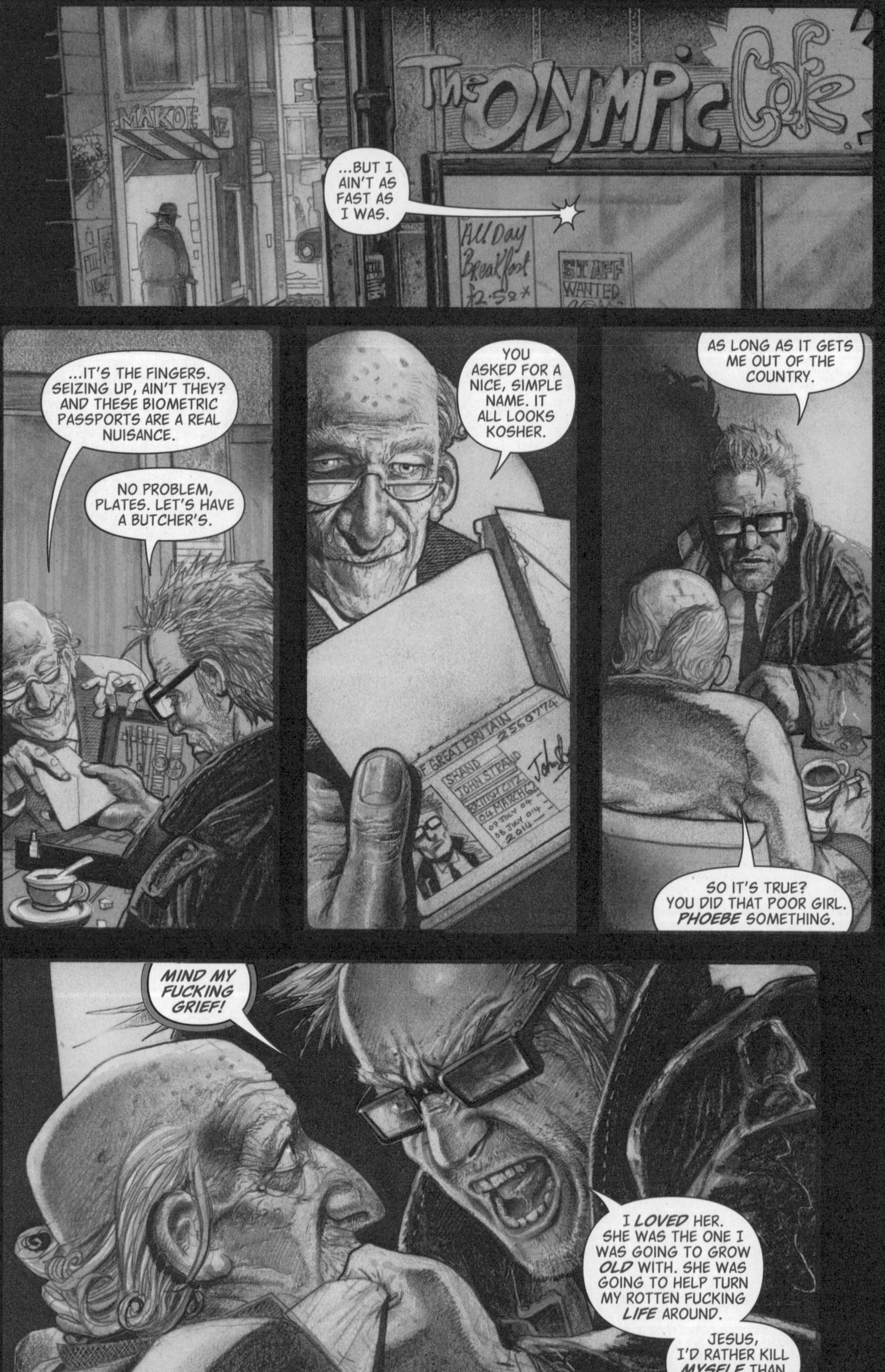

The OLYMPIC Cafe
...BUT I AIN'T AS FAST AS I WAS.
All Day Breakfast £2.50*
STAFF WANTED
...IT'S THE FINGERS. SEIZING UP, AIN'T THEY? AND THESE BIOMETRIC PASSPORTS ARE A REAL NUISANCE.
NO PROBLEM, PLATES. LET'S HAVE A BUTCHER'S.
YOU ASKED FOR A NICE, SIMPLE NAME. IT ALL LOOKS KOSHER.
AS LONG AS IT GETS ME OUT OF THE COUNTRY.
SO IT'S TRUE? YOU DID THAT POOR GIRL. PHOEBE SOMETHING.
MIND MY FUCKING GRIEF!
I LOVED HER. SHE WAS THE ONE I WAS GOING TO GROW OLD WITH. SHE WAS GOING TO HELP TURN MY ROTTEN FUCKING LIFE AROUND.
JESUS, I'D RATHER KILL MYSELF THAN KILL HER.

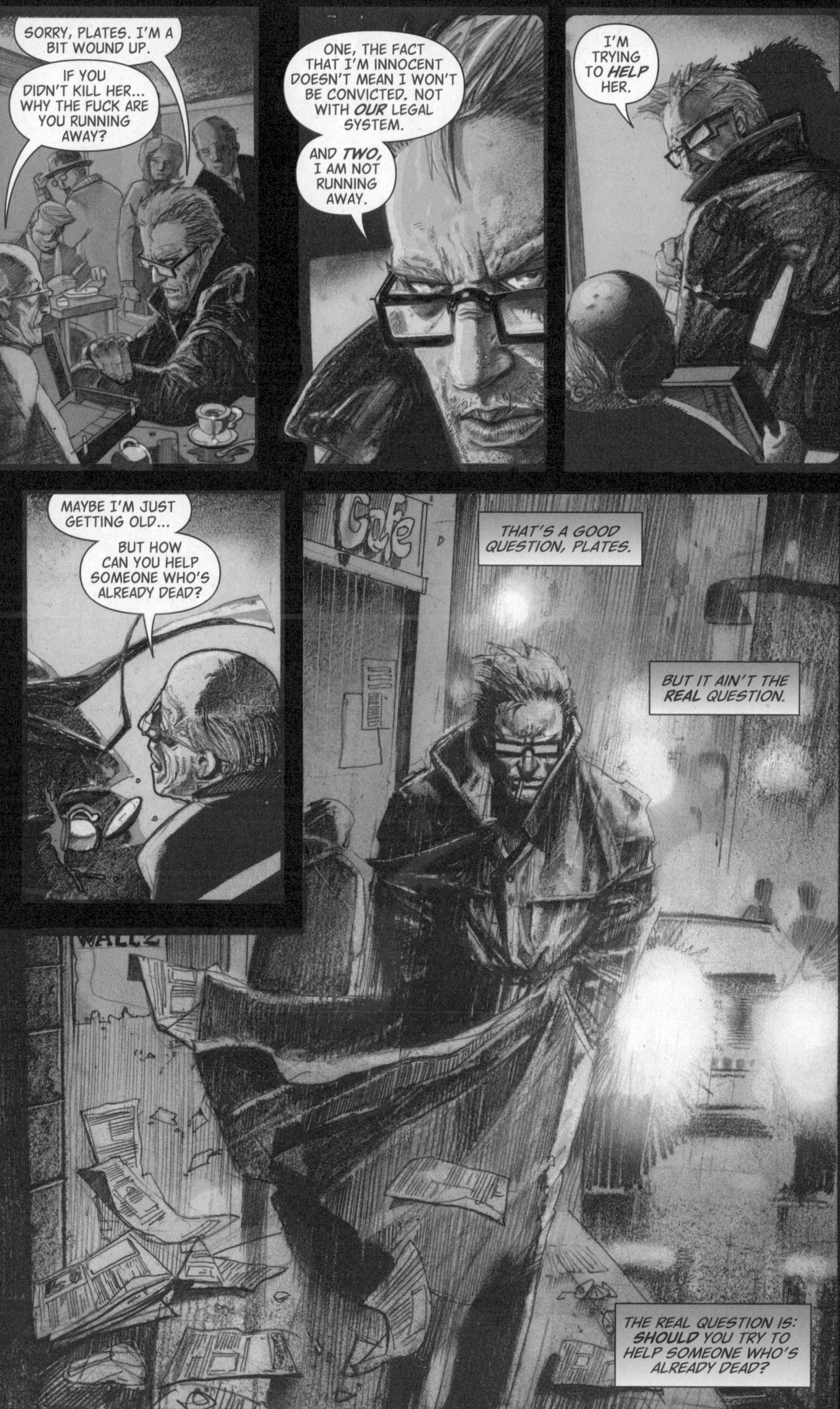
SORRY, PLATES. I'M A BIT WOUND UP.
IF YOU DIDN'T KILL HER... WHY THE FUCK ARE YOU RUNNING AWAY?
ONE, THE FACT THAT I'M INNOCENT DOESN'T MEAN I WON'T BE CONVICTED. NOT WITH OUR LEGAL SYSTEM.
AND TWO, I AM NOT RUNNING AWAY.
I'M TRYING TO HELP HER.
MAYBE I'M JUST GETTING OLD...
BUT HOW CAN YOU HELP SOMEONE WHO'S ALREADY DEAD?
Cafe
THAT'S A GOOD QUESTION, PLATES.
BUT IT AIN'T THE REAL QUESTION.
THE REAL QUESTION IS: SHOULD YOU TRY TO HELP SOMEONE WHO'S ALREADY DEAD?

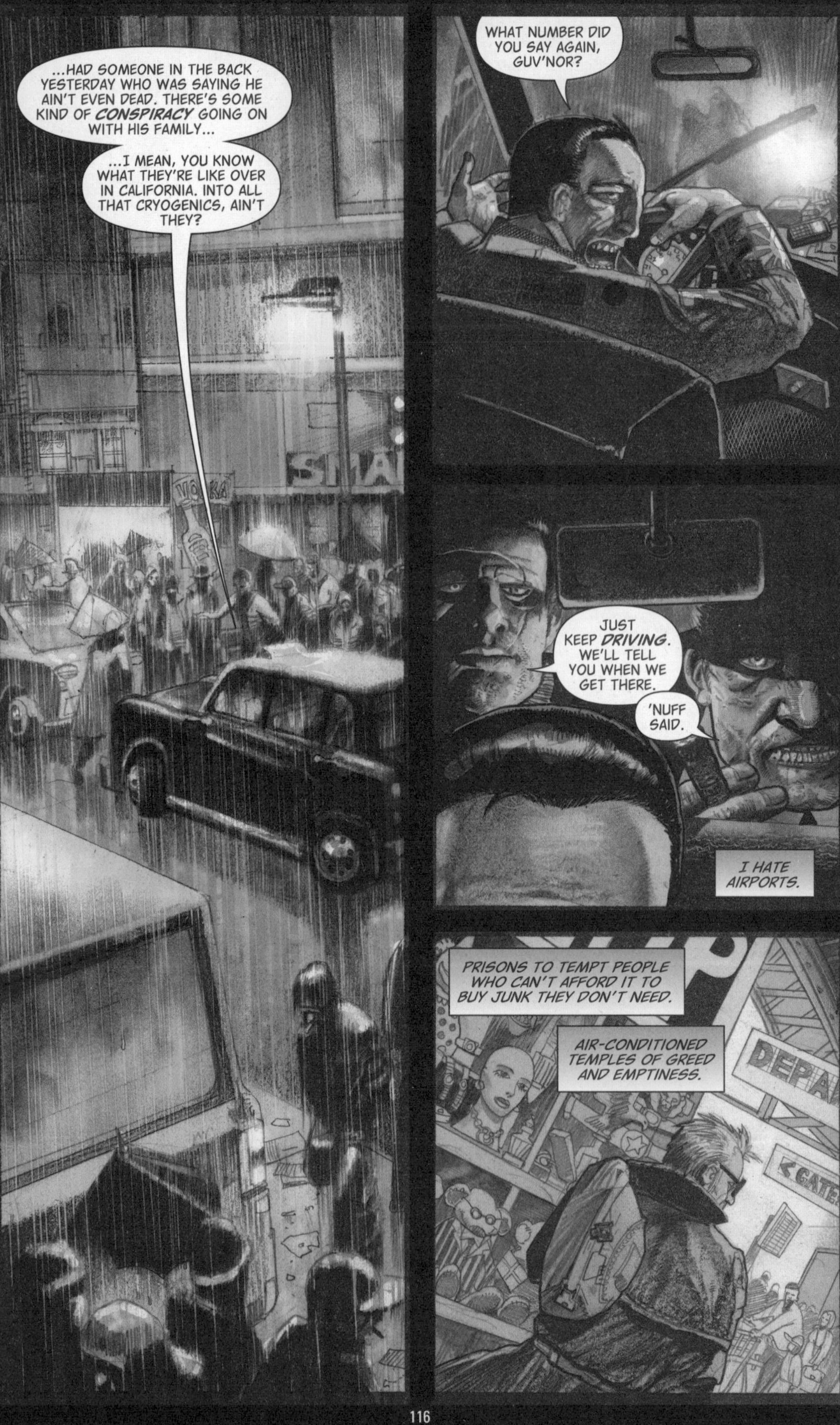
...HAD SOMEONE IN THE BACK YESTERDAY WHO WAS SAYING HE AIN'T EVEN DEAD. THERE'S SOME KIND OF CONSPIRACY GOING ON WITH HIS FAMILY...
...I MEAN, YOU KNOW WHAT THEY'RE LIKE OVER IN CALIFORNIA. INTO ALL THAT CRYOGENICS, AIN'T THEY?
WHAT NUMBER DID YOU SAY AGAIN, GUV'NOR?
JUST KEEP DRIVING. WE'LL TELL YOU WHEN WE GET THERE.
'NUFF SAID.
I HATE AIRPORTS.
PRISONS TO TEMPT PEOPLE WHO CAN'T AFFORD IT TO BUY JUNK THEY DON'T NEED.
AIR-CONDITIONED TEMPLES OF GREED AND EMPTINESS.

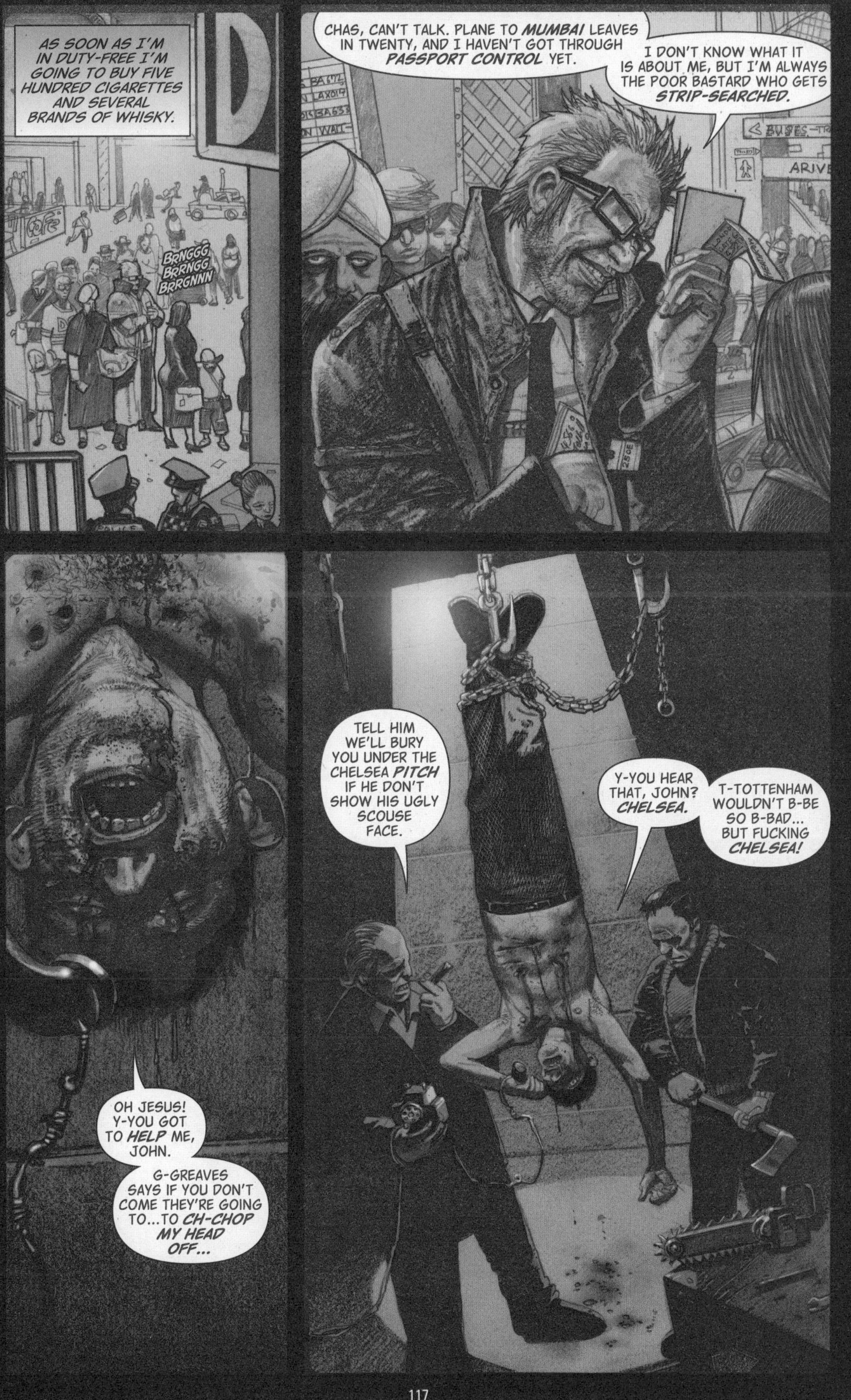
AS SOON AS I'M IN DUTY-FREE I'M GOING TO BUY FIVE HUNDRED CIGARETTES AND SEVERAL BRANDS OF WHISKY.
BRNGGG BRRNGG BRRGNNN
CHAS, CAN'T TALK. PLANE TO MUMBAI LEAVES IN TWENTY, AND I HAVEN'T GOT THROUGH PASSPORT CONTROL YET.
I DON'T KNOW WHAT IT IS ABOUT ME, BUT I'M ALWAYS THE POOR BASTARD WHO GETS STRIP-SEARCHED.
OH JESUS! Y-YOU GOT TO HELP ME, JOHN.
G-GREAVES SAYS IF YOU DON'T COME THEY'RE GOING TO...TO CH-CHOP MY HEAD OFF...
TELL HIM WE'LL BURY YOU UNDER THE CHELSEA PITCH IF HE DON'T SHOW HIS UGLY SCOUSE FACE.
Y-YOU HEAR THAT, JOHN? CHELSEA.
T-TOTTENHAM WOULDN'T B-BE SO B-BAD... BUT FUCKING CHELSEA!

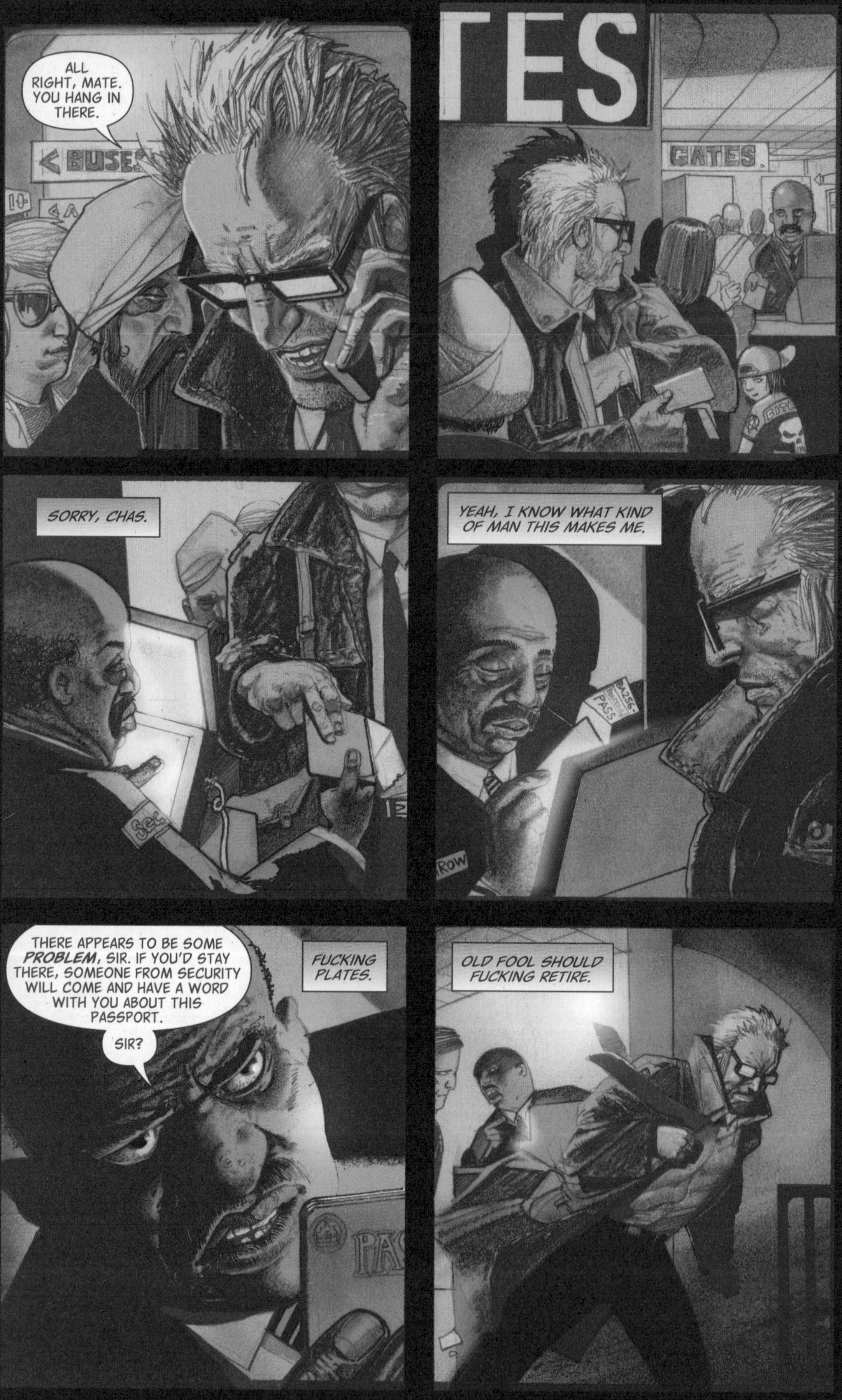
ALL RIGHT, MATE. YOU HANG IN THERE.
TES
GATES
SORRY, CHAS.
YEAH, I KNOW WHAT KIND OF MAN THIS MAKES ME.
THERE APPEARS TO BE SOME ***PROBLEM***, SIR. IF YOU'D STAY THERE, SOMEONE FROM SECURITY WILL COME AND HAVE A WORD WITH YOU ABOUT THIS PASSPORT.
SIR?
FUCKING PLATES.
OLD FOOL SHOULD FUCKING RETIRE.

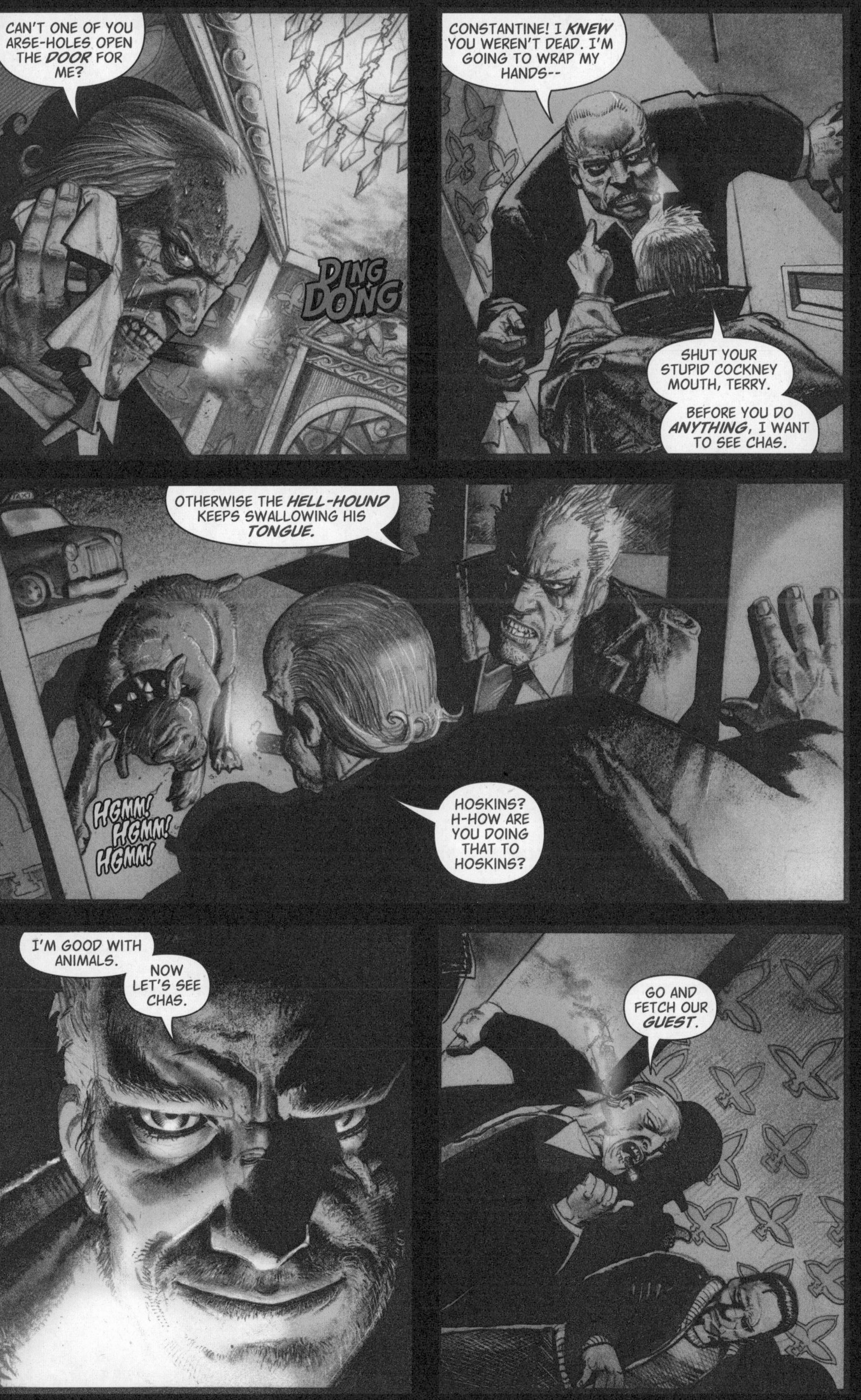
CAN'T ONE OF YOU ARSE-HOLES OPEN THE DOOR FOR ME?
DING DONG
CONSTANTINE! I KNEW YOU WEREN'T DEAD. I'M GOING TO WRAP MY HANDS--
SHUT YOUR STUPID COCKNEY MOUTH, TERRY.
BEFORE YOU DO ANYTHING, I WANT TO SEE CHAS.
OTHERWISE THE HELL-HOUND KEEPS SWALLOWING HIS TONGUE.
HGMM! HGMM! HGMM!
HOSKINS? H-HOW ARE YOU DOING THAT TO HOSKINS?
I'M GOOD WITH ANIMALS.
NOW LET'S SEE CHAS.
GO AND FETCH OUR GUEST.

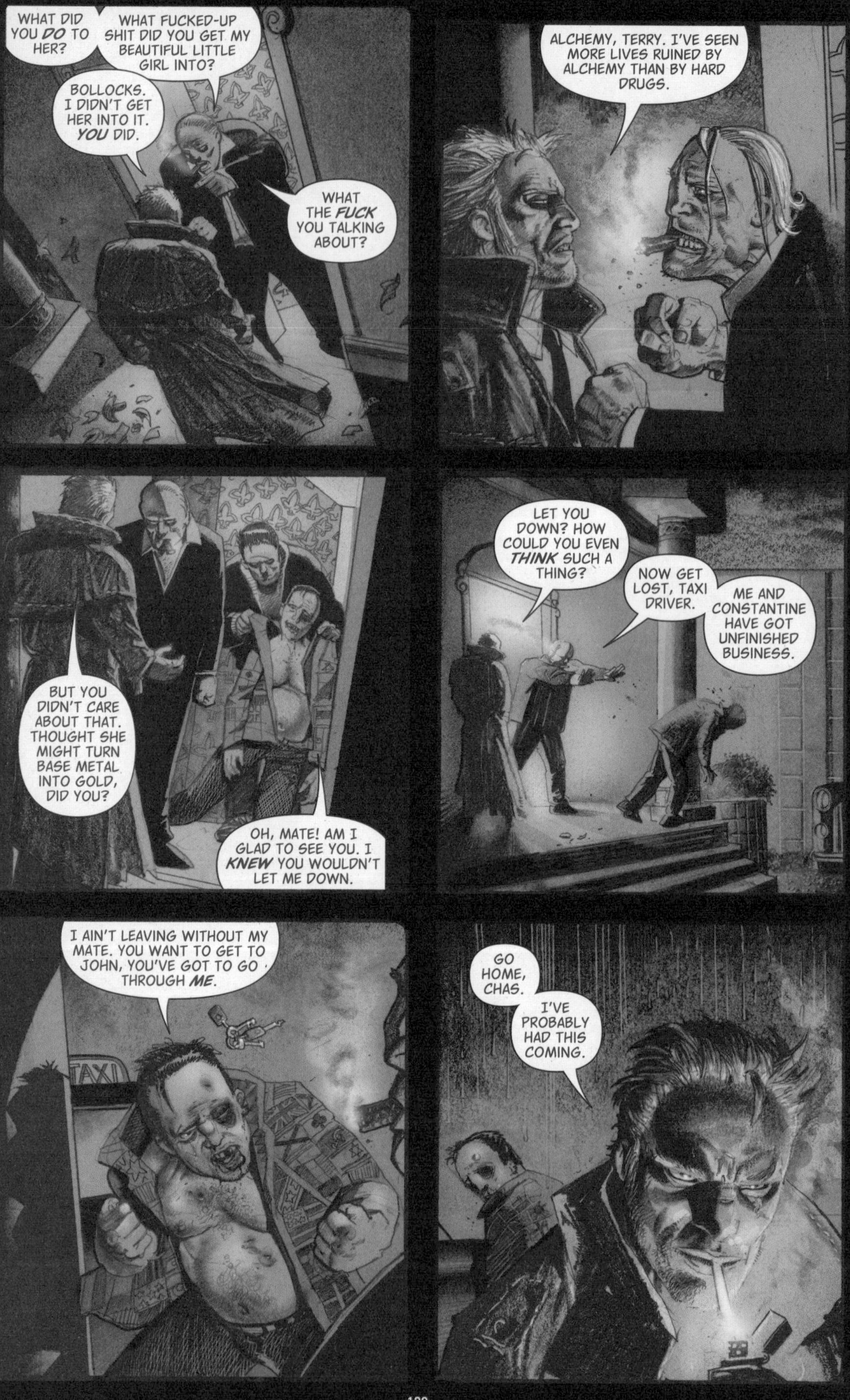
WHAT DID YOU *DO* TO HER?
WHAT FUCKED-UP SHIT DID YOU GET MY BEAUTIFUL LITTLE GIRL INTO?
BOLLOCKS. I DIDN'T GET HER INTO IT. *YOU* DID.
WHAT THE *FUCK* YOU TALKING ABOUT?
ALCHEMY, TERRY. I'VE SEEN MORE LIVES RUINED BY ALCHEMY THAN BY HARD DRUGS.
BUT YOU DIDN'T CARE ABOUT THAT. THOUGHT SHE MIGHT TURN BASE METAL INTO GOLD, DID YOU?
OH, MATE! AM I GLAD TO SEE YOU. I *KNEW* YOU WOULDN'T LET ME DOWN.
LET YOU DOWN? HOW COULD YOU EVEN *THINK* SUCH A THING?
NOW GET LOST, TAXI DRIVER.
ME AND CONSTANTINE HAVE GOT UNFINISHED BUSINESS.
I AIN'T LEAVING WITHOUT MY MATE. YOU WANT TO GET TO JOHN, YOU'VE GOT TO GO THROUGH *ME*.
TAXI
GO HOME, CHAS.
I'VE PROBABLY HAD THIS COMING.

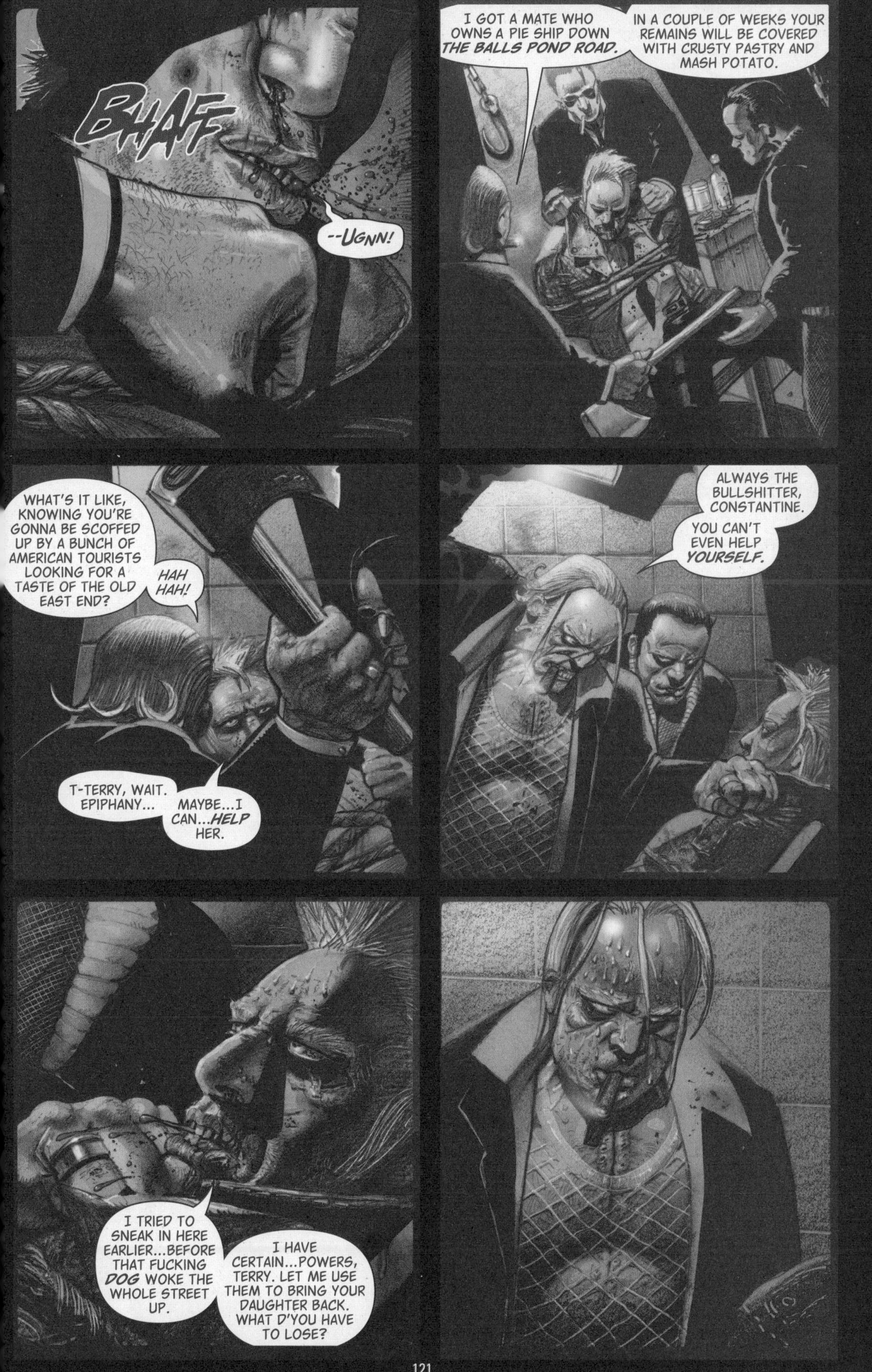
BHAFF
--UGNN!
I GOT A MATE WHO OWNS A PIE SHIP DOWN THE BALLS POND ROAD.
IN A COUPLE OF WEEKS YOUR REMAINS WILL BE COVERED WITH CRUSTY PASTRY AND MASH POTATO.
WHAT'S IT LIKE, KNOWING YOU'RE GONNA BE SCOFFED UP BY A BUNCH OF AMERICAN TOURISTS LOOKING FOR A TASTE OF THE OLD EAST END?
HAH HAH!
T-TERRY, WAIT. EPIPHANY...
MAYBE...I CAN...HELP HER.
ALWAYS THE BULLSHITTER, CONSTANTINE.
YOU CAN'T EVEN HELP YOURSELF.
I TRIED TO SNEAK IN HERE EARLIER...BEFORE THAT FUCKING DOG WOKE THE WHOLE STREET UP.
I HAVE CERTAIN...POWERS, TERRY. LET ME USE THEM TO BRING YOUR DAUGHTER BACK. WHAT D'YOU HAVE TO LOSE?

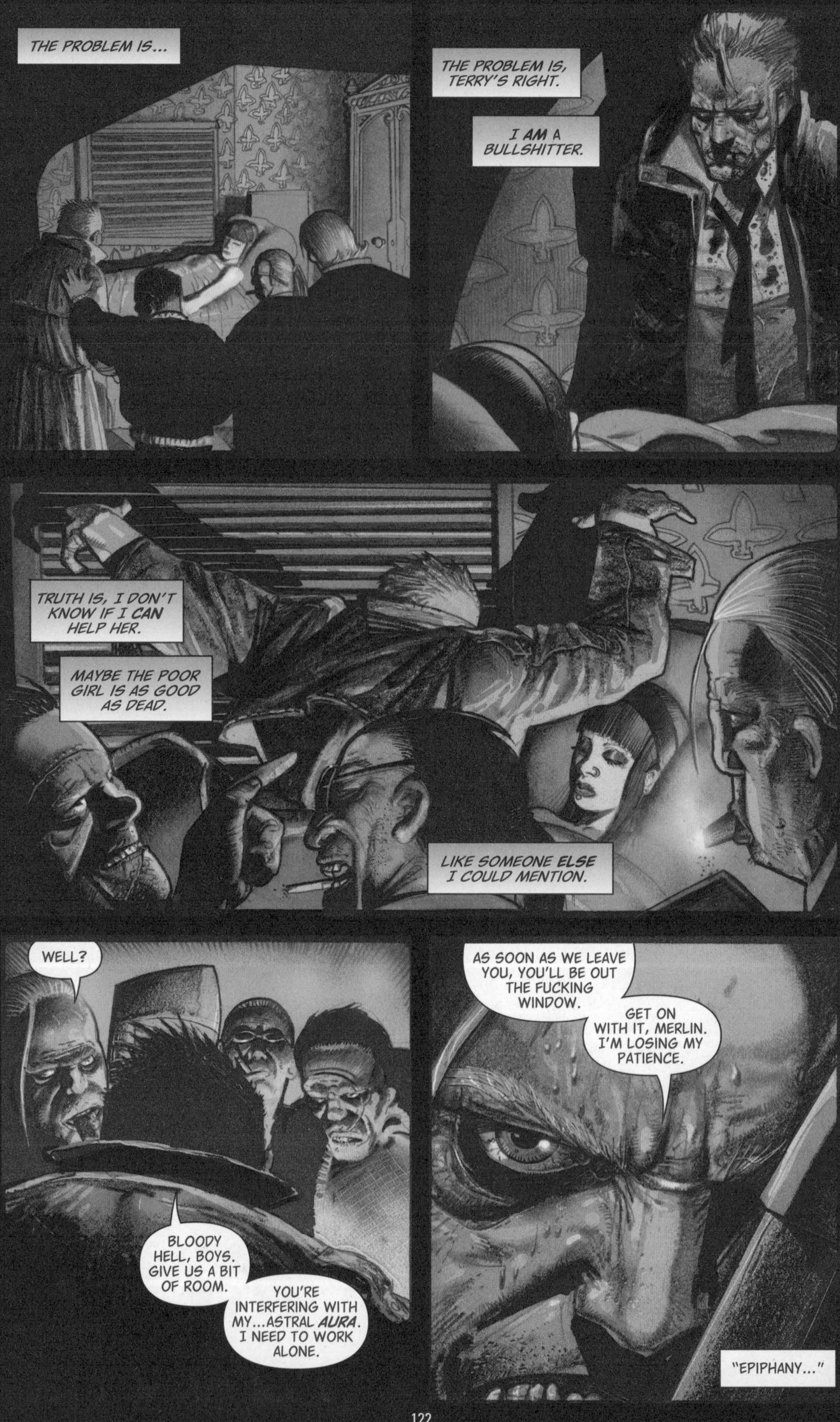
THE PROBLEM IS...
THE PROBLEM IS, TERRY'S RIGHT.
I AM A BULLSHITTER.
TRUTH IS, I DON'T KNOW IF I CAN HELP HER.
MAYBE THE POOR GIRL IS AS GOOD AS DEAD.
LIKE SOMEONE ELSE I COULD MENTION.
WELL?
BLOODY HELL, BOYS. GIVE US A BIT OF ROOM.
YOU'RE INTERFERING WITH MY...ASTRAL AURA. I NEED TO WORK ALONE.
AS SOON AS WE LEAVE YOU, YOU'LL BE OUT THE FUCKING WINDOW.
GET ON WITH IT, MERLIN. I'M LOSING MY PATIENCE.
"EPIPHANY..."

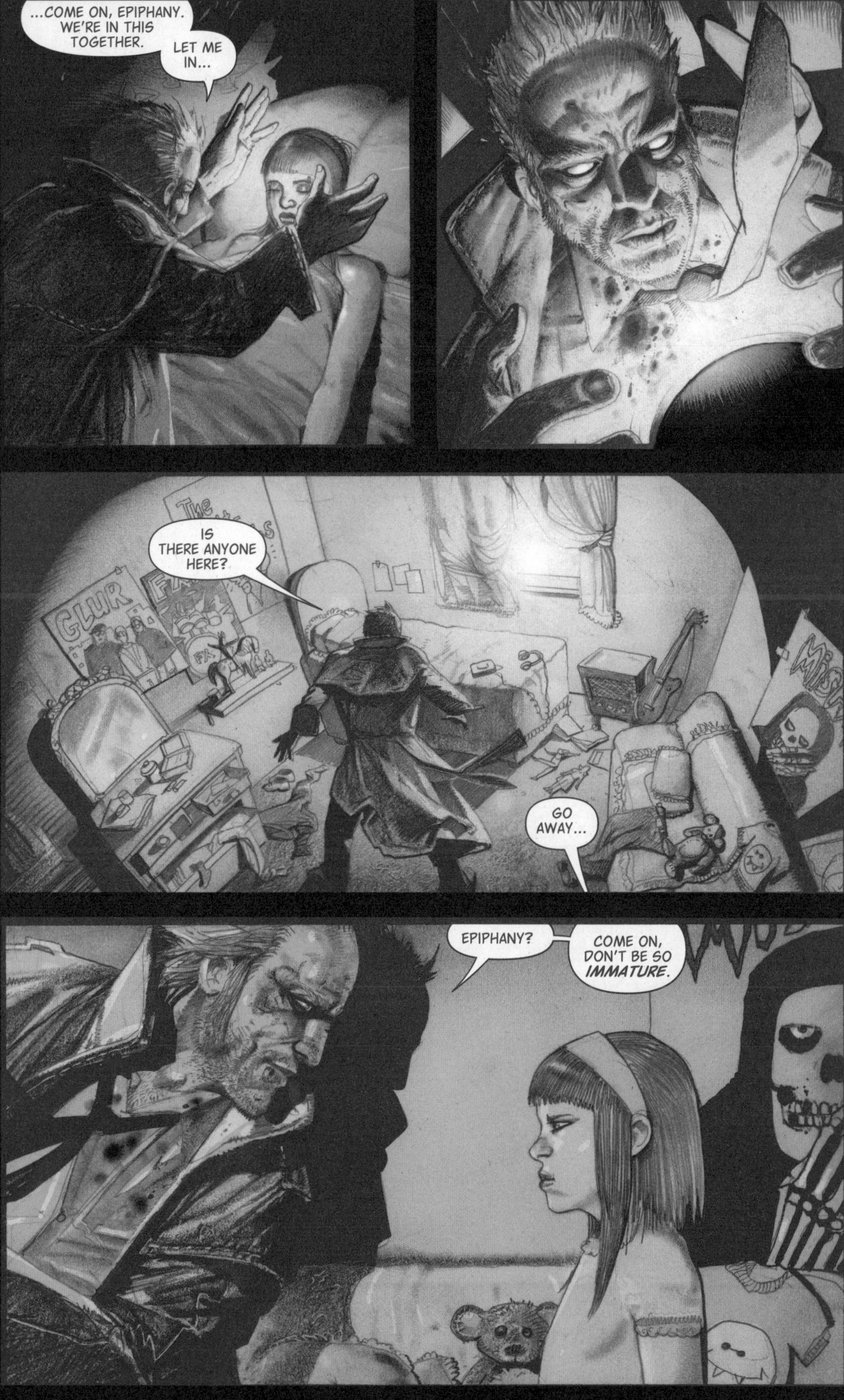

...COME ON, EPIPHANY. WE'RE IN THIS TOGETHER.
LET ME IN...
IS THERE ANYONE HERE?
GO AWAY...
EPIPHANY?
COME ON, DON'T BE SO *IMMATURE*.

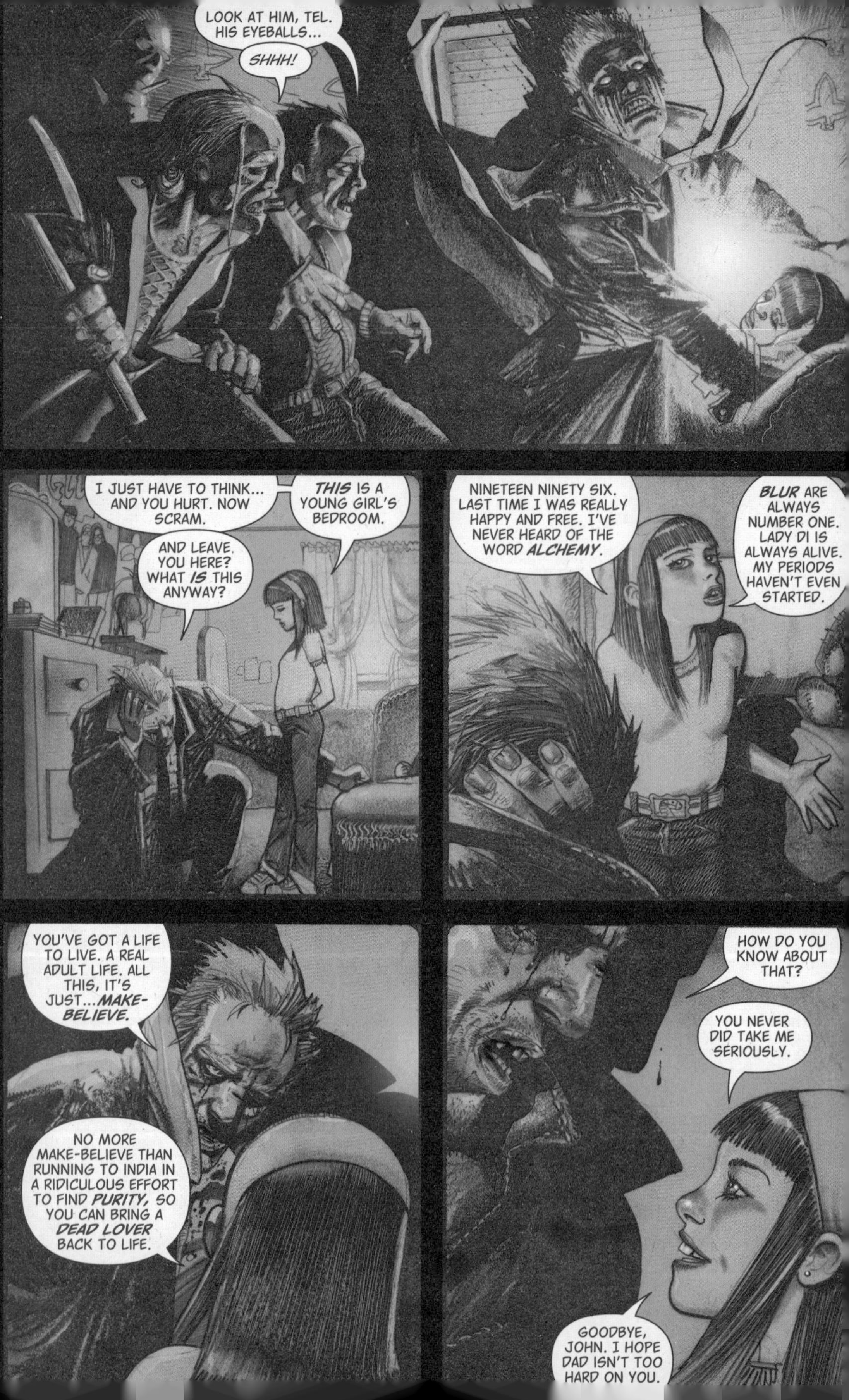

LOOK AT HIM, TEL. HIS EYEBALLS...
SHHH!
I JUST HAVE TO THINK... AND YOU HURT. NOW SCRAM.
THIS IS A YOUNG GIRL'S BEDROOM.
AND LEAVE. YOU HERE? WHAT IS THIS ANYWAY?
NINETEEN NINETY SIX. LAST TIME I WAS REALLY HAPPY AND FREE. I'VE NEVER HEARD OF THE WORD ALCHEMY.
BLUR ARE ALWAYS NUMBER ONE. LADY DI IS ALWAYS ALIVE. MY PERIODS HAVEN'T EVEN STARTED.
YOU'VE GOT A LIFE TO LIVE. A REAL ADULT LIFE. ALL THIS, IT'S JUST...MAKE-BELIEVE.
NO MORE MAKE-BELIEVE THAN RUNNING TO INDIA IN A RIDICULOUS EFFORT TO FIND PURITY, SO YOU CAN BRING A DEAD LOVER BACK TO LIFE.
HOW DO YOU KNOW ABOUT THAT?
YOU NEVER DID TAKE ME SERIOUSLY.
GOODBYE, JOHN. I HOPE DAD ISN'T TOO HARD ON YOU.

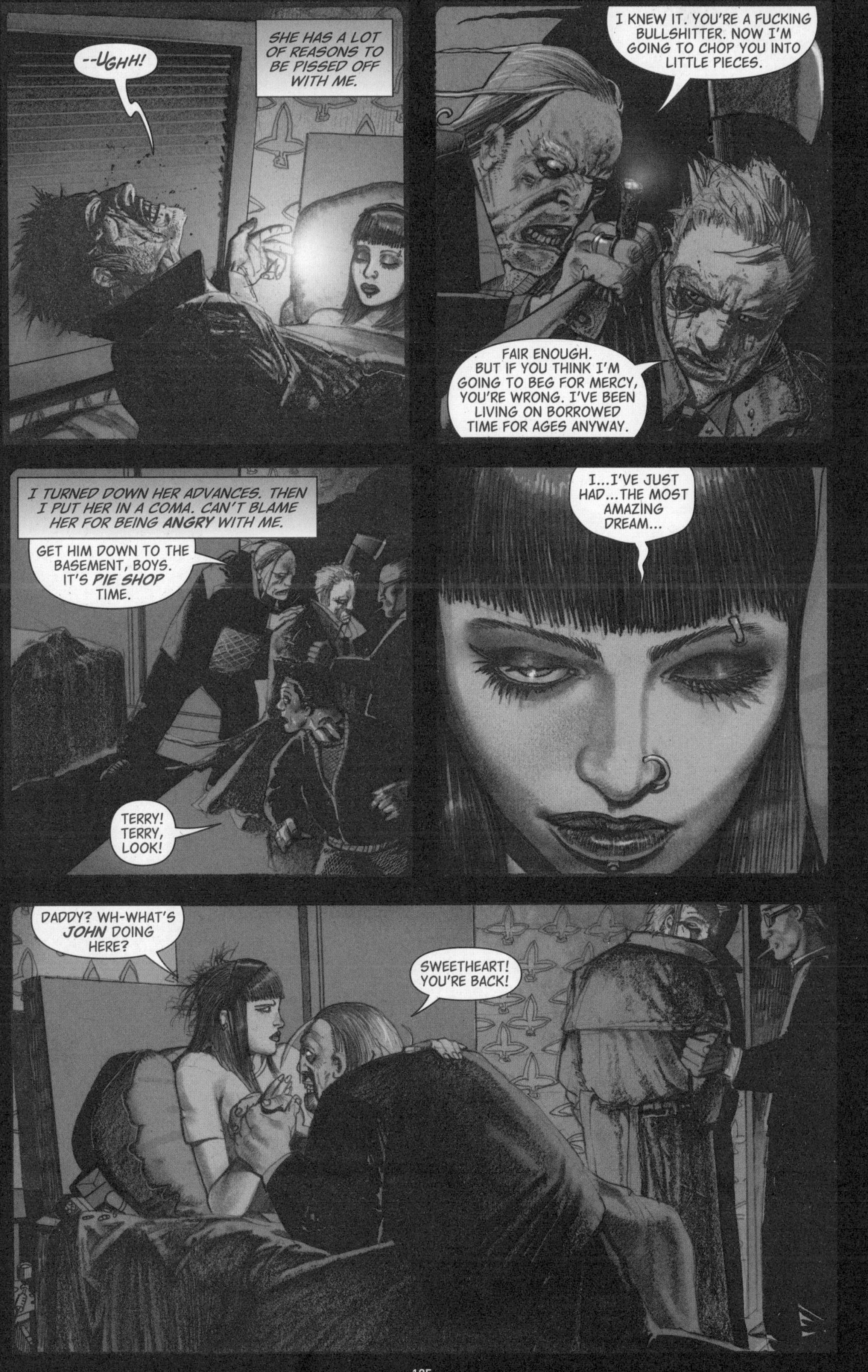

SHE HAS A LOT OF REASONS TO BE PISSED OFF WITH ME.
--UGHH!
I KNEW IT. YOU'RE A FUCKING BULLSHITTER. NOW I'M GOING TO CHOP YOU INTO LITTLE PIECES.
FAIR ENOUGH. BUT IF YOU THINK I'M GOING TO BEG FOR MERCY, YOU'RE WRONG. I'VE BEEN LIVING ON BORROWED TIME FOR AGES ANYWAY.
I TURNED DOWN HER ADVANCES. THEN I PUT HER IN A COMA. CAN'T BLAME HER FOR BEING ANGRY WITH ME.
GET HIM DOWN TO THE BASEMENT, BOYS. IT'S PIE SHOP TIME.
TERRY! TERRY, LOOK!
I...I'VE JUST HAD...THE MOST AMAZING DREAM...
DADDY? WH-WHAT'S JOHN DOING HERE?
SWEETHEART! YOU'RE BACK!

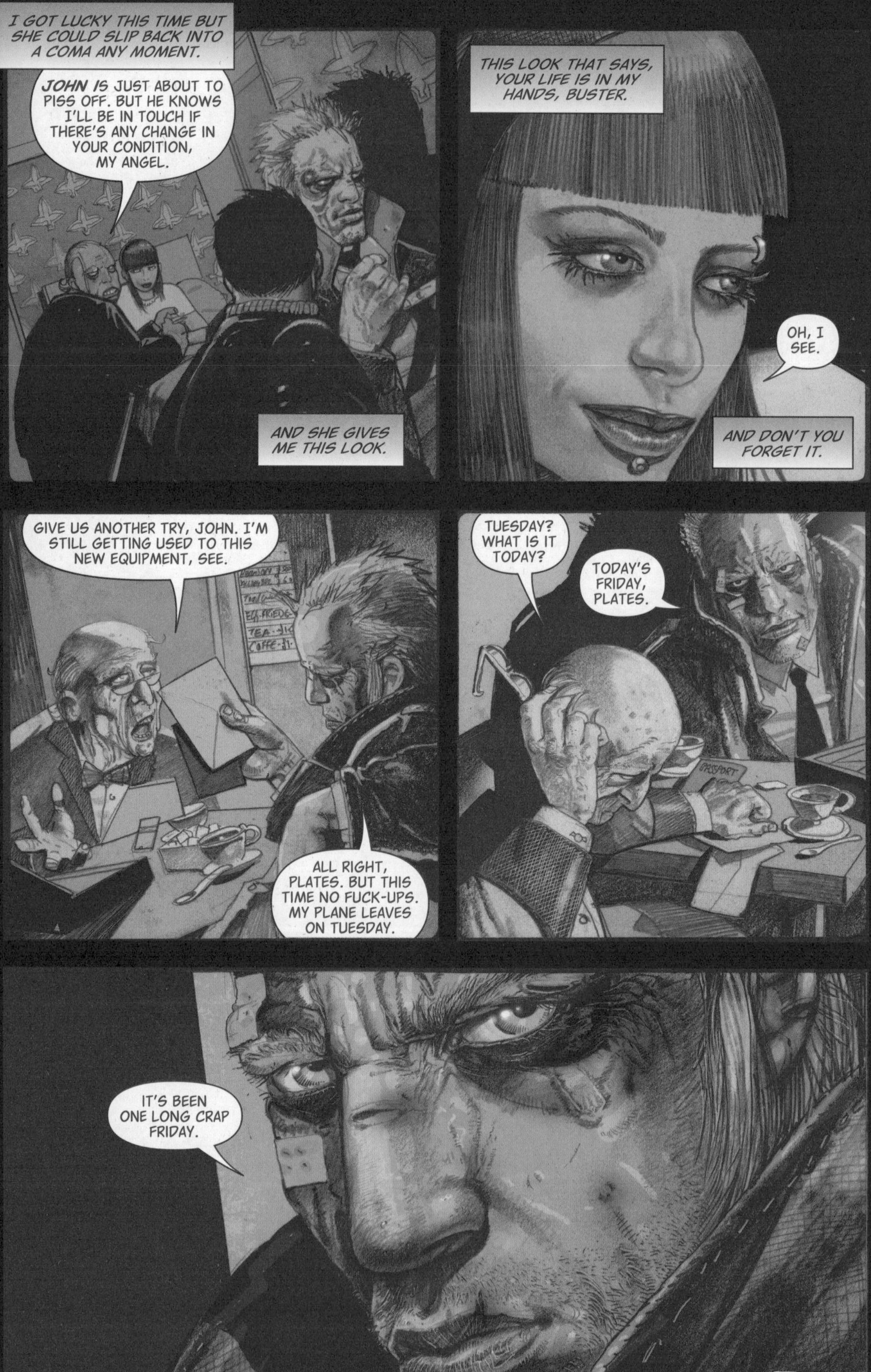
I GOT LUCKY THIS TIME BUT SHE COULD SLIP BACK INTO A COMA ANY MOMENT.
JOHN IS JUST ABOUT TO PISS OFF. BUT HE KNOWS I'LL BE IN TOUCH IF THERE'S ANY CHANGE IN YOUR CONDITION, MY ANGEL.
AND SHE GIVES ME THIS LOOK.
THIS LOOK THAT SAYS, YOUR LIFE IS IN MY HANDS, BUSTER.
OH, I SEE.
AND DON'T YOU FORGET IT.
GIVE US ANOTHER TRY, JOHN. I'M STILL GETTING USED TO THIS NEW EQUIPMENT, SEE.
ALL RIGHT, PLATES. BUT THIS TIME NO FUCK-UPS. MY PLANE LEAVES ON TUESDAY.
TUESDAY? WHAT IS IT TODAY?
TODAY'S FRIDAY, PLATES.
IT'S BEEN ONE LONG CRAP FRIDAY.
THE END

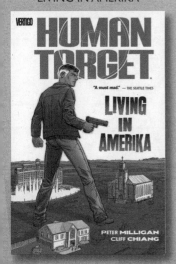

FROM THE WRITER OF
LUCIFER

MIKE CAREY

HELLBLAZER: RED SEPULCHRE

HELLBLAZER: BLACK FLOWERS

HELLBLAZER: STARING AT THE WALL

HELLBLAZER: STATIONS OF THE CROSS

HELLBLAZER: REASONS TO BE CHEERFUL

HELLBLAZER: THE GIFT

HELLBLAZER: ALL HIS ENGINES

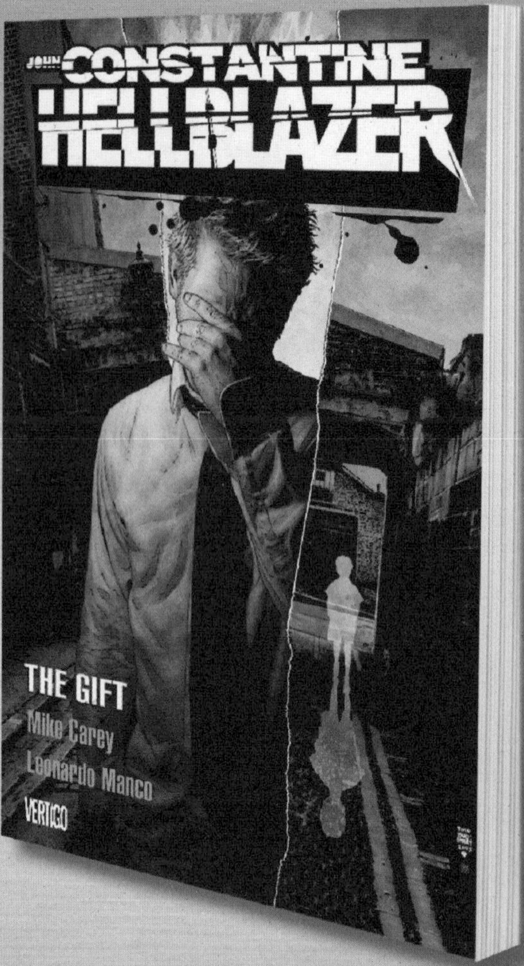
JOHN CONSTANTINE
HELLBLAZER
THE GIFT
Mike Carey
Leonardo Manco
VERTIGO

HELLBLAZER:
RED SEPULCHRE

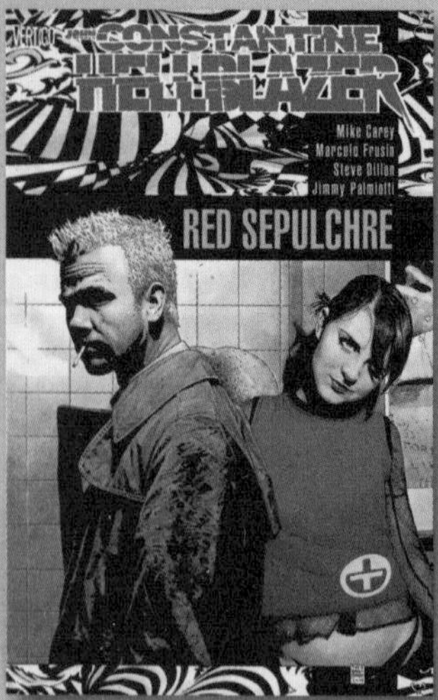
VERTIGO
JOHN CONSTANTINE
HELLBLAZER
Mike Carey
Marcelo Frusin
Steve Dillon
Jimmy Palmiotti
RED SEPULCHRE

with
MARCELO FRUSIN
STEVE DILLON

HELLBLAZER:
BLACK FLOWERS

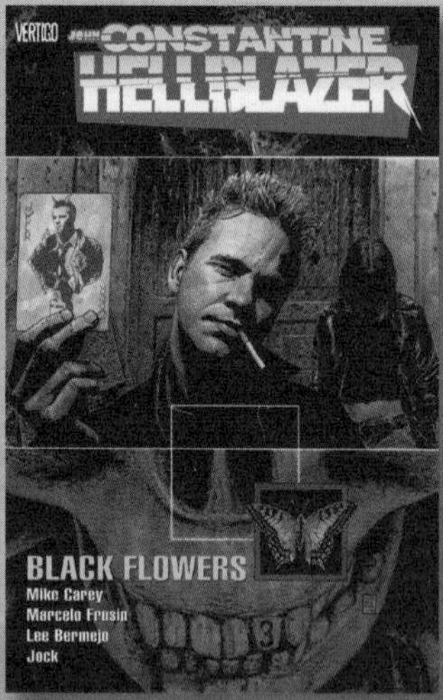
VERTIGO
JOHN CONSTANTINE
HELLBLAZER
BLACK FLOWERS
Mike Carey
Marcelo Frusin
Lee Bermejo
Jock

with
MARCELO FRUSIN
LEE BERMEJO
JOCK

HELLBLAZER:
ALL HIS ENGINES

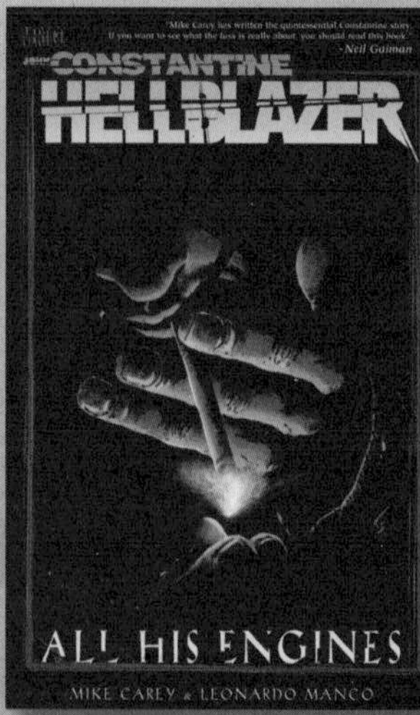
"Mike Carey has written the quintessential Constantine story. If you want to see what the fuss is really about, you should read this book."
- Neil Gaiman
JOHN CONSTANTINE
HELLBLAZER
ALL HIS ENGINES
MIKE CAREY & LEONARDO MANCO

with
LEONARDO MANCO

GO TO
VERTIGOBOOKS.COM
FOR FREE SAMPLES OF THE FIRST ISSUES OF OUR GRAPHIC NOVELS

Suggested for Mature Readers